DISCOVERING AMERICAN ENGLISH:
READING

DISCOVERING AMERICAN ENGLISH: READING

Harriet Krantz   **Joan Kimmelman**   **Sandra Seltzer**
Charles Martin   **Regina Sackmary**   **Sue Lantz-Goldhaber**

Queensborough Community College
The City University of New York

MACMILLAN PUBLISHING CO., INC.
New York
Collier Macmillan Publishers
London

MACMILLAN PUBLISHING CO., INC.
866 Third Avenue, New York, New York 10022

COLLIER MACMILLAN CANADA, LTD.

Library of Congress Cataloging in Publication Data

Main entry under title:

Discovering American English, reading.

  Includes index.
  1. College readers.   2. English language—Grammar—
1950–   I. Krantz, Harriet.
PE1122.D53   428.6   80-16007
ISBN 0-02-366150-X

Printing: 2 3 4 5 6 7 8   Year: 2 3 4 5 6 7

ACKNOWLEDGMENTS

All dictionary entries from The Random House Dictionary, revised edition © 1979. Reprinted by permission of Random House Inc.

PREFACE

Discovering American English: Reading is a text intended for use by students of English as a second language who are at the beginning or intermediate level in their reading and writing skills. These students may have lived in the United States for many years, or they may have arrived here only a short time ago; they may have studied English formally, in schools in their native lands, or they may have acquired English informally, in work and social experiences; what they have in common is the need to master, in a short time, the reading skills that will enable them to succeed in their college careers. This book has been designed to help them achieve their goals.

Discovering American English: Reading is composed of eight Units, each of which explores a different aspect of the American experience, ranging from the kinds of food which Americans enjoy to their attitudes about the cities, towns, and suburbs in which they live. The themes of the earlier Units are generally simpler than those of the later Units, which take advantage of the students' increasing ability to express themselves in class discussion and in reading.

Each Unit contains three original essays of increasing length and complexity, which present and develop the Unit's theme. Interesting, informative, and with a carefully controlled vocabulary, these essays present the students with real approaches to current American concerns. The more difficult vocabulary items for each essay are found in the margin of the page on which they appear, so that instructors can preview the terms with their students, and students can learn the meanings of new words immediately. Vocabulary and idioms are learned not in a vacuum, but in a context of direct application. Not only the essays but the instructional materials as well—examples, exercises, and practices—help to develop the theme of each Unit. The result is a consistently supported thematic environment which invites students, in class discussions and in reading assignments, to share their own experiences of life in the United States.

Each reading Unit is divided into major sections, and different skills are presented in each. The skills are presented in sequence, so that students move in a logical way from easy skills to more complex ones, building on what they have already learned; no skill is ever presented without reference to another. Concepts are introduced inductively, by questions and answers; an abundance of imaginative exercises allows students to practice the skill both in class and independently, and screened summaries and rules provide students with quick reference, reinforcement, and review.

Three major sections in each Unit cover the development of basic vocabulary skills, beginning in the first Unit with the use of correct homonyms. The second Unit begins the presentation of dictionary use skills;

here the emphasis is on understanding the basic parts of a dictionary entry, which is continued and developed in Unit III, where the student is introduced to the skill of syllabication. Syllabication is further developed in Unit IV, and becomes the foundation, in Units V, VI, and VII, for the skills of recognizing prefixes, suffixes, and roots. Unit VIII draws all these skills together and focuses the student's attention on the dictionary once again. In this Unit, previously mastered skills are presented as the basis for determining the correct meanings of words in context.

Each Unit of the text also contains three sections devoted to comprehension and/or study skills. Beginning with understanding sentences and paragraphs in Unit I, comprehension skills are developed in Unit II, and the focus is on understanding topics in paragraphs of varied length. Unit III develops the skill of relating topics to main idea sentences, and Unit IV introduces the technique of highlighting main idea sentences and details. In Unit V the relationship between highlighting and outlining is established. The skill of outlining paragraph selections of varying lengths is continued in Unit VI. Units VII and VIII introduce the techniques of following directions and taking tests. Specific instruction focuses on understanding directional words, answering objective test items, and following essay test directions.

ACKNOWLEDGMENTS

It is a pleasure to be able to thank the many people who gave us aid and comfort during the writing, testing, editing, and production of this book. We must first acknowledge the unflagging support and understanding of our families—husbands, children, and wife. We also owe a special debt of gratitude to Paul Panes, James Shepherd, Michael Elkin, Celeste Berner, Bonnie Semon, and Myra Waldinger, our colleagues at Queensborough Community College, and to Michael Melody, Robert L. Allen, Doris A. Allen, Amy Sonka, and Rosalind Sackoff for their thoughtful evaluations of our manuscript. We are also grateful to Edith Grossman, Francine Stavas, and Barbara Grable, members of the staff of the Department of Basic Educational Skills, for their many kindnesses. At Macmillan, Anthony English was the gentle shepherd of this venture, never losing patience with his occasionally unruly flock. We are also indebted to Pat Cabeza, our production editor, for the care with which she guided our manuscript—and its authors—through the many stages of production. Finally, we must thank our students, without whom this book would have been neither possible nor necessary.

CONTENTS

UNIT III
AMERICAN PLAYGROUNDS

UNIT IV
WOULD YOU BUY A USED CAR
FROM THESE AUTHORS?

UNIT V
GROWING UP IN SPITE OF IT ALL

UNIT VI
IF I HAD IT TO DO ALL OVER AGAIN . . .

UNIT VII
WHO REALLY WEARS THE PANTS?

UNIT VIII
URBAN, SUBURBAN, AND RURAL:
Where We Live Now

DISCOVERING AMERICAN ENGLISH:
READING

UNIT I
WE ARE WHAT WE EAT:
From Apple Pie to Baked Zucchini

Reprinted by permission of The Panasonic Company.

The sentences, paragraphs, essays,° and exercises that follow are designed to help you improve your reading comprehension and, at the same time, to describe an aspect° of American life to you. Like all people, Americans are intensely° interested in food: buying it, cooking it, tasting it, testing it, enjoying it, and trying not to eat too much of it. It is helpful to know something about how Americans feel about food. The information in each series of exercises is loosely organized around the following food subjects: supermarkets, consumerism,° health foods, dining out, preparing foods, dieting, and regional° cooking.

DISCUSSION

Where do you do your shopping for food? Why? What are some differences between shopping for food in the United States and in other countries? What are some advantages of shopping in supermarkets? What are some disadvantages of shopping in supermarkets?

INITIAL READING

Visiting a Supermarket

Visiting a supermarket is like taking a trip around the world. Over here is a mountain of oranges from sunny Florida. Over there are heads of lettuce from California. The frozen crab meat comes all the way from Alaska. There are also sardines from Norway and Portugal. In the next aisle° there is mustard from Germany, soy sauce from Hong Kong, and wine from Chile and Argentina.

A young Haitian student discovers a pile of mangoes from the Caribbean. They are so expensive here! A Korean man is carefully examining a small piece of ginger. Two women from Lebanon are looking for dried chickpeas. An elderly Italian man finds a can of olive oil from Italy. What will they do with these things?

CHAPTER 1

UNDERSTANDING LITERAL MEANINGS:
Sentences

*_{*}

To understand the world you live in, you must understand what you are seeing, hearing, feeling, and reading. Every day you read labels on food products, directions on street signs, headlines in newspapers, and chapters in textbooks. When you understand things literally, you can shop wisely, follow directions, understand the day's events, and comprehend course work. Look at the following picture.

EXAMPLE

Reprinted by permission of the Campbell's Soup Company.

QUESTIONS

1. What is the brand name of the soup? _____Campbell's_____

2. What kind of soup is mentioned on the label? _____Noodle_____

3. What is the weight of the can in ounces? _____ 10 ³/₄ _____

4. What is the weight of the can in grams? _____ 305 _____

5. Is the soup condensed? _____ good idea _____

These questions ask you to recall written information. The can of Campbell's Chicken Noodle Soup weighs 10¾ ounces or 305 grams and is condensed.

Literal comprehension means understanding and recalling the facts.

Often you answer questions from other kinds of written material.

EXAMPLE

Bob buys a dozen eggs.

QUESTIONS

1. How many eggs does Bob buy? _____ 12 eggs _____

2. Who buys the eggs? _____ Bob _____

3. Does Bob buy twelve eggs? _____ yes _____

Bob buys twelve, or one dozen, eggs. Again, the questions ask for a recall of facts. Remember that the question may have a different word than appears in the sentence. In the example, "a dozen" is the same as twelve eggs.

Recalled facts may often be stated in different words.

EXERCISE The following exercises present simple statements. Read each pair of sentences carefully. Compare the second sentence with the first sentence. Answer <u>Same</u> (S) if the second sentence says the same thing as the first sentence. Answer <u>Different</u> (D) if the second sentence says something different. The first two are done for you.

  D 1. The lines in supermarkets are long on Friday night.
         Supermarket lines are long on Tuesday.

  S 2. Bargain hunters watch for sales in their markets.
         Supermarket sales attract people looking for bargains.

  S 3. Food coupons help homemakers save money on their groceries.
         Grocery coupons do little to help homemakers.

_S_ 4. Some cakes sold in supermarkets have no real food substances in them.
Some supermarket cakes contain no real food substances.

_D_ 5. Watch the cash register at the checkout counter because you can be overcharged.
Overcharging at the checkout counter never happens.

PRACTICE Answer <u>Same</u> (S) if the two sentences say the same thing. Answer <u>Different</u> (D) if they are different.

_S_ 1. Most Americans are constantly on diets.
All Americans are usually on diets.

_S_ 2. The dinner meal is usually the big meal of the day for Americans.
Dinner is always the main meal for Americans.

_D_ 3. Americans are concerned about their eating habits.
Americans are not interested in their diets.

_S_ 4. Americans are always trying to lose weight.
Americans don't want to be overweight.

_S_ 5. Each American consumes gallons of soda every year.
Americans drink a lot of soda.

EXERCISE Here is another exercise to help you improve literal comprehension. In this exercise read the pairs of sentences carefully. The second sentence has a word or group of words missing. Complete the second sentence with the facts from the first sentence. The first one is done for you.

1. Service is one difference between a fast-food restaurant° and a diner.   °a restaurant with inexpensive, quickly prepared food

   Fast-food restaurants and diners differ in ___service___.

2. Fast-food restaurants are money savers for consumers.

   Consumers can save _____*money*_____ by eating at fast-food places.

3. Pizza parlors are crowded on Friday nights.

   There are many people at ____*Pizza parlors*____ on Friday nights.

4. Fish and chips are easy to eat but hard to digest.

   I love to eat fish and chips, but they are ___*hard to digest*___.

5. Fast-food restaurants like McDonald's and Burger King are popular in the United States.

   ____*McDonald's*____ and ____*Burger King*____ are popular U.S. restaurants.

PRACTICE Read these pairs of sentences. Complete the second sentence with the correct information from the first sentence.

1. Lunch for a busy person might be a hot dog at the nearest stand.

   A ___lunch for a busy___ person might be found at a hot dog stand.

2. Many restaurants have special menus for children.

   Children get ___special___ menus at many restaurants.

3. Fried chicken is a popular take-out item.

   A popular take-out food is ___fried chicken___.

4. Eating too many hot dogs can give you a stomach ache.

   You can get a stomach ache from eating ___too many hot dogs___.

5. At any coffee counter, most people will order muffins, doughnuts, rolls, or coffecake for breakfast.

   ___Muffins, doughnuts, rolls, or coffecake___ people eat cake products for breakfast at coffee counters.

EXERCISE Here is another exercise to help you improve literal comprehension. Using the information in the first sentence, choose the best answer for each statement. Write your choice (a, b, c, or d) in the space. Part of the first one is done for you.

1. You must pay the full sales tax on the price of a product even when you use a coupon.

   _a_ A coupon lowers
      a. the price of the product.
      b. the tax on the product.
      c. both the price and the tax.

   _a_ With a coupon, you pay sales tax on
      a. the discount price of the item.
      b. the full price of the item.
      c. the tax on the item.

2. The produce section of a supermarket displays lettuce, tomatoes, other vegetables, and fruit.

   _d_ One item not found in the produce section is
      a. apples.
      b. string beans.
      c. lettuce.
      d. cheese.

_a_ Lettuce, tomatoes, and vegetables are
  a. kept in the produce section.
  b. not found in the produce section.
  c. found in the dairy° section.

°of or from milk

3. A picnic in the park is a lovely way to spend a Sunday afternoon.

_c_ On a Sunday afternoon it is lovely to
  a. eat at home.
  b. have a picnic in the backyard.
  c. have a picnic in the park.

_b_ Sunday afternoons are great for
  a. parking.
  b. picnicking.
  c. sleeping.

4. The cost of a Saturday night dinner at a restaurant is getting higher and higher.

_a_ Prices are rising for
  a. Saturday dinners.
  b. all dinners.
  c. Friday lunches.

_c_ Restaurant prices are
  a. getting higher for breakfasts.
  b. getting lower for Saturday night dinners.
  c. getting higher for Saturday night dinners.

5. We can cut down on the sweets we eat by using sugar substitutes.

_b_ Sugar substitutes cut down on
  a. the food we eat.
  b. some sweets.
  c. only candy.

_c_ Sugar substitutes can help us
  a. do away with sweets.
  b. increase our sweets.
  c. reduce our sweets.

Understanding Literal Meanings:
Identifying Who and What

Good comprehension includes three things: who does the action, what the action is, and what the purpose of the action is.

EXAMPLE

Pierre meets Marie for a date.

QUESTIONS

1. Who meets Marie? _____ *Pierre* _____

2. What does Pierre do? _____ *meets Marie* _____

3. Why does Pierre meet Marie? _____ *A date* _____

In this example, "Pierre meets Marie for a date." Pierre does the action. The action is "meets Marie." The purpose of the action is "a date."

> **Literal comprehension** means knowing **who** does the action, **what** the action is, and **what** the purpose of the action is.

EXERCISE Read each statement and answer each question. The first one is done for you.

1. Jacques meets Kim for coffee after work. They always go to a coffee house.

   What do Jacques and Kim do after work? They meet for coffee.

   Where do they always go? They go to the local coffee house.

2. Rose is not responsible for the burned toast. Her brother left the toaster on while he played outside.

   Who is responsible for the burned toast? _____ *Rose brother* _____

   Who was playing outside? _____ *her brother* _____

3. Marco enjoys cooking Italian food. Every Saturday night he prepares spaghetti for all his friends.

   What does Marco like to do? _____ *cooking Italian Food* _____

   On the weekend Marco _____ *prepares* _____ spaghetti for his friends.

   For whom does Marco cook? _____ *all his friends* _____

4. The best place to buy cereal is in a health food store where the cereals are prepared without artificial° ingredients.° °not natural / °contents

What is the name of the best place to buy cereal? __health food store__

What is left out of health food cereals? __artificial ingredients__

5. Roger is driving his car to the restaurant. His friend Mimi is going with him.

Who is driving with Roger? __Mimi__

Where is Roger driving? __to the restaurant__

Who is driving the car? __Roger__

PRACTICE The following statements tell about who does an action and what the action is. Using these facts, answer the questions or fill in the sentences following each statement.

1. "Alma, bring me a chair," said Juanita to her sister.

Who is Alma? __sister of Juanita__

What does Juanita ask? __bring her a chair__

2. The children eat chocolate pudding for breakfast. This does not please their mother.

Who is not pleased? __their mother__

What do the children eat? __chocolate pudding__

What displeases their mother? __for breakfast__

3. The supermarket manager decides when to have a sale. He lowers prices on certain items.

Who reduces prices? __supermarket manager__

Name two things the manager does: __when to have a sale__ and __lower prices on certain items__.

4. Cooking meals for a large family is hard work. Whoever cooks the meal must prepare a lot of food and wash many pots and pans.

What is hard about cooking for a large family? __whoever cooks the meal meal must prepare a lot of food__

What does the cook wash? __many pots and pans__

5. Eating out with friends is fun. It is less enjoyable to eat alone.

What is fun to do with friends? _eating out_

What is it like to eat alone? _less enjoyable_

6. It is difficult to cook frozen hamburgers. They usually burn on the outside and stay raw on the inside.

What part of the hamburger is raw? _inside_

What part of the hamburger is burned? _outside_

7. A typical American breakfast may include juice, toast, eggs, bacon, cereal, and coffee. Breakfast may vary from person to person.

What varies from person to person? _breakfast_

What is a typical breakfast like? _juice, toast, eggs, bacon, cereal and coffee_

8. Frost kills oranges easily. They need warm weather to ripen.

What will warm weather do for oranges? _to ripen_

What does frost kill? _oranges_

9. The thirsty child drinks his milk shake. He loves sweet-tasting drinks.

Who loves sweet drinks? _child_

What happens to the milk shake? _The thirsty child drinks the milk shake_

10. Americans adopt foods from other cultures. Each new group of immigrants brings a dish or two. Americans adopt these dishes.

What do new immigrants do? _brings a dish or two_

Who adopts the dishes? _Americans_

What do Americans do with food from other cultures? _adopt food from other cultures._

Understanding Literal Meanings: Single Paragraphs

It is necessary to understand single paragraphs before you can make sense of longer selections. In this section, you will practice reading single paragraphs to understand who is doing the action, what is happening, and what the result of the action is.

EXAMPLE

"Being overweight is no fun," complains Jamie. "All the kids at school say things behind my back."° She continues, "I never find clothing as nice as all the other girls wear."

°secretly

QUESTIONS

1. Who is overweight? _____ *Jamie* _____

2. Who talks secretly about Jamie? _____ *All the kids at school* _____

3. Describe the clothing of the other girls. *Never find clothing as nice as all the other girls wear.*

4. Jamie can't find _____ *clothing* _____.

5. [True or False] Only boys talk about Jamie. _____ *False* _____

"Jamie" is overweight. "All the kids talk behind her back." The other girls have nice clothing. Jamie wants to find "clothing as nice as the other girls have." Each of these questions tests your literal understanding of an entire paragraph. You are now ready to answer questions about literal meanings in paragraphs.

> **Literal comprehension** of paragraphs often means knowing who does or says something, what the action is, and what happens as a result of the action.

EXERCISE Each exercise has several statements after it. If the statement is correct according to the passage, mark it True (T). If it is not correct, mark it False (F). Write your answers on the lines. The first one is done for you.

1. Arturo and Jeanne are waiting for me so we can buy popcorn at the movies.

   _F_ I am buying popcorn.

   _F_ Arturo and Jeanne are watching the movie.

   _T_ Arturo, Jeanne, and I will buy popcorn.

2. In some states wine is sold in supermarkets. In other states it is not.

Officials argue that selling wine in supermarkets will put smaller liquor stores out of business.

F Some parents argue against selling wine in markets.

F Most states allow wine to be sold in supermarkets.

F Some small stores have liquor for sale.

°arguments against

F Opposition to° wine sales comes from states where wine is sold in supermarkets.

3. "Our favorite treat," say the children, "is to go shopping for food with Mom and Dad when he gets paid."

F The children get paid.

T Mom and Dad tell about a special treat.

F The children wait until Mom gets paid.

T The children enjoy shopping with their parents.

4. "Carla, how can I bake a chocolate cake as good as yours?"
She answers, "It's easy, but you must remember the big secret."
"What's that?" asks Raoul.
"Use only real chocolate bits and real butter along with the other ingredients."

F Carla asks how to bake a good cake.

T Carla has a big secret.

F Raoul tells the secret of the cake.

F Chocolate alone makes the difference in the cake.

5. Do you start diets all the time? Most people say they will begin tomorrow, right after that big piece of apple pie. Of course, that doesn't mean much. The time to start a diet is right now.

F The best time to start a diet is tomorrow.

F Most people begin a diet right away.

T Most people start diets tomorrow.

PRACTICE Read each short passage. The statements after each passage are either True (T) or False (F). Write your answer on the line next to each statement.

1. Unlike other cultures, Americans eat their main meal of the day in the evening. At noon they usually have a light lunch of a sandwich or salad.

F Americans eat sandwiches and salads for dinner.

F All over the world, people eat their main meal in the evening.

F Americans are like other cultures in their eating patterns.

2. Many teenagers do not eat chocolate or fried foods. They do not want to suffer from the common teenage skin problem called acne.

    F Teenagers never eat chocolate.

    F Teenagers eat fried foods.

    T Teenagers do not want acne.

    F Acne is a bone disease.

3. "I'm on a diet," says Marie. "I eat little during the day. I do not eat between meals, and I do not eat after dinner."
    "Aren't you hungry?" asks Harry.
    "I am."

    F Marie cuts out snacks when dieting.

    T Marie does not eat snacks at each meal.

    F Marie asks, "Aren't you hungry?"

    T Harry is usually hungry when on a diet.

4. At about 10:30 A.M. office workers take their first coffee break of the day. The second one comes at about 3:00 P.M. At these times a coffee wagon arrives with coffee, tea, cakes, and sandwiches. Workers buy their snacks right on the job.

    T Workers take two coffee breaks a day.

    F The coffee wagon contains only drinks.

    F Workers drive their cars to nearby coffee shops.

    F There are two morning coffee breaks in most offices.

5. Supermarkets are very well organized. Meats and dairy products are always in different sections. All frozen foods are in large freezers. Breads and cakes are in another section. Each section has a display sign hanging above the aisle.

    F Breads and meats are usually in the same section.

    T Frozen foods must be refrigerated.

    F Foods are located by looking at the signs above the aisles.

    F Supermarkets organize their products into groups.

6. More and more people are returning to a basic, healthy way of life. Farm communities are springing up in uninhabited areas. Community members grow all their own foods and follow a simple way of life. They sell surplus° produce to raise money for the community.   °extra

_F_ People are turning to a healthy life-style.

_F_ People move to farms every spring.

_F_ People in farming communities sell basic foods to raise money.

_F_ Extra produce is helpful to the farming community.

_T_ Money from selling extra produce helps the farming community.

_F_ The new farming communities force settlers out of the land.

PRACTICE Now that you are able to answer True–False questions, you can move to another type of question. In this exercise the questions focus on who does an action, what the action is, and what the aim of the action is. Read each passage carefully. Place your answers on the lines.

1. "Why don't you take your vitamin pills as the doctor suggests?" Susanna's mother asks her.
     "I always forget them," she replies.

Who says that she forgets? ___Susanna___

What does the doctor suggest? ___vitamin pills___

Who should take the pills? ___Susanna___

Who asks about the vitamins? ___Susanna's mother___

2. "Will we be seeing you after class in the cafeteria? Carl! Answer us! Why don't you listen when we ask you a question?" shouted John.

Who asks, "Will we be seeing you?" ___John___

Who is not listening? ___Carl___

3. Rice is an important part of the diet for many people of the world. Most Americans, however, eat rice only as a side dish. It should be included in the American diet. It is certainly a healthy addition. It is inexpensive and easy to cook.

Do the majority of Americans eat rice? ___side dish___

Name three reasons for adding rice to the American diet.

___Healthy___

___inexpensive___

___easy to cook___

How do most Americans eat rice? ___In diet___

4. A glass of lemonade is a typical American drink on a hot summer day. Its cool taste is refreshing and gives relief from the heat. Everyone enjoys lemonade, and anyone can make it easily, with lemons, water,

and sugar. Adding mint leaves to the drink makes it even better. Served with ice in tall glasses, lemonade can make a hot afternoon more pleasant.

What is a typical summer drink in the United States? _____Lemonade_____

Who can make the drink? _____Anyone can_____

What makes the drink even better? _____Adding mint leaves_____

What can one serve with ice? _____lemonade_____

PRACTICE You are now ready to practice literal comprehension in longer passages. Some questions require a True (T) or False (F) answer, and some questions require more information. Make sure that your answers show factual recall of the passage.

1. Shopping for a party is fun. However, one must plan every detail. I am planning a surprise party for my boyfriend, and I am inviting twenty people. I have a lot of soda and party snacks. I have napkins, plastic dinnerware, and tablecloths. I already have the ice for the soda. Can you suggest an easy, tasty dinner menu?

   What is fun? _____shopping for a party_____

   How many people are invited? _____20_____

   What does the writer need? _____food_____

   What kind of party is it? _____surprise_____

   The writer already has _____soda_____, _____snacks_____, _____napkins_____, and _____ice_____.

2. Outdoor cooking is a popular American pastime. Barbecuing in the backyard is fun. Everyone enjoys the aroma° of food cooking over hot coals. Many foods taste delicious when they are cooked on an outdoor grill.°

   °a pleasant smell or odor

   °a metal screen for broiling food

   Answer True (T) or False (F):

   _F_ Few foods can be cooked outdoors.

   _F_ Americans rarely barbecue their foods.

   _F_ Food cooking on an open fire smells terrible.

   _T_ Food cooked outdoors is tasty.

   _F_ Outdoor cooking is fun only for the cook.

3. Tofu, a staple° of many oriental diets, is a traditional natural food. Today it is widely available in American health food stores, fruit and vegetable markets, and some supermarkets. Tofu, a soybean product, is both inex-

   °a basic food

°a substance necessary for
the growth and repair of
body tissue

pensive and healthy. Americans are beginning to include tofu in their
diets because it is a good source of vegetable protein.° Tofu is also low in
fat, calories, and salt.

Answer True (T) or False (F):

_F_ Tofu is expensive to buy.

_F_ You can find tofu in most supermarkets.

_T_ Tofu is an important part of oriental diets.

_F_ Americans are eating tofu because it is tasty.

_F_ Tofu is a dairy product.

_F_ Although high in calories, tofu is low in salt and fat.

_F_ High amounts of animal protein make tofu healthy.

4. Good nutrition and fast-foods are enemies. Fast-food restaurants offer
hamburgers, french fries, and soda. Vegetables and fruits are missing
from fast-food menus. Therefore, a steady diet of only fast-food meals
cannot supply essential° vitamins and minerals, and this can cause
health problems for children and adults alike. Although fast-food restaurants are convenient and inexpensive, they just <u>might lead</u> to inconvenient and expensive doctors' bills later on.

Answer these questions in complete sentences.

1. What do fast-food places serve? _Fast food places serve hamburgers, french fried and soda_

2. Why do total diets of fast-foods become a problem? _Total diet of fast food become a problem because cannot have vitamins and minerals_

3. How can a person avoid expensive doctors' bills? _a Person can avoid expensive doctors' bills by eating a little meat and a lot of vegetables and fruits_

4. How can fast-food places be convenient and inconvenient, expen-
sive and inexpensive at the same time? _Fast food places serve convenient and inexpensive_

5. What is missing from fast-food menus? _Vegetables and fruits_

CHAPTER 2

USING THE CORRECT HOMONYM

* *
*

Maria has just arrived in this country. She is in an English class with Suly. Maria is having a lot of trouble with her spelling. She finds that many words in English sound alike but have different meanings and different spellings. Suly offers to explain such words to her.

MARIA: Suly, can you help me with my spelling? I'm really confused.

SULY: What's the problem?

MARIA: Every time I write my compositions I misspell words. When Professor English corrects the errors, I find that the sound of the correct word and the misspelled word are the same.

SULY: You must be having a problem with homonyms. **Homonyms are two or more words that sound the same but have different meanings and different spellings.** Sometimes you have the right sound and you know the right meaning, but you use the incorrect spelling. Once you connect the meanings and the spellings of the homonym pairs, you'll be able to use the correct one.

MARIA: Look at this Suly. Here's one of the corrections that Professor English made. He crossed out "there" and wrote "their."

SULY: That's not too difficult. The word "there" usually refers to a place away from where you are.

> EXAMPLE We are sitting here in our seats, and Professor English is over **there** at the blackboard.

The same word "there" can also introduce a sentence.

> EXAMPLE **There** are five ways to preserve fresh fruit.

MARIA: That's easy. But I spelled the word "their." What does that homonym mean?

SULY: The homonym "their" shows ownership or possession.

> EXAMPLE The three little kittens lost **their** mittens. **Their** home is beautiful.

MARIA: Now I understand. "There–their" is a homonym pair with two meanings, two spellings, and the same sound.

SULY: So far, so good. But sometimes a homonym group can consist of three. "Their–there" is a good example. Look at this sentence.

> EXAMPLE **They're** playing our song.

In this sentence, "they're" is a shorter way of writing "they are."

MARIA: I see. Let me practice some groups of homonyms so that I'll know their different spellings and different meanings.

You can practice recognizing homonym meanings and spellings. Look at the following:

EXAMPLE

1A. The best **way** to make pizza is in a baker's oven.
1B. Do you **weigh** meat in pounds or in grams?

QUESTIONS

1. What is the meaning of "way" in 1A? _____

2. What is the meaning of "weigh" in 1B? _____

Both "way" and "weigh" are pronounced alike. But in 1A the word "way" means a method, and in 1B the word "weigh" means to measure according to a specific weight standard.

Homonyms are two or more words that sound the same but are spelled differently and have different meanings.

EXERCISE Select the correct homonym in each sentence and circle it. Use the Glossary of Homonyms to help you.

1. (Right Write) a shopping list for next week's party.
2. My house is located on the (right write) side of the street.
3. There are (to too two) many rich foods on the table.
4. We are going (to two too) buy (to two too) puppies.
5. Everyone ate a (piece peace) of fudge cake.
6. The generals are signing a (peace piece) treaty.
7. There is a space (hear here) at the table.
8. Do you (hear here) the soup bubbling in the pot?
9. (Your You're) the only one who ate five pieces of pie.
10. (Your You're) recipe won first prize.
11. Every day at the cafeteria we have to (weight wait) in line for our lunch.
12. I am gaining (to two too) much (weight wait).
13. (Hour Our) family always drinks soda.
14. The milkman delivers milk at an early (hour our).
15. There is (no know) food in our picnic basket.
16. Do you (no know) the price of tomatoes this week?

17. I (passed) past) the weekly quiz.
18. In the (passed past) housewives spent their days in the kitchen.
19. Many people recognize the skyscraper (seen scene) from the movie *King Kong*.
20. Have you (seen) scene) the latest style of dress?

PRACTICE Use the Glossary to help you complete each sentence. Place the correct homonym in the blank space.

1. (Whose, Who's) __who's__ the man __whose__ coat is hanging here?

2. (I'll, Aisle, Isle) __I'll__ walk down the __Aisle__ singing with the rest of the chorus.

3. (Whether, Weather) __Whether__ we take our trip to Vermont or not depends on the __weather__.

4. (It's, Its) __It's__ a pity that Jimmy's restaurant has lost __its__ customers.

5. (Their, There, They're) __They're__ having __theirs__ appetizers in the small dining room over __there__.

6. (tale, tail) We are telling the children the __tale__ of the lion with the golden __tail__.

7. (so, sew) Alice is going to __sew__ some curtains tonight, __so__ she can't go out to dinner with us.

8. (pear, pair, pare) My mother is asking me to __pare__ the apples, to slice the __pear__, and to bring her __pair__ of brown shoes to the shoemaker.

9. (for, four) There are __four__ guests visiting us __for__ the weekend.

10. (fair, fare) The __fare__ for the ferry is two dollars, and we don't think that's a __fair__ price.

PRACTICE Here are some of the homonyms used in the previous exercise and practice. Match the words on the left with their correct definitions on the right. The first one is done for you.

_h_	1. piece	a.	possessive form of who or which
_j_	2. your	b.	to understand
_i_	3. here	c.	an open space between sectioned areas
_g_	4. weight	d.	local atmospheric condition
_b_	5. know	e.	a time before the present
_d_	6. weather	f.	to communicate on a surface, usually on paper
_c_	7. aisle	g.	a measurement of heaviness
_a_	8. whose	h.	a portion or a section
_f_	9. write	i.	a location close to the speaker
_e_	10. past	j.	belonging to you

PRACTICE READING

The Diner

The diner is only a humble restaurant, but it has a special place in American life. Diners appear in our novels, plays, poems, and movies. Many artists have used diners as scenes for their paintings. Why are diners so fascinating to us?

The diner attracts many different kinds of people. It is a haven° for lonely truck drivers far away from home. Construction workers learn about new jobs in distant cities. Traveling salesmen exchange gossip with one another. Teenagers sit in their booths, hunched over° Cokes and hamburgers.

The people who work in diners are also interesting. Where did the new waitress come from? Will she remain here, or will she suddenly run off one day, as the last one did? And is the short-order° cook really an escaped convict, fleeing° from the law?

Everyone comes to the diner for a different reason. Some want to work there, and some want to eat there. Some stay for years, and others stay only for a few minutes. But, for all of them, the diner is a bright, warm stopover° between the endless stretches of open road.

°a safe place or shelter

°bent

°food quickly prepared and served
°running away

°a brief stop or stay during a trip

VOCABULARY EXERCISE Choose one of the words just defined that best completes each of the following sentences.

1. A Salvation Army shelter is frequently a ___haven___ for people with no place to live.

2. Joe is a great ___short order___ cook.

3. Escaping prisoners are often caught while ___fleeing___ from the police.

4. Elyse had a ___stopover___ in Chicago before arriving in Los Angeles.

VOCABULARY PRACTICE Use the new words in your own sentences.

1. _The trees bend when the wind blew_
2. _A house is a haven for us after a hard work day_
3. _A rest area is a warm stopover for a long trip._
4. _____
5. _____

LITERAL COMPREHENSION EXERCISE Decide which of the answers best completes the statement. Write the letter on the line.

_c_ 1. Why do truck drivers like a diner?
    a. It's a place to gossip.
    b. It's a place for a Coke and a hamburger.
    c. It's a haven against loneliness.
    d. It's a place to learn about new jobs.

_b_ 2. Diners attract
    a. only truck drivers.
    b. many different kinds of people.
    c. novelists.
    d. escaped convicts.

_d_ 3. Diners are
    a. gloomy.
    b. unpleasant.
    c. luxurious.
    d. fascinating.

LITERAL COMPREHENSION PRACTICE Decide if these statements are True (T) or False (F) according to the passage.

_F_ 1. In diners, teenagers learn about new jobs.

_F_ 2. The short-order cook is an escaped convict.

_T_ 3. Diners are places to stop on the open road.

_F_ 4. Diners are important in American life.

_F_ 5. Most people come to diners for the same reason.

CLASS DISCUSSION The following exercise will help you practice spoken English. With several classmates, use the menu provided and take the part of a waiter, waitress, or family member. Order breakfast, lunch, dinner, or a snack.

M E N U

Sandwiches

BACON, LETTUCE, TOMATO	1.10	ROAST BEEF SANDWICH	2.80
TURKEY AND TOMATO	2.85	GRILLED HAM AND CHEESE	1.60
CHICKEN SALAD	2.25	GRILLED CHEESE	1.20
TURKEY SALAD	2.00	GRILLED HAM AND TOMATO	1.35
TUNA SALAD	2.05	HAMBURGER	1.95
CORNED BEEF	2.35	HAMBURGER DELUXE	2.60
		CHEESEBURGER	2.40

Steaks & Chops

Choice of Cup of Soup of the Day, Chilled Tomato Juice or Grapefruit Juice

SIRLOIN STEAK	8.00	MINUTE STEAK, Mushrooms	7.25
CLUB STEAK	7.00	TWO PORK CHOPS, Applesauce	5.85
GROUND BEEF STEAK, Fried Onions	5.50	RIB EYE STEAK	6.75

Seafood

RAINBOW TROUT	5.50	GRILLED HALIBUT STEAK	5.50
BROILED FRESH RED SNAPPER	5.50	ASSORTED SEAFOOD PLATTER	5.95
FRIED DEEP SEA SCALLOPS	5.25	FISH AND CHIPS	4.75
FRIED FRESH SHRIMP	5.50	HALF DOZEN GOLDEN FRIED JUMBO OYSTERS	5.00

Above served with salad, potatoes and assorted bread basket

Side Orders

Tossed Salad	.70
Cole Slaw	.55
Cottage Cheese	.60
Small Greek Salad	1.50
French Fries	.50
Onion Rings	.85
Potato Salad	.75

Desserts

Pecan Pie	.85
Homemade Pie	.75
Pie a La Mode	1.00
Ice Cream	.65
Cheese Cake	.95
Rice Pudding	.65
Sundae	.85
Applesauce	.60
Fruit Cup	.70

Beverages

Coffee	.40
Tea	.30
Milk	.25
Hot Chocolate	.30
Iced Tea or Coffee	.40
Sanka	.30
Chocolate Milk	.25
Soft Drinks	.35

Breakfast Specials

TWO FRESH EGGS, any style	
with Toast & Jelly	.95
with Fried Ham, Bacon, or Sausage	1.55
PANCAKES,	
with Syrup & Butter	.80
with Fried Ham, Bacon, or Sausage	1.40
ONE EGG	.75

Omelettes

HAM	1.50
HAM AND CHEESE	1.65
MUSHROOM AND CHEESE	1.65
WESTERN	1.65
CHEESE	1.35

Served with Toast and Jelly

We Are What We Eat

PRACTICE READING

A Candy Shop

A candy shop is a lovely place to visit. The counters are filled with an as-
sortment° of chocolates. Some are cream-filled, and some contain sweet
cherries or caramel.° Other counters show different kinds of nuts and dried
fruit and toffees.° Often a candy shop has special treats from foreign countries, such as anise° chocolate wafers from Holland, orange-drop candies
from Israel, or macaroon° chocolates from Germany. For anyone with a
sweet tooth, a candy shop is heaven.

°variety
°a chewy candy
°soft, sugar or molasses
 candies
°a licorice-flavored herb
°an almond or coconut-
 flavored cookie

VOCABULARY EXERCISE   Circle the word that best completes each of
the following sentences.

1. We are watching the bubbling (coffee   toffee   anise) become soft and
   sticky.
2. Chocolates come in many (assortments   boxes).
3. The new (candy   macaroon) shop offers fifty kinds of chocolate.
4. What a (sweet   chewy) tooth you have.
5. Pour some (toffee   anise) over the ice cream for a sweet liqueur *very sweet*
   flavor.   *desert*

LITERAL COMPREHENSION EXERCISE   Decide which choice best completes the sentence. Write the letter on each line.

_c_ 1. You must not count _____ calories/treats _____ in a candy shop.
    a. a sweet-tooth
    b. special treats
    c. calories

_a_ 2. The passage talks about _____ anise _____ chocolate.
    a. anise
    b. raisin
    c. bitter

_c_ 3. A variety of fruit includes _____ raisins and prunes _____
    a. caramels.
    b. chocolate-covered wafers.
    c. raisins and prunes.

_c_ 4. _____ Orange-drop candies _____ are from Israel.
    a. Cream-filled candies
    b. Apricots
    c. Orange-drop candies

_c_ 5. You can enjoy heavenly treats from _____ any candy shop _____.
    a. Canada.
    b. the United States.
    c. any candy shop.

Using the Correct Homonyms   23

CHAPTER 3

UNDERSTANDING LITERAL MEANINGS:
Longer Selections

***

°more than one

In this section you will practice literal comprehension in multiple° paragraph passages. After each passage is a variety of questions: vocabulary, True–False, matching, multiple choice, or completion. Pay attention to new vocabulary words circled in the passages. Vocabulary instruction will appear later on. However, you can work with these vocabulary words as they appear in the selections.

EXERCISE Read the following passages and answer the questions.

°healthful

°healthful
°whitened / °with nutrients
 added
°chemicals used to keep
 food fresh
°relating to a specific
 culture
°large-scale selling

Passage 1 Small neighborhood bakeries are being replaced by large bread factories. As a result, the fine art of making tasty, nutritious° bread is also fading away.

The flour used in making bread is no longer whole and wholesome.° Instead, it is bleached° white, enriched° with unnecessary vitamins, and made flavorless. Added chemicals and preservatives° give it a fresh look.

A few traditional bakeries remain, usually in the ethnic° neighborhoods of larger cities, but even they now use the same kind of flour as the commercial° bakeries do. The old kind of bread, once an important part of our diet, is disappearing.

VOCABULARY EXERCISE Use the words in parentheses ( ) to complete the sentences.

(commercial) 1. _wholesome_ bread is hard to find these days.

(nutritious) 2. _commercial_ bakeries produce most of our bread.

(wholesome) 3. Today's bread is _nutritious_ with vitamins.

(bleached) 4. _enriched_ bread is tasty.

(enriched) 5. _Bleached_ flour is white in color.

(preservatives) 6. Chemicals and _preservatives_ give bread a fresh look.

LITERAL COMPREHENSION EXERCISE Choose the best answer according to the passage. Place your answers on the lines.

We Are What We Eat

___b__ 1. The art of making nutritious bread is
   a. an ethnic tradition.
   b. fading away.
   c. replacing commercial baking.

___c__ 2. Vitamins added to bread
   a. give it a fresh look.
   b. bleach it white.
   c. are unnecessary.

___c__ 3. Commercial bakeries
   a. use old-fashioned flour.
   b. are found in ethnic centers.
   c. use bleached white flour.

___b__ 4. Wholesome bread
   a. was once an important part of our diet.
   b. is enriched with unnecessary vitamins.
   c. was always flavorless.

___a__ 5. Large bread factories
   a. add chemicals and preservatives to bread.
   b. are slowly fading away.
   c. continue the tradition of old-fashioned baking.

Passage 2 Schools are beginning to substitute wholesome foods in place of junk foods° in cafeterias. Instead of colas, they serve juice or milk. Fruits replace cake. They serve balanced meals instead of starch-filled lunches. These starches are nothing but fillers.

°foods with little health value

Some schools are hiring companies to provide balanced lunches for students. There are fewer starchy foods such as bread and spaghetti on the menu. Instead, meat dishes, salads, fruits, soups, juices, and milk are now the main offerings. They are served attractively and provide a varied and balanced lunch.

LITERAL COMPREHENSION EXERCISE Decide if the following statements are True (T) or False (F) according to the passage.

___F__ 1. Students have a choice of colas in most cafeterias.

___F__ 2. Fruits are now replacing balanced meals.

___F__ 3. Schools are offering a substitute to starch-filled lunches.

___F__ 4. Parents are providing the new selection of food.

___T__ 5. Cakes are no longer offered.

LITERAL COMPREHENSION PRACTICE Complete the following statements by selecting the correct answer. Write the letter of your choice on the line.

_a_ 1. Cakes
   a. replace fruit.
   b. are considered junk food.
   c. are a nutritious dessert.

_b_ 2. Lunches now include
   a. hamburgers and spaghetti.
   b. fruit and milk.
   c. cake and burgers.

_c_ 3. Starch-filled lunches
   a. contain fruit and salad.
   b. are wholesome and filling.
   c. fill you up.

_c_ 4. Companies provide lunches for
   a. parents.
   b. restaurants.
   c. students.

_b_ 5. What is replacing cake in the cafeteria?
   a. juice
   b. fruit
   c. milk

Passage 3 Americans eat too much fat, and the problem with fat is that it is fattening. Ounce for ounce, fat contains twice as many calories as protein and carbohydrates° do. Being overweight is one of the most common health problems in the United States. Nearly one out of every three Americans is overweight or obese.° Obesity increases the risk of many serious diseases, including heart disorders and diabetes.°

°foods made of sugar and starch

°extremely fat

°a disease of too much sugar in the blood

°a kind of bean

We can cut down on our fat intake in a number of ways. For one thing, we can replace fatty meats like beef and pork with leaner meats like veal and chicken. We can eat smaller portions, too. We can also use more vegetable sources of protein, such as peas, beans, lentils,° nuts, potatoes, and rice. Finally, we can use low-fat dairy products such as skimmed milk and pot cheese in place of whole milk and high-fat cheeses. Even a small change in our fat intake can make an enormous difference in our general health over a period of years.

VOCABULARY EXERCISE Choose the best word in parentheses ( ) to complete each statement. Circle that word.

1. People should eat smaller (sizes   portions).
2. (Obese   Thin) people should be concerned about their health.
3. Too much fat in the diet causes body (health   problems).
4. It is easy to (replace   intake) fats in our diet.
5. (Foods   Fats) contain twice as many calories as proteins.

LITERAL COMPREHENSION EXERCISE Answer the following statements by putting True (T) or False (F) on the lines.

T 1. Fat contains twice as many calories as sugar.

T 2. Obesity is related to serious diseases.

T 3. One-third of all Americans are overweight.

F 4. Only large changes in fat intake can affect our health.

T 5. Smaller servings of meat can reduce fat intake.

F 6. Whole milk products usually have low-fat content.

F 7. Veal and chicken are high in fat content.

T 8. Chicken is a good replacement for fatty meats.

T 9. Vegetables are a good source of protein.

F 10. Being overweight is not a cause for concern.

Passage 4 Fast-food is becoming a way of life in America. There are pizza shops, hamburger stores, fish and chips stores, and a variety of take-out places. They sell such foods as tacos, egg rolls, papaya drinks, and cookies.

Take the hamburger places, for example. Pedro and his family want a fast burger dinner. Will they have to search for a quick meal? To their surprise, there are four places within a two-block area.

Pedro's father isn't sure which one is the best. He asks, "What are the burgers at Joe's Burger Palace like?" Only one person knows. Jorge says, "They are okay." So they all agree to go there. He is right, and the family gets a quick, good meal. They are finished in half an hour and have plenty of time for their evening's plans.

LITERAL COMPREHENSION EXERCISE Decide whether each statement is True or False based on the passage. Write "T" or "F" on the line.

F 1. Pedro knows Joe's Burger Palace.

F 2. Pedro's family wants a slow, relaxed dinner.

T 3. Only Jorge eats at Joe's.

F 4. Pedro's father says, "They are okay."

F 5. There are two burger places to choose from.

T 6. The family does not want a slow dinner.

T 7. Pedro is a member of the family.

F 8. The family has much afternoon shopping to do.

F 9. It only takes one half hour to find a place to eat.

F 10. The family does not go to a burger place.

LITERAL COMPREHENSION PRACTICE Complete the following statements by choosing the best answer according to the story. Place your answers on the lines.

_c_ 1. Who says, "What are the burgers at Joe's Burger Palace like?"
  a. Pedro
  b. Jorge
  c. Pedro's father

_a_ 2. Who is surprised to find so many burger places?
  a. Pedro's family
  b. Pedro and his father
  c. Jorge and his father

_b_ 3. The story does not mention
  a. pizza.
  b. roast beef.
  c. cookies.
  d. fish.

_c_ 4. Which of the fast-foods do they find quickly?
  a. tacos
  b. pizza
  c. burgers
  d. fish and chips

IDIOM EXERCISE The term fast-food is used several times in the story. Examples are given. Can you now define fast-food?

1. Fast-food means: _popular food + fast_

2. Two fast-foods I enjoy are _Hamburger_ and _Pizza_.

3. Explain why you enjoy each of the fast foods. _Hamburger is fast + good tast Pizza also._

Passage 5 The hamburger is the most popular food item in the United States. Every year Americans consume° billions of them. They are sold in expensive restaurants and in humble° diners. They are cooked at home on the kitchen stove or over a barbecue grill in the backyard. Why are they so popular?

First, a hamburger is extremely easy to prepare. It is nothing more than a piece of ground beef, cooked for a few minutes. Then it is placed in a sliced bun. Nothing could be simpler. Even an unskilled cook can turn out hundreds of them in an hour.

°eat
°modest

Besides that, the simple hamburger can be varied in many ways. You can melt some cheese on top of the beef to create a cheeseburger. You can also add some grilled bacon for an interesting flavor contrast. In addition, you can garnish° the hamburger with other things such as lettuce, tomato, °decorate onion, mushrooms, avocado, pickles, hot peppers, ketchup, relish, mayonnaise, mustard—or whatever you wish!

VOCABULARY EXERCISE Name several garnishes you like on:

PIZZA   HOT DOGS   ICE CREAM CONES

LITERAL COMPREHENSION EXERCISE According to the passage, are the following statements True or False? Write "T" or "F" on the line.

_F_ 1. Hamburgers are mainly cooked on barbecues.

_F_ 2. Hamburgers are put in buns before cooking.

_F_ 3. Almost anyone can easily prepare thousands of hamburgers per hour.

_F_ 4. Lettuce, tomato, and onion make a tasty cheeseburger.

_T_ 5. Humble diners serve hamburgers.

_T_ 6. Hamburgers are the most popular food in the United States.

_T_ 7. Hamburgers need a short time for cooking.

_T_ 8. Billions of hamburgers are eaten every year.

_F_ 9. The plain hamburger is ungarnished.

_F_ 10. You can put anything on a hamburger.

LITERAL COMPREHENSION PRACTICE Show your understanding of the story by filling in the correct response.

1. _Every year Americans_ consume billions of hamburgers.

2. Hamburgers are _____ simple _____ to fix.

3. _Cheese burger_ is a simple hamburger garnish.

4. A good contrast to cheeseburgers is a hamburger with _lettuce_ _and tomato_ .

5. Garnished hamburgers are sold in _fast-foods_ .

Seasoning the American Palate°

°sense of taste

People from other countries often find American food dull and tasteless. In their countries, they use a variety of seasonings, such as garlic, chili powder, oregano, and ginger to flavor their foods. Americans, however, use few spices besides salt, pepper, and ketchup to liven up their lunches and dinners.

There are also differences in the kinds of foods served at these meals. An American dinner often consists of a large portion of meat with a few smaller portions of vegetables. Many foreigners prefer a well-seasoned portion of grains and vegetables and a little meat.

°people who plan healthful meals

Now, however, the American diet is being attacked by nutritionists.° They say that we eat more meat, especially fatty beef, than is good for us. They also say that we should eat more grains and vegetables.

As a result, Americans are trying foods of other nations. In more and more American cities, people find not only Chinese and Italian restaurants, but also Lebanese, Mexican, Korean, and Japanese restaurants. In the

We Are What We Eat

future such foods as bean curd,° stuffed grape leaves, and tacos° will become as American as apple pie.°

°an oriental soybean vegetable product / °a folded Spanish pancake
°typically American

VOCABULARY EXERCISE Circle the word or words that make the sentence correct.

1. You make meals (<u>tasty</u>   tasteless) by adding spices.
2. (<u>Liven up</u>   Apple pie) the tasteless vegetables.
3. (<u>Hamburgers</u>   Tacos) are American favorites.
4. (Beef   <u>Oregano</u>) is on the spice shelf.
5. A good Mexican dish is (bean curd   <u>tacos</u>).

LITERAL COMPREHENSION EXERCISE Use the information in the passage to decide which answer best completes the statement. Write the letter on the line.

_a_ 1. Soon ~~stuffed grape leaves~~ will be as American as apple pie.
    a. stuffed grape leaves
    b. hamburger
    c. steak

_c_ 2. Two seasonings used by most Americans are
    a. salt and chili.
    b. oregano and ketchup.
    c. pepper and ketchup.
    d. garlic and salt.

_d_ 3. Who criticizes American diets?
    a. teenagers
    b. Americans
    c. doctors
    d. nutritionists

_d_ 4. Experts say that
    a. Americans eat too many vegetables.
    b. Americans should eat more beef.
    c. fatty beef is good for us.
    d. Americans eat too much beef.

LITERAL COMPREHENSION PRACTICE Use the information in the passage to complete these sentences.

1. _People from other countries_ feel that American food is dull.

2. A large helping of meat is common in ___ _American_ ___ dinners.

3. ___ _Many foreigners_ ___ prefer vegetables and grains as the main part of the meal.

4. Americans eat too much ___ _fatty_ ___ beef.

Understanding Literal Meanings   31

5. Spices used by Americans include _____ *pepper* _____ and salt.
6. Spices used by foreigners include _____ *ginger* _____ and garlic.
7. According to nutritionists, _____ *the American diet* is not good for you.
8. Foreigners prefer _____ *vegetable* _____ to meat.

WRITING PRACTICE On separate paper, write ten sentences about foods from your country.

WRITING PRACTICE Choose two of the following main idea sentences and write a list of details for each. Then turn the main idea and the list into a paragraph. Write the paragraphs on separate paper.

MAIN IDEA SENTENCES

Many American foods are popular in foreign countries.
Eating on an airplane is not pleasant.
In my country different foods are prepared for different holidays.
Many popular American foods are fattening.
The college cafeteria is an unpleasant place to eat lunch.
My diet consists of many healthful (or non-healthful) foods.

UNIT II
BEING, BELONGING, BECOMING:
Getting Together in America

Photo by Eugene Luttenberg. Reprinted by permission of Queensborough Community College.

All over the world people have special customs and forms of behavior. The sentences, paragraphs, essays, and exercises in this unit will help you to develop your reading and dictionary skills, and at the same time, describe many aspects of how Americans live. You will learn how they celebrate holidays, how they socialize, what activities they enjoy, and how interested they are in ways of self-improvement.

DISCUSSION

What are some of the special customs in your country? What are some important holidays you celebrate? How are American customs and behavior similar to those of people in other countries? Have you found any new interests in the last few years?

INITIAL READING

Better and Better

In America, self-improvement is a national pastime. Every year, more and more Americans spend their leisure° time trying to improve themselves in one way or another.

One popular form of self-improvement is the search for physical fitness. Thousands of Americans who never exercised are now out on the streets, jogging in fashionable° running suits and expensive sneakers. They boast° of how many miles they run each day and of how many pounds they lose each week. Others are turning to swimming, tennis, dance, and the martial arts° to improve their physical fitness.

Instead of running around the park in the morning or evening, other Americans are studying yoga° or are meditating° quietly in their homes. They are seeking to improve themselves by finding peace and tranquility.°

Adult education is another form of self-improvement. After a hard day's work, many Americans take evening courses at a local high school or college. There they can study a variety of subjects. Often these people are preparing to return to the job market or trying to qualify themselves for better jobs. A mother busy raising her children might attend night school to learn secretarial skills. A secretary might return to study accounting. Some retired people go back for the education they missed at an earlier age.

°free time

°stylish / °praise oneself

°skills of self-defense

°exercises to attain physical and mental well-being / °doing exercises in concentration
°peacefulness; quiet

QUESTIONS

1. Are any of these activities helpful to others? _____

2. Do you enjoy any of the activities mentioned? _____

3. How do you spend your leisure time? _____

CHAPTER 4

UNDERSTANDING TOPICS

* *
*

In Unit I you wrote lists of details for main idea sentences. Now you will have a chance to create topics for lists of details. Look at the picture.

QUESTIONS

1. List the items in the picture. _____

   Running out in the street

   Tennis

   baseball

2. Each of these items is a type of ___*exercises*___.

3. ___*Sports*___ is the topic of this picture.

Identifying the Topic

The topic is the name of the group to which all the items belong. Good comprehension depends on recognizing the topic in whatever you read.

Look at the following list. All the items on the list except one are specific items. One is not a specific item but, rather, the topic that includes the others. Circle it.

> practicing yoga
> jogging
> swimming
> jumping rope
> (exercises)

The topic that includes the others is "exercises." All the other items—"practicing yoga," "jogging," "swimming," and "jumping rope"—are types of exercises. "Exercises" is the general **subject** or **topic** that includes all other items on the list.

> The **topic** is the name of the group to which all of the items belong.

EXERCISE   One item in each list is the topic. Circle it. The first one is done for you.

New Hampshire	toasters	exams
Massachusetts	irons	papers
(New England states)	vacuums	discussions
Rhode Island	blenders	(classwork)
Maine	can openers	exercises
Vermont	(appliances)	quizzes
Connecticut		
hitting a ball	(lounge chair)	textbook
(playing baseball)	bench	novel
striking out	sofa	nonfiction
pitching a fast ball	couch	mystery
walking	chairs	(books)
hitting a foul	rocker	biography
(jewelry)	New York	pediatricians
bracelet	Idaho	radiologists
anklet	California	(doctors)
earring	(states)	cardiologists
cuff link	New Mexico	orthopedists
charm	Florida	psychiatrists
pin	Washington	

PRACTICE What is the topic of the following? _Three kinds of dancing._

Naming Topics

In the previous exercises, the topic was included in each list or was given in the pictures. In the following exercises, only the details are presented. Each of the details in the list is a part of a general subject. Look at each item or detail in the following example.

EXAMPLE

> Christmas
> Easter
> Halloween

QUESTION What do all of these have in common? _____

_____

"Christmas," "Easter," and "Halloween" are all holidays. The topic of the list is holidays. The word "holidays" includes all of the details in the list.

EXERCISE Consider the following groups of details. Decide what each group of details has in common. Write the topic for the details in each group on the line. The first one is done for you.

1. sports
   bowling
   soccer
   tennis

2. _American Cars._
   Chevrolet
   Dodge
   Ford

3. _American manufacturers_
   General Motors
   Ford Motor Company
   American Motors

4. _Professions or occupations_
   law
   accounting
   medicine

5. _Liquor_
   martini
   scotch sour
   gin and tonic

6. _Shopping_
   suit
   dress
   shoes

7. _Distractions_
   movies
   concerts
   theater

8. _Exercises_
   jogging
   swimming
   martial arts

9. _Physical_
   EST
   meditation
   yoga

PRACTICE Make up a topic for each of the following lists. Make sure that each item fits the subject you choose.

1. _Dances_
   disco
   ballroom
   ballet

2. _Schedule_
   9:00 to 5:00
   9:00 to 3:00
   Mon. to Fri.

3. _Mental education_
   politeness
   thoughtfulness
   patience

4. *Meal time* (handwritten)
8:00 A.M.
12:00 noon
6:00 P.M.

5. *Christmas decoration* (handwritten)
fir tree
tinsel
ornaments

6. *Credit card* (handwritten)
American Express
Master Card
VISA

PRACTICE Write a topic for each group of details. Make sure each item on the list is part of the topic.

1. *Hobbits* (handwritten)
chess
stamp collecting
astronomy
bridge

2. *celebrations* (handwritten)
weddings
proms
graduations
engagements

3. *Partys* (handwritten)
cocktail
surprise
anniversary
birthday

4. *Cars auto* (handwritten)
station wagon
sedan
convertible
jeep

5. *Workers* (handwritten)
printer
carpenter
plumber
mechanic

6. *Houses* (handwritten)
split level
bungalow
ranch
colonial

7. *Apartment* (handwritten)
studio
penthouse
one bedroom
duplex

8. *American holidays* (handwritten)
Thanksgiving
Christmas
Easter
Columbus Day

9. *Lovers* (handwritten)
kissing
hugging
smiling
holding hands

10. *Dances* (handwritten)
disco
hustle
waltz
tango

11. *Circus* (handwritten)
acrobats
clowns
lion tamers
high-wire per-
    formers

12. *School Courses* (handwritten)
evening classes
correspondence
    courses
craft workshops
independent studies

PRACTICE Consider what the following people are talking about. Can you tell what the topic of each conversation is? Write the topic on the line.

1. Juan and Maria are discussing intersession, finals' week, orientation, and midterms. They are discussing _____.

2. Jean is telling someone about typewriters, ditto machines, computers, and dictaphones. She is telling him about *short hand* (handwritten).

3. The class is discussing democracy, communism, monarchy, fascism, and dictatorship. The class is discussing *history* (handwritten).

Selecting the Correct Topic

Look at the list of details on the right and decide what they have in common. Choose the topic that includes all the details in the list and put a check next to it.

EXAMPLE

TOPIC	DETAILS
___ American holidays	1. Thanksgiving
___ parades	2. Mother's Day
___ holidays	3. July Fourth

"Holidays" is too broad an answer because each of the details is specifically an American holiday. Although each of these American holidays usually has a parade as part of the celebration, "parades" is one small part of the holiday. That answer is too specific. The correct answer is "American holidays." Each detail—"Thanksgiving," "Mother's Day," and "July Fourth"—is an example of an American holiday.

> When **selecting a topic,** make sure that the topic includes all the details in the group. Do not choose a topic that is either too general or too specific.

EXERCISE Read each list of details. Choose the topic that includes all the details in the list and put a check next to it. The first one is done for you.

TOPIC	DETAILS
1. ✔ American political parties	Liberal
___ worldwide political parties	Democrat
___ movements	Republican
2. ___ affairs	bride
✔ weddings	maid of honor
___ members of a wedding party	best man
3. ___ airlines	Eastern
✔ American airlines	TWA
___ planes	United

4. _✓_ international airlines   Alitalia

 _____ airlines   Pan American

 _____ planes   El-Al

5. _✓_ children   scraped knees

 _✓_ childhood events   a new tooth

 _____ teenage problems   fist fights

6. _____ improvements   deep-knee bends

 _✓_ exercises   push-ups

 _____ gymnastics   sit-ups

7. _____ cities   Atlantic City

 _✓_ vacation beaches   Las Vegas

 _____ gambling casinos   Acapulco

8. _____ religions   Cherokee

 _✓_ Indians   Apache

 _____ American Indian tribes   Sioux

9. _____ New York State   Syracuse

 _✓_ U.S. cities   Albany

 _____ N.Y.S. cities   New York

10. _____ naming bridges   ribbon cutting

 _____ gatherings   ground breaking

 _____ dedications   breaking bottles of champagne

PRACTICE Choose the best topic for each group of details on the right. Be sure that the topic is neither too broad nor too specific. Check each correct answer. The first one is done for you.

TOPIC	DETAILS
1. _✓_ celebrations	birthday
_____ dates	anniversary
_____ yearly parties	graduation

2. ✓ drinking places   singles' bars

     ____ businesses   saloons

     ____ Saturday entertainment   nightclubs

3. ____ school programs   Little League

     ✓ children's organizations   Boy Scouts

     ____ boys' clubs   girls' clubs

4. ____ buildings   arena

     ____ racing   stadium

     ✓ sports areas   track

5. ✓ diet plans   counting calories

     ____ exercises   Weight Watchers

     ____ eating   low carbohydrate

6. ✓ baseball equipment   bat

     ____ toys   ball

     ____ catcher's equipment   mitt

PRACTICE Match the details on the right with the correct topics on the left. Next to each detail write the number "1" if it is a dessert or the number "2" if it is a type of soda.

TOPIC	DETAILS
1. Desserts	2 sherbet
	2 cola
2. Sodas	1 cream
	1 cake
	1 cookies
	1 pudding
	2 ginger ale

CHAPTER 5

USING THE DICTIONARY TO IDENTIFY PARTS OF SPEECH

* *
*

Using the dictionary is an important skill to develop. Read the dialogue between Suly and Maria.

MARIA: Suly, I'm learning so many new things about English each day. I can hardly keep track of them all.

SULY: It's difficult at first, but you'll get used to it. Are you having any trouble with your classwork?

MARIA: Well, just a little. Professor English suggested that I use a dictionary to help me better understand the new words I come across.

SULY: He's given you some very good advice. The dictionary has been so helpful that I still carry it after all these months.

MARIA: Maybe you can help me then. When I look at an entry in my dictionary, there are usually many symbols and abbreviations I don't understand. I'm sure I could use the dictionary better if I knew what the abbreviations mean.

SULY: Let's look at an entry together. Here is a good example:

fast[1] (fast, fäst), *adj.* **1.** moving or able to move, operate, function, or take effect quickly; quick; swift; rapid: *a fast horse; a fast pain reliever.* **2.** done in or taking comparatively little time: *a fast race.* **3.** (of time) indicating in advance of the correct time, as a clock. **4.** adapted to, allowing, productive of, or imparting rapid movement: *a hull with fast lines.* **5.** characterized by unrestrained conduct or lack of moral conventions. **6.** characterized by extreme energy or activity, esp. in the pursuit of pleasure. **7.** resistant: *acid-fast.* **8.** firmly fixed in place; not easily moved. **9.** held or caught firmly, so as to be unable to escape or be extricated. **10.** firmly tied, as a knot. **11.** closed and made secure. **12.** such as to hold securely: *to lay fast hold on a thing.* **13.** firm in adherence; loyal: *fast friends.* **14.** permanent, lasting, or unfading: *a fast color.* **15.** deep or sound, as sleep. **16.** *Photog.* **a.** (of a lens) able to transmit a relatively large amount of light in a relatively short time. **b.** (of a film) requiring relatively little exposure to attain a given density. **17.** *Horse Racing.* **a.** (of a track condition) completely dry. **b.** (of a track surface) very hard. **18. pull a fast one,** *Slang.* to play an unfair or unscrupulous trick; practice deceit. —*adv.* **19.** tightly; firmly: *to hold fast.* **20.** soundly: *fast asleep.* **21.** quickly, swiftly, or rapidly. **22.** in quick succession. **23.** in a wild or dissipated way. **24.** ahead of the correct or announced time. **25.** *Archaic.* close; near: *fast by.* **26. play fast and loose.** See **play** (def. 56). [ME; OE *fæst;* c. D *vast,* Icel *fastr* firm, G *fest;* akin to FAST[2]] —**Syn. 1, 2.** fleet, speedy. See **quick.** **5.** dissolute, immoral; wild. **8.** secure, tight, firm. **9.** inextricable. **13.** faithful, steadfast. **14.** enduring. **19.** securely, tenaciously. **23.** recklessly, wildly. —**Ant. 1, 2.** slow. **8.** loose.
fast[2] (fast, fäst), *v.i.* **1.** to abstain from all food. **2.** to eat only sparingly or of certain kinds of food, esp. as a religious observance. —*n.* **3.** an abstinence from food, or a limiting of one's food, esp. as a religious observance; fasting. **4.** a day or period of fasting. [ME *faste(n),* OE *fæstan;* c. G *fasten,* Goth *fastan,* Icel *fasta*]
fast[3] (fast, fäst), *n.* a chain or rope for mooring a vessel [ME *fest* < Scand; cf. Icel *festr* mooring rope; akin to FAST[1]]

Suly: As you can see, there are different kinds of information included in the entry. In addition to the correctly spelled word divided into syllables, the entry consists of the pronunciation, definitions, and etymology or history of the formation of the word from other languages. Certain terms in the entry appear in their abbreviated form. They are the parts of speech, the terms of special usage, or historical terms. Dictionaries usually contain a key or explanation of the abbreviations near the beginning.

Maria: That's a lot to remember.

Suly: Let's look at them separately. We can start with the abbreviations. They are the lowercase letters that are usually followed by a period and are recognized or accepted shortened versions of longer words.

Maria: Let's use the entry you just showed me.

fast¹ (fast, fäst), *adj.* **1.** moving or able to move, operate, function, or take effect quickly; quick; swift; rapid: *a fast horse; a fast pain reliever.* **2.** done in or taking comparatively little time: *a fast race.* **3.** (of time) indicating a time in advance of the correct time, as a clock. **4.** adapted to, allowing, productive of, or imparting rapid movement: *a hull with fast lines.* **5.** characterized by unrestrained conduct or lack of moral conventions. **6.** characterized by extreme energy or activity, esp. in the pursuit of pleasure. **7.** resistant: *acid-fast.* **8.** firmly fixed in place; not easily moved. **9.** held or caught firmly, so as to be unable to escape or be extricated. **10.** firmly tied, as a knot. **11.** closed and made secure. **12.** such as to hold securely: *to lay fast hold on a thing.* **13.** firm in adherence; loyal: *fast friends.* **14.** permanent, lasting, or unfading: *a fast color.* **15.** deep or sound, as sleep. **16.** *Photog.* **a.** (of a lens) able to transmit a relatively large amount of light in a relatively short time. **b.** (of a film) requiring relatively little exposure to attain a given density. **17.** *Horse Racing.* **a.** (of a track condition) completely dry. **b.** (of a track surface) very hard. **18. pull a fast one,** *Slang.* to play an unfair or unscrupulous trick; practice deceit. —*adv.* **19.** tightly; firmly: *to hold fast.* **20.** soundly: *fast asleep.* **21.** quickly, swiftly, or rapidly. **22.** in quick succession. **23.** in a wild or dissipated way. **24.** ahead of the correct or announced time. **25.** *Archaic.* close; near: *fast by.* **26. play fast and loose.** See **play** (def. 56). [ME; OE *fæst;* c. D *vast,* Icel *fastr* firm, G *fest;* akin to FAST²] —**Syn. 1, 2.** fleet, speedy. See **quick.** **5.** dissolute, immoral; wild. **8.** secure, tight, firm. **9.** inextricable. **13.** faithful, steadfast. **14.** enduring. **19.** securely, tenaciously. **23.** recklessly, wildly. —**Ant. 1, 2.** slow. **8.** loose.
fast² (fast, fäst), *v.i.* **1.** to abstain from all food. **2.** to eat only sparingly or of certain kinds of food, esp. as a religious observance. —*n.* **3.** an abstinence from food, or a limiting of one's food, esp. as a religious observance; fasting. **4.** a day or period of fasting. [ME *faste(n),* OE *fæstan;* c. G *fasten,* Goth *fastan,* Icel *fasta*]
fast³ (fast, fäst), *n.* a chain or rope for mooring a vessel [ME *fest* < Scand; cf. Icel *festr* mooring rope; akin to FAST¹]

Suly: Let me ask you some questions to see whether you understand the entry.

1. What is one meaning of "fast" used as an adjective? _____
   quick, rapid

2. What is one meaning of "fast" used as an adverb? _quickly_
   firmly, tightly

3. What is one meaning of "fast" used as a verb? _____
   to abstain from all food

4. What is one meaning of "fast" used as a noun? _____

a chain or rope for mooring a vessel

The meaning of "fast" as an adjective appears first in the entry. It is followed by the meaning of "fast" as an adverb, then as a verb, and finally as a noun.

5. What is the connection between the order of meanings in the entry and the use of the word "fast" in English? _____

_____

MARIA: Could it be that people use the word "fast" most often as an adjective? The word "fast" is probably used as an adverb less frequently, and so on.

SULY: Great! You're really beginning to see the relationship between the parts in a dictionary entry.

Some abbreviations in a dictionary entry show the function of a word in terms of the **parts of speech.** They also show how the form and meaning of a word change as its function changes. Abbreviations provide help in using the word correctly in a sentence and in determining which part of speech is necessary for the definition.

SULY: Here is a chart I made up to help remember the dictionary definitions. All dictionaries have these abbreviations, but they may vary somewhat.

DICTIONARY ABBREVIATIONS INDICATING PARTS OF SPEECH

ABBREVIATION	MEANING	ILLUSTRATION IN A SENTENCE
adj.	adjective	He is a **fast** runner.
adv.	adverb	She held **fast** to the oars.
v.i. or v. intrans.	verb intransitive	The teenager lost five pounds after she **fasted** for a week.
n.	noun	He remained on a **fast** until the doctor ordered him to eat.

Remember that, in English, the same form of a word can function differently in sentences.

MARIA: Are those the only abbreviations in an entry?

SULY: No, there are many more. Here are some other important ones.

DICTIONARY ABBREVIATIONS INDICATING PARTS OF SPEECH

ABBREVIATION	MEANING	ILLUSTRATION IN A SENTENCE
conj.	conjunction	I will ski **and** I will skate.
interj.	interjection	**Oh!** I didn't see you standing there.
pl.	noun plural	In the morning I do **exercises**.
prep.	preposition	This morning, I jogged **around** the park.
pron.	pronoun	**She** studied yoga for six years.
v.t. or v. trans.	verb transitive	**Read** this sign.

EXERCISE Write a sentence illustrating the stated function of each of the words.

	WORD	FUNCTION	SENTENCE
1.	strong	adj.	He is a strong men
2.	quickly	adv.	I must make quickly my test.
3.	but	conj.	I want to buy a beautiful car but I dont have enough money
4.	blah!	interj.	
5.	club	n.	
6.	clubs	n. pl.	
7.	after	prep.	I eat dinner after take a shower.
8.	him	pron.	I told him "don't do that again"
9.	enlist in	v.i.	
10.	join	v.t.	

PRACTICE READING

Antonia

Antonia left Athens and came to America to make her fortune.° She wanted to be a famous actress, so she went to live in Hollywood, California.

At first, Antonia had very little money, so she was forced to watch every penny° while making the rounds° of movie agents' offices. For over a year, she worked only in small parts. She found life extremely hard. She had to take buses or walk everywhere, and she ate only one meal a day. Even though she worked nights as a waitress, Antonia could not really make ends meet.°

°become rich; make a lot of money

°budget carefully; have no extra expenses or luxuries / °visiting in search of jobs

°spend only what you earn

Using the Dictionary to Identify Parts of Speech   **47**

Suddenly, one day, the star of the film became ill, and the director asked Antonia to take the part. Her acting was superb.° After the premiere° of the film, she became an overnight success.° Everyone gave her rave notices,° and she received many offers for future starring roles.

Since then, Antonia has changed her whole way of life. Now she wears expensive furs and drives a Rolls-Royce. She lives in a twenty-seven room mansion in Beverly Hills, with seven servants. All her needs are cared for. For Antonia, America was truly the land of streets paved with gold.° Through her hard work, she had earned the fame she desired so much.

°excellent; outstanding /
°first performance of a film
 or play
°instant recognition as a
 star/°good reviews of a
 performance

°a place where riches
 await you

DICTIONARY EXERCISE Using your dictionary, give the correct meaning for each of the following words.

1. agent   *n.*   _____

2. act   *n.*   _____

      v.   _____

3. star   *n.*   _____

      v.t.   _____

4. film   *n.*   _____

      v.   _____

IDIOM EXERCISE The meanings of six idioms used in the story are in the right-hand column. Look back at the story to understand the meaning of each idiom. Match the idiom with its meaning.

Idiom	Meaning
____ overnight success	1. good reviews of a performance
____ making the rounds	2. budget carefully; have no extra expenses or luxuries
____ rave notices	3. spend only what you earn
____ make ends meet	4. instant recognition as a star performer
____ watch every penny	5. calling on employers in the hope of getting a job
____ streets paved with gold	6. a place where riches await you

LITERAL COMPREHENSION EXERCISE Antonia came to America and did many things here. Look at the following list. Which things did Antonia do? Mark "Yes" next to the things she did and "No" next to the things she did not do.

_____ 1. Antonia paved the streets with gold.

_____ 2. She saw all the movie agents in town.

_____ 3. She received poor reviews for her performance.

_____ 4. She drove a Cadillac.

_____ 5. She became an overnight sensation.

_____ 6. She was careful of her spending before she became a star.

_____ 7. She went home to Athens.

_____ 8. She starred in films for one year.

_____ 9. She ate three good meals every day before she became a star.

_____ 10. She took buses or walked after she became a star.

CHAPTER 6

NAMING TOPICS
IN PARAGRAPHS

* *
*

In previous sections, you identified topics for lists of details and also created your own topics. In those exercises you were the writer. Now you are going to read someone else's paragraphs.

EXAMPLE

In modern society, it is often difficult for people to meet one another. Men and women of similar interests or needs may be separated from one another by their jobs or by great distances. As a result, they must advertise. Open any newspaper, and you will find personal ads of all sorts. Lonely men and women advertise for husbands, wives, lovers, traveling companions, and partners both in business and in personal relationships. There are also ads for services that provide computer-chosen dates or escorts. Are you looking for someone new in your life? Try looking in the personal ads section of your newspaper. It is filled with opportunity.

QUESTIONS

1. What are the details in this paragraph?

_____

_____

_____

_____

2. What general topic does each detail talk about? _____

_____

The details are "Open any newspaper, and you will find personal ads of all sorts"; "Lonely men and women advertise for husbands, wives, lovers, traveling companions, and partners". "There are also ads for services that provide computer-chosen dates or escorts." Each of these details refers to the general topic of **meeting people through the newspaper.**

athiest = person doesn't beleive.
goth

The **topic of a paragraph** includes all the details that the paragraph discusses.

EXERCISE Read each paragraph. What is the common subject or topic of the sentences? Write the topic on the line.

Paragraph 1 Topic ___ *Blind date* ___
Blind dates can be exciting and nerve-wracking.° Each person can only imagine what the other will be like. Will they both enjoy the same kinds of food, music, and movies? What will their conversation be like? Will he be good-looking? Will she be pretty? All these thoughts go through their minds as the doorbell rings.

°tension-causing

Paragraph 2 Topic ___ *Giving cards: Valentine's Day* ___
On February 14, we celebrate Valentine's Day. On this day, men, women, and even boys and girls present each other with cards or notes saying, "Be My Valentine." Through the cards they show affection for someone they care about. There are cards for mothers, fathers, best friends, and even teachers. Believe it or not, there are even cards for pets. Everyone looks forward to receiving a card on Valentine's Day.

Paragraph 3 Topic ___ *Secular holidays* ___
Most holidays in the United States are secular° rather than religious. We celebrate important people, movements, and events in our history. For example, we celebrate the birthdays of such figures as George Washington, Abraham Lincoln, and Martin Luther King, Jr. On the Fourth of July, we celebrate the signing of the Declaration of Independence, and we celebrate the end of the First and Second World Wars on Memorial Day. The struggle of workers to organize is celebrated on Labor Day. Americans take a special pride in all the holidays that they celebrate.

°non-religious

close thorough your clothes

Paragraph 4 Topic ___ *Annual vacation* ___
Every year millions of Americans look forward to the largest holiday of all: a two- or three-week summer vacation! During these periods of freedom, they try to forget their jobs and escape for a little recreation. Families pack clothes, toys, and sometimes utensils° and furniture into the car. They head for a bungalow,° hotel, wilderness campsite,° or beach house. What could be more fun! Everyone is out of doors enjoying the sun and fresh air. No one thinks about school or work. The annual vacation is a time to forget the weekly routines and to celebrate relaxation.

°tools used for a specific purpose
°a cottage / °an outdoor area for temporary living

Paragraph 5 Topic _____

°days reserved for special emotions, tenderness or feeling

Compared with the number of religious holidays, the number of sentimental holidays° celebrated by Americans is large. Americans celebrate people on Mother's Day and Father's Day, events on Labor Day and Memorial Day, products during National Pickle Week, and animals during Be Kind to Your Pet Week. In recent years the trend has been to add more and more holidays. Americans may eventually find themselves celebrating a different holiday every day of the year.

PRACTICE You have had practice in determining the topic for a paragraph. Now practice the same skill in the following paragraphs.

Paragraph 1 Topic _____

°make attractive and charming

°body positions showing the male form / °bend
°body positions showing the female form
°participants in an event
°freedom movement

Many people glamorize° beautiful women and strong men. All over the world there are yearly contests for Miss Universe, Mr. America, Miss Galaxy, Mr. Body Beautiful, and many more. Men parade down runways, strike masculine poses,° and flex° their muscles. Women also parade down runways, sing, dance, and strike feminine poses° in bathing suits and gowns. The contestants° ignore protests from women's and men's liberation° groups and continue to seek top prizes and a crown for their good looks.

Paragraph 2 Topic _____

There has been a recent revolution in footwear. I see people wearing sneakers instead of leather shoes. This is not because they are cheaper than leather shoes. My sneakers are more expensive than my street shoes. In fact, some of my sneakers are made of leather. I have special sneakers for jogging, walking, and playing basketball or tennis. My children wear sneakers instead of shoes to school every day. I am more comfortable in sneakers. I have concluded that sneakers are today's most popular shoes.

Paragraph 3 Topic _____

On my first trip to the United States, I was surprised to see how casually everyone dressed. Men went to work wearing slacks and shirts. Very few wore business suits or ties. I saw women and men wearing jeans to theaters, restaurants, and offices. Even teachers wore jeans to school. At first I thought this was true in just one city, but I found it was the same in almost every city and town that I visited. Dungaree jeans and denim° were the common American uniform.

°a strong cotton material used to make jeans

Paragraph 4 Topic _____

Many Americans are volunteering° their time and efforts to help others. These volunteers do unpaid work in schools, hospitals, and charity organizations. Some of them help raise funds for nonprofit° organizations such as medical research hospitals, cultural associations, and social change groups. Others work with underprivileged,° sick, or handicapped° people. These volunteers often work long hours, get no pay, and receive little or no recognition for their efforts. All over the United States there are thousands of these silent heroes working each day for the good of others.

°working for free

°not in business to make money

°socially or economically deprived / °physically disabled

Paragraph 5 Topic _____

Last week I made my shopping rounds° without getting out of my car. Monday morning I drove around looking for gas. I passed the carwash and noticed a Monday-only special.° I drove in. Next, I withdrew $50.00 from my account at the drive-in bank. I shopped with this money. I bought milk and cheese at the drive-in dairy. On Tuesday and Wednesday I went to the drive-in cleaners, drive-in photo store, and finally, the drive-in hamburger place. I ended the week at the drive-in movie. Never once did I leave my car. I may have saved a lot of walking, but I spent a lot of money on gas.

°travel to different stores

°reduced prices offered only on Monday

Selecting the Correct Paragraph Topic

You have just practiced the skill of naming a paragraph topic. In each exercise, you first read the paragraph, decided what the details had in common, and then wrote a topic. Now, you will practice the skill of choosing the best topic from among several given topics. This is more difficult than writing your own topic. You must be sure that the topic you choose is not too general nor too specific. Read this paragraph.

EXAMPLE

°tolerate

Last year I started preparing for Christmas in July. I began shopping in the summer. I could not bear° the Christmas rush. At Christmas there are too many lines, too many people pushing and shoving, and too many crowded stores. In July there is no snow, no Santa, and no cold weather, but otherwise, everything is perfect for starting my Christmas shopping.

QUESTION What is the best topic for this paragraph?

1. Christmas shopping
2. Crowded stores
3. Early Christmas Shopping

Answer _____

Answer 1, "Christmas shopping," is too general. This paragraph specifically gives the reasons for starting Christmas shopping as early as July. Answer 2, "Crowded stores," is too specific. Crowded stores are mentioned in the paragraph, but they are presented as one reason for shopping in July. The best topic for this paragraph is answer 3, "Early Christmas shopping." All the sentences discuss reasons for starting Christmas shopping early. This topic includes all the details in the paragraph.

> The **topic of a paragraph** includes all of the details that the paragraph discusses.

EXERCISE Read the following paragraphs and choose the best topic. Write the number of your answer on the line.

°announced publicly

°the acting out of historical events

Paragraph 1 July Fourth is America's annual birthday. It is called Independence Day. America proclaimed° its independence from England on July 4, 1776. Traditionally, Americans celebrate the Fourth by having parties, barbecues, picnics, parades, and reenactments° of the struggle for freedom. At night there are displays of fireworks. The skies are filled with bursts of color.

The best topic for this paragraph is

1. Fireworks explode in the night skies

2. Fourth of July celebrations

3. Independence

Answer _____

Paragraph 2   Like many Americans I am a nut for cleanliness.° I bathe twice a day, brush my teeth after every meal, comb my hair many times, and carry all sorts of makeup and perfumes to use at the office. Like me, each day millions of Americans deodorize° every part of their bodies with the newest and best-smelling products on the market. As a result, items like deodorants are no longer considered drug items. They now have a special place in the cosmetic areas of stores. Most Americans are now worshippers° of the clean body, mind, and life, and I am too.

°overly concerned with being clean

°conceal body odors with chemical products

°those who show great devotion for something or someone

The best topic for this paragraph is

1. Deodorants

2. Good health is wonderful

3. Americans are superclean

Answer _____

Paragraph 3   John Wayne died, but he did not leave us. America and the world lost a film giant when he died, but his spirit and his film contributions will remain for years to come. Wayne's appeal was great in all countries. He represented the tough hero, the frontiersman,° and the adventurer. Even when the odds were against him,° Wayne stood up and fought. He was the strong father who protected his children, his troops, and his friends. He spoke out in films and in politics for his beliefs. Even though people disagreed with him, they respected his integrity.°

°someone who lived in the American wilderness
°he was in a difficult situation

°honesty; uprightness

The best topic for this paragraph is

1. John Wayne

2. John Wayne's death

3. John Wayne's appeal

Answer _____

Paragraph 4   Have you ever seen children in costumes and masks ringing doorbells and crying out, "Trick or Treat?" This is a very common sight every year on October 31. The children are celebrating Halloween. On this holiday children dress up as witches, ghosts, goblins,° and other characters. They ring doorbells and ask for a piece of candy or some bubble gum or

°evil spirits

even a few pennies. If they do not receive a treat, they may play a trick on the person or on the house.

The best topic for this paragraph is

1. Spooks, goblins, and witches

2. An annual holiday on October 31

3. Celebrating Halloween

Answer _____

PRACTICE Here are additional paragraphs for practice in choosing a topic. Once again, select the best topic for the paragraph and write your answer on the line.

Paragraph 1 Last week, I became the best volunteer in town. I got a phone call from the secretary of the local school board. He asked me to organize a food drive on my block, and I accepted. Then I agreed to donate used clothing to the bazaar.° I volunteered to spend five hours at the bazaar's clothing booth. I became chairperson° of the cake sale for the hospital building fund. In addition, I drove the children to Little League° practice. I am now eligible° to enter the Volunteer-of-the-Year Contest.

°a sale of various articles to raise money for an organization
°someone in charge of a meeting
°baseball teams for children
°qualified

The best topic for this paragraph is

1. Becoming a volunteer

2. Helping

3. How to win a contest

Answer _____

Paragraph 2 A month ago I wrote to a computerized° dating service. I wanted to find the perfect mate, and I decided to give the computer a chance to help me. I filled out a five-page questionnaire° about my social, educational, physical, and religious background. Within two weeks the dating service sent three names to me. Each one of these people was supposed to be a match for me. Can you guess what happened when I met my first date?

°controlled by electronic computers

°a written or printed list of questions used in gathering information

The best topic for the paragraph is

1. Filling out a questionnaire

2. Going out on dates

3. Using a computerized dating service

Answer _____

Paragraph 3   Years ago people started programs to keep America beautiful. They placed ads in magazines and ran special commercials on television. Everyone applauded this wonderful cause. However, the effort did not last. Many began to let their streets get dirty again. Some let their towns and cities get run-down too. Some even showed a lack of respect for their public buildings and parks. Still the majority of Americans agreed to a continuation of the "Keep America Beautiful" program and work hard to keep it alive.

The best topic for this paragraph is

1. Keeping America beautiful

2. American's differing values

3. Filth in the cities

Answer _____

PRACTICE   Read the following conversations aloud. After reading the dialogue, decide what the conversation is about. Write the topic of the conversation on the line following each dialogue.

Conversation 1

ALEX: Let's check the paper to see what's playing.
MIKE: There's something starting at 8:00.
ALEX: Is it close enough to walk to, or should we take the bus?
MIKE: We can walk there. We'll buy candy and drinks before we go in. It's cheaper to buy those things at the candy store.
ALEX: How late will we get out?
MIKE: According to the time schedule in the newspaper, it will be over at 11:30.
ALEX: Why is it so late?
MIKE: It's a double-feature. *two movies the same show*

What topic are the boys talking about? _Going to the movie._

Conversation 2

FABIANA: Where are you going this year?
MOHAMMED: I don't have any definite plans yet. I'm looking through brochures° and talking to agents. *person*   °small booklets
FABIANA: Do you like warm southern climates or do you prefer the cold northern areas?
MOHAMMED: I prefer the warm climates so I can relax and enjoy the sun. Besides, it reminds me of home.

What are the two people talking about? _Vacation plans._

Naming Topics in Paragraphs   **57**

Conversation 3

°tap a baseball lightly with a bat

°a baseball thrown with a twist

REGGIE: What did you say?

BILLIE: I said play ball! Run on any hit!

REGGIE: He'll try to bunt° the next one.

BILLIE: Don't take any chances. The play is to second base.

REGGIE: I have to watch their pitcher. He has a fast curve ball.°

The topic of this conversation is _Play baseball._

Conversation 4

°the female leader of a marching band

°large flat vehicles carrying an exhibit in a parade

MOTHER: Watch the band members marching and playing. Look at the drum majorette.°

CHILD: I can't see! There are too many people in front of me.

MOTHER: Stand near the curb. Then you'll see everything.

CHILD: Now I see the band! I see the beautiful floats° and funny clowns.

What is the topic of this conversation? _Marching band_

CHAPTER 7

USING THE DICTIONARY
TO DETERMINE RESTRICTIVE
LABELS, SYNONYMS,
AND ANTONYMS

* *
*

MARIA: There are some words in *italics* in the dictionary entries that I have been using. Every time the italics appear, they are followed by an unusual definition of the word.

SULY: Those *italicized* words signal a restrictive° use of the word that °limited you are defining. When you see an *italicized* word numbered among the definitions, consider it carefully. It signals a special meaning of the word apart from the word's general definition.

MARIA: But, Suly, isn't a general definition of a word enough?

SULY: Usually, a general definition of a new word is all you need. But many words have additional meanings that relate to a particular subject. Also, some words have important informal or even slang meanings. To understand these special meanings, you must know the *italicized* and abbreviated signals to those meanings. Let me give you an example.

EXAMPLE

The word **pitch** has several general meanings. Here are two from a typical dictionary entry.

1. to throw or toss **2.** to erect or set up (a tent)

The word **pitch** also has several restrictive uses. Here are some of those uses.

3. *Baseball. a.* to deliver or serve the ball to the batter *b.* to fill the position of pitcher in the game **4.** *Music.* to set at a particular pitch (a particular tonal standard) **5.** *Obs.* to arrange **6.** *Informal. a.* to contribute *b.* to begin work vigorously **7.** *Accoustics.* the apparent predominant frequency sounded by an accoustical source **8.** *Cricket.* the central part of the field **9.** *Slang. a.* a high-pressured sales talk *b.* a specific plan of action (angle).-**SYN.** see **THROW**

MARIA: This is becoming complicated.

SULY: I think that placing the definitions of some of the restrictive labels on paper will help you understand them more easily.

RESTRICTIVE DICTIONARY LABELS AND THEIR MEANINGS

TERM	MEANING
Archaic	rare in present usage
Informal	casual use in spoken and written English
Obs., Obsolete	no longer used no used anymore
Slang	very informal usage in vocabulary and idioms, characterized by socially unacceptable vocabulary and idiomatic expressions
-SYN., Synonym	a word having the same or nearly the same meaning as another word
-ANT., Antonym	a word having the opposite or nearly opposite meaning to another word

A LIST OF ADDITIONAL TERMS

Cricket
Baseball
Tennis
Eccles., Ecclesiastical
Judaism
Theol., Theology
Brit., British,
chiefly British
U.S.
U.S. Army

Acct., Accounting
Anat., Anatomy
Archaeol., Archaeology
Archit., Architecture
Art
Banking
Biol., Biology
Bot., Botany
Chem., Chemistry
Economics
Elect., Electricity
Geol., Geology
Gram., Grammar

Hist., History
Journalism
Law
Med., Medicine
Mil., Military
Music
Pharm., Pharmacology
Photog., Photography
Physics
Printing
Psychol., Psychology
Rhet., Rhetoric
Sociol., Sociology

EXERCISE Each of the following words has a restrictive meaning in its dictionary entry. Look up each word in your dictionary and in the blank space write one special or restrictive meaning.

WORD	RESTRICTIVE LABEL	MEANING
1. strike	*Geology*	_____
		_____
	Law	_____
		_____
	Baseball	_____
		_____
	Printing	_____
		_____
	U.S. Army	_____
		_____
2. stress	*Phonetics*	_____
		_____
	Physical	_____
		_____
3. honor	*Cards*	_____
		_____
	Golf	_____
		_____
	-SYN.	_____
		_____
4. agree	*Chiefly Brit.*	_____
		_____
	-SYN.	_____
		_____
	-ANT.	_____
		_____

5. neat   *Slang* _____

                  _____

               Informal _____

                  _____

               (of liquor) _____

6. bite   *Slang* _____

                  _____

               Archaic _____

                  _____

               Angling _____

                  _____

               Machinery _____

7. break   *Archaic* _____

                  _____

               Law _____

                  _____

               Pool _____

                  _____

               Music _____

               Electricity _____

                  _____

               Informal _____

                  _____

               -SYN. _____

                  _____

               -ANT. _____

                  _____

               Boxing _____

                  _____

Jazz _____

8. blow   Slang _____

    U.S. Slang _____

    Music _____

    Photography _____

    Archaic _____

9. large   Obsolete _____

    Nautical _____

10. gas   Physics _____

    U.S. Informal _____

    Slang _____

CHAPTER 8

RECOGNIZING TOPICS:
Longer Passages

⁎
⁎

In this section, you will practice writing topics for longer reading passages. Each selection is followed by exercises in vocabulary, dictionary, and literal comprehension. Read each passage and decide on its topic. Remember, the topic must cover the entire selection. First, read the passage and write the topic on the line; then answer the questions.

°ideas about right and
wrong that influence a
person's actions
°praises
°in trouble

Selection 1 One of the great problems that troubles the conscience° of each individual is the question of getting involved. Everyone applauds° the efforts of those few citizens who risk their personal safety by coming to the aid of those in distress.° Their photographs appear on the front pages of newspapers, and they are justly admired. Despite this, many people turn away from personal involvement. They pretend not to notice others in trouble.

What will happen when you are faced with the choice between helping a person in distress or turning away? Will you jump into the situation, or will you knowingly turn your back saying, "I don't want to get involved?"

Topic _____

DICTIONARY EXERCISE Using your dictionary, find the correct meaning for each word.

WORD	SPECIAL USE	MEANING
1. back	*Sports*	_____
		_____
	adj.	_____
		_____
	Nautical	_____
		_____
	n.	_____
		_____

2. distress   *n.*   _____

                          _____

         Law   _____

                          _____

         v.t.   _____

                          _____

         -ANT.   _____

                          _____

LITERAL COMPREHENSION EXERCISE   Answer these questions according to facts in the passage.

1. What do few citizens risk? _____

2. Whose photographs appear in the newspapers? _____

_____

3. What choice do you have when you see someone in trouble? _____

_____

4. Why might a person need your help? _____

5. If a person is in trouble, you will be faced with

    a. a chance to help him.

    b. two possible choices: to help or to stay away.

    c. a chance to stay away from the trouble.

    d. admiration.

    Answer _____

Selection 2   Americans need to do everything bigger and better than anyone else. Look at the cars that they drive. Each year new, small models appear. In no time, what happens to them? They grow into medium-sized versions of the original car. Every time a new compact° car appears, it soon   °fitting into a small space
stretches into a larger, shinier one.

    Also, Americans have a reputation for spending a lot on luxury° items.   °expensive; not necessary
Every time a new appliance appears on the market, Americans have to
have it. Similar versions are developed with different buttons and gadgets°   °an item that does a
attached, and these too are snapped up.° People sometimes buy one, two, or   specific job
more of the same appliance because the newer versions are bigger, better,   °bought quickly
and more attractive.

Topic _____

DICTIONARY EXERCISE   Using your dictionary, find the correct meaning for each word listed.

1. model   *v.i.*   _____

                    _____

              v.t.   _____

                    _____

2. luxury   *Archaic*   _____

                    _____

              n.   _____

                    _____

3. medium   *Biology*   _____

                    _____

              Painting   _____

4. button   *Slang*   _____

                    _____

              Fencing   _____

              Boxing   _____

              v.t.   _____

                    _____

              n.   _____

                    _____

LITERAL COMPREHENSION EXERCISE   Answer each question based on information in the passage.

1. What kinds of cars appear every year? _____

2. What prices do Americans tend to pay for items? _____

_____

3. What does a compact car turn into? _____

4. Why do people purchase similar versions of new gadgets? _____

_____

5. How many television sets do you have?_____

6. Do you agree that most Americans spend more money and buy newer and bigger items than other people do? Explain. _____

_____

TOPICS EXERCISE Answer these questions according to the passage.

1. What is the topic of the first paragraph? _____

2. What is the topic of the second paragraph? _____

Selection 3 The cocktail party° is a curious° American event. Millions of people follow this ritual° every year, yet many complain about how awful or frightening it can be.

For some, the cocktail party is a pleasant way of getting together with friends for a social evening of drinks, food, and conversation. For others, it means spending time with strangers, talking about dull subjects, and viewing behavior that is often distasteful.°

At some point in the evening, one or more of the guests usually drinks too much and reaches a state of intoxication.° Some people say or do things that they may regret° later. Most guests do not reach this stage. They simply loosen up,° laugh, and become instant friends.

Toward the end of the party, guests begin to leave, some with pleasant memories, and others with the beginnings of the headache that will soon become tomorrow's hangover.° Each drifts° homeward knowing that next week it will be someone else's turn to host a cocktail party.

°a social gathering where alcoholic drinks are served / °strange and unusual
°the observance of a set form for a ceremony

°unpleasant; offensive; disagreeable

°being drunk
°feel sorry about something said or done
°relax

°the unpleasant after-effect of heavy use of liquor / °moves slowly

Topic _____

DICTIONARY EXERCISE Using your dictionary, find the meanings for each word listed.

1. host   *n.*   _____

                         _____

       -SYN.   _____

                         _____

2. party   *Informal*   _____

                         _____

        Slang   _____

                         _____

        adj.   _____

                         _____

Law	_____
	_____
3. stage	*Radio*	_____
	_____
	v.t.	_____
	_____
	Geology	_____
	_____
	n.	_____
	_____
4. guest	**-SYN.**	_____
	_____
	Informal	_____
	_____
	Zoolology	_____
	_____
	n.	_____
	_____

LITERAL COMPREHENSION EXERCISE Here are some statements based on information in the story. If they give the same information as the story, write Same (S). If they are different from the story, write Different (D).

____ 1. All the guests at the party leave with pleasant memories.

____ 2. One or more guests usually get drunk.

____ 3. Cocktail parties can be dull and distasteful.

____ 4. Cocktail parties offer drinks, food, and pleasant talk.

____ 5. The parties usually happen once a year.

____ 6. Everyone loves the American cocktail party.

____ 7. Most people have nothing to regret after the party.

Selection 4 An afternoon ballgame in the United States is like no other sporting event. Fans arrive in the early morning with radios, television sets, lunches, and binoculars.° Usually, they attend warm-up° and team practice. Next comes the feast. The parking lots are filled with picnickers

°special lenses for seeing distances / °a practice exercise before an actual game

Being, Belonging, Becoming

eating lunches in station wagons or at tables. When they finish everything they have brought with them, they buy hot dogs, soda, beer, popcorn, pretzels, ice cream, and peanuts.

Television sets and radios give instant replays and report what's going on. At the same time, the ballgame is going on in front of them. Why do they also need a photographic image? Some fans behave in very unusual ways. Suddenly a six-foot chicken dances through the stands to cheers and waving banners. In some ballparks, the show-off° may dress up as a dancing lion or a man with his hair dyed orange. Cheers of delight greet these performers. In addition, youngsters and grownups parade banners and signs stating their love for player 7 or for the whole team. It's no wonder that the fans are sometimes more fun to watch than the game.

°someone who performs to attract attention

Topic _____

DICTIONARY EXERCISE Using your dictionary, find the meaning of each word listed.

1. fan   *Agriculture* _____

　　　　　　　　　　　　　　_____

　　　　v.t. _____

　　　　　　　　　　　　　　_____

2. banner   *adj.* _____

　　　　　　　　　　　　　　_____

　　　　n. _____

　　　　　　　　　　　　　　_____

3. player   *n.* _____

　　　　　　　　　　　　　　_____

　　　　n. _____

　　　　　　　　　　　　　　_____

　　　　n. _____

　　　　　　　　　　　　　　_____

4. game   *Archaic* _____

　　　　　　　　　　　　　　_____

　　　　Informal _____

　　　　　　　　　　　　　　_____

LITERAL COMPREHENSION EXERCISE   Use information from the passage to complete these sentences.

1. A _____ might be waving a banner in the stands.

2. Youngsters and grownups alike love _____ .

3. Fans arrive in the morning carrying _____ .

4. Five things eaten by viewers in the stands are _____

   _____ , _____ ,

   _____ , _____ , and

   _____ .

5. Three things eaten by baseball fans before the game are _____

   _____ , _____ , and

   _____ .

6. Television sets give _____ of the game.

CHAPTER 9

USING THE DICTIONARY
TO IDENTIFY ETYMOLOGY

.
*

The dictionary can be used for more than locating the correct meanings, parts of speech, and special uses of words. Read the following dialogue between Suly and Maria about the meanings of symbols and language abbreviations found in some dictionaries.

MARIA: I've been using the dictionary to help me identify the functions of words. Now I know which meaning and form to use in writing, and I know which meaning can help me to understand the passages I read. But there are some abbreviations, for example, L, Gk, and ME, that I don't understand.

SULY: I can explain them to you. Those abbreviations stand for the languages from which words come. Many words in English have come from other languages such as Latin (L), Greek (Gk), or even an earlier version of English like Middle English (ME). This was what the English people spoke and wrote around 1300.

MARIA: Let's look at an entry. It might be fun to trace the history of some words.

SULY: Here's a good example. It has most of the symbols you'll need to know.

    order [ME *ordre* < OF < L *ordin-* (*s. of ordō*) row, rank, regular arrangement]

SULY: Let's take this step by step. First, the etymology or word history is included in brackets [ ]. The first language listed after the beginning bracket is the language that gives us the word in a form closest to its current form.

    order [ME   comes to us from Middle English

Next, the symbol < tells you from what language the Middle English meaning comes.

    order [ME < OF   comes from Old French to Middle English to us

If you follow the symbol < to the end of the bracket], you will find the language in which the first form of the word appeared.

    order [ME < OF < L]   comes from the Latin to Old French to Middle English to us

Finally, the words written in *italics* tell the form of the word in the language from which it comes. The abbreviations "s." and "pl." tell you whether your word comes from English through a singular or plural word form. This information is usually placed in parentheses ( ) within the bracket.

[　(*s.*)　]

MARIA: Let me try to put all of this together with the example you gave me.

order [ME *ordre* < OF < L *ordin-* (*s.* of *ordō*) row, rank, regular arrangement]

The word "order" comes into English through the Middle English word *ordre*. *Ordre* is descended from an Old French word that comes from the singular form *ordō* of the Latin root *ordin-*, meaning row, rank, or regular arrangement. How was that?

SULY: Great! Let's list some of these symbols on paper.

UNDERSTANDING ETYMOLOGY SYMBOLS IN THE DICTIONARY

SYMBOL OR ABBREVIATION	MEANING
ME	Middle English
F	French
OF	Old French
L	Latin
Gk	Greek
<	descended from
=	equivalent to
?	origin unknown
[ ]	brackets used to set off the derivation of the word
( )	parentheses to set off an explanation within the brackets.

Dictionaries usually have an **Etymology Key** near the front of the book. In this key you will find a complete listing of the symbols used in that dictionary. Also included in dictionaries is a **Language Key.** The key contains a listing of all languages used to show the history of words in that dictionary.

MARIA: How can an understanding of etymology help me?

SULY: In lots of ways! First, it's interesting to know how words comes into English. For example, I discovered that many words comes into English from my grandparents' native languages. Second, I found this skill helpful when I began studying prefixes, suffixes, and roots. You'll probably be learning them in the next few weeks, and you will see what I mean.

EXERCISE Read each dictionary entry and answer the questions about it.

1. **universal** [ME *universal* < MF < L *universal* (is)]

   a. What is the original source of **universal?** _____

   b. Through how many languages did **universal** come before it entered current usage? _____

2. **manipulation** [F = *manipule* handful (of grains, etc; see Maniple) + -ation -ATION]

   a. From what language is **manipulation** descended? _____

   b. What was the meaning in that language? _____

3. **colony** [late ME *colonie* < L *colōnia*]

   a. In what language does the earliest form of **colony** appear? _____

   b. From what language does **colony** come into current usage? _____

4. **hover** [ME *hoveren*, freq. of *hoven* to hover < ?]

   a. What is the earliest origin of the word **hover?** _____

5. **splurge** [? b. SPLASH and SURGE]

   a. What language gives us the word **splurge?** _____

6. **dialogue** [ME *dialoge* < OF < L *dialog* (us) < Gk *diālogos*]

   a. What is the oldest form of the word **dialogue?** _____

   b. What is the form of the word that comes directly into current use? _____

FINAL PRACTICE READING

Untitled

Yesterday my Uncle Jose told us that he was taking the whole family on a car trip across the United States. He said this, and it made us happy indeed.

74   *Being, Belonging, Becoming*

He also told us to pack a lot of clothes, for we would be traveling across very hot deserts and cold mountains.

Two years ago Uncle Jose made this trip by himself. As a newcomer to America, he wanted to experience the great American adventure of going West. First, he went to the Carolinas and saw the red clay of the fields. Then he went to Texas, and he visited an oil tycoon.° The tycoon lived in a forty-two room house with gold faucets° in every one of its twelve bath rooms.

°a wealthy and important person
°a metal fixture controlling the flow of water

Later Uncle Jose drove to Colorado, and he took a canoe ride down the Colorado River through the Grand Canyon. It was a dangerous and scary ride, but he said that climbing up the steep paths of the canyon on a donkey was more frightening.

Two weeks after that, he arrived at Death Valley, a desert region. An Indian guide from a nearby reservation° took him across the sandy plains to the California coast.

°a piece of land set aside for the Indians

For Uncle Jose, California was the most exciting place of all. The panorama° of beautiful beaches, the giant redwood forests, and the homes of the movie stars were brand new sights for him.

°a wide view of the scenery

After listening to all my uncle's descriptions, my mother told me something interesting. She knows that Uncle Jose is going west to show us the beauty of America, but she says that he has also caught the American fever of being on the move.° Uncle Jose, she says, has discovered that he's an American, too!

°traveling; moving about constantly

VOCABULARY EXERCISE Look at the definitions of the new words in the story. Using the definitions, decide if the words are used correctly in the following sentences. Write "Yes" if the word is used correctly or "No" if it is used incorrectly.

_____ 1. The **tycoon** borrowed a quarter to pay for his newspaper.

_____ 2. Turn off the **faucet** to stop the dripping.

_____ 3. The **reservation** was dotted with teepees.

_____ 4. I can't see through this small **panorama.**

DICTIONARY EXERCISE Use your dictionary to locate the meanings of each word listed.

1. beach   *n.*   _____

_____

Nautical   _____

_____

2. oil   *Painting* _____

       adj. _____

       v.t. _____

       n. _____

3. pack   *Hunting* — a group of animals

       Slang _____

4. guide   **-SYN.** _____

       -ANT. misguide.

5. brand   *Archaic* _____

       n. _____

       v.t. _____

LITERAL COMPREHENSION EXERCISE Answer the statements True (T) or False (F) according to the story.

____ 1. Uncle Jose thought that the most exciting place was Colorado.

____ 2. As a newcomer, Uncle Jose traveled across the United States.

____ 3. The most frightening event was a canoe ride down the Colorado River.

____ 4. Uncle Jose saw redwood trees, red clay fields, and gold faucets.

____ 5.. The story tells of taking the family to the Carolinas, Texas, Colorado, Death Valley, and California.

LITERAL COMPREHENSION PRACTICE Match the place Uncle Jose visited with the sight he saw there.

_____ Texas   1. Grand Canyon

_____ Death Valley   2. beaches and redwoods

_____ Colorado   3. red clay fields

_____ California   4. desert

_____ Carolinas   5. the oil man's house

GENERAL COMPREHENSION EXERCISE Answer the questions according to the information in the story.

1. What is the best title for the entire selection? _____

_____

2. What is the topic of paragraph 2? _____

3. What is the topic of paragraph 4? _____

WRITING PRACTICE Write four details for each main idea sentence provided below.

Main Idea Sentence 1 There are several popular sports in my country.

_____

_____

_____

_____

Main Idea Sentence 2 School can help me improve myself in many ways.

_____

_____

_____

_____

Main Idea Sentence 3 Buying on credit has advantages.

_____

_____

_____

_____

Main Idea Sentence 4 Before I attended college, I had many incorrect ideas about it.

_____

_____

_____

_____

Now select two of your lists and write a paragraph for each on a separate sheet of paper. Be sure to indent the first sentence and to follow the margins.

UNIT III
AMERICAN PLAYGROUNDS

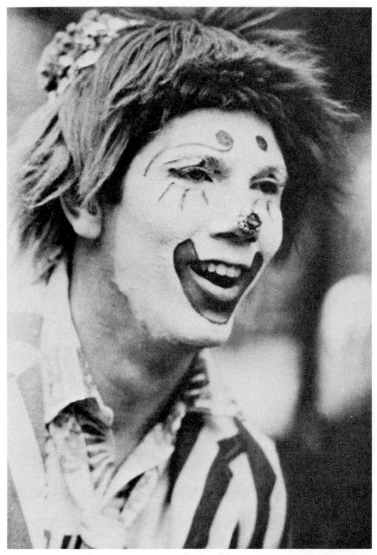

Reprinted by permission of Harry Greenberger.

Americans spend their leisure time in many different ways. In this unit you will read about some typical American pastimes. In addition, you will have a chance to improve your skills in identifying main ideas and using the dictionary to locate word meanings.

DISCUSSION

Do you think most Americans prefer playing sports or being spectators? How do people that you know use their leisure time?

INITIAL READING

American Playgrounds

°is a more powerful force than

An amusement park is a place where fantasy triumphs over° reality. We can't take the afternoon off to visit one since our next class will begin in just a few minutes. But, while we are waiting for class to start, let's use our imagination and build our own amusement park.

First, we will need rides, and the rides must be exciting. Let's begin with a roller coaster, with a long, steep climb to a dizzying height—and a sudden, terrifying drop. Everyone who rides it will shriek with excitement. We will also need a ferris wheel for the timid,° a brightly painted carousel for children, and bumper cars for aggressive° drivers.

°easily frightened
°bold; active; energetic

We will need more than rides to keep people happy. Let's build a tunnel of love and a haunted house. Let's set up shooting galleries and games of chance where everyone can win fabulous prizes. And, of course, we must have plenty of refreshment stands where people can grab a quick snack before running off to the next attraction.

Have we forgotten anything? Have we left anything out? Do we need a swimming pool? Should we have a crazy house, where down is up and up is down? Is there anything that **you** want to include in our amusement park?

QUESTIONS

1. Have you ever been to an amusement park? _____ What was your experience like? _____

_____

2. How do people in other countries spend their leisure time? _____

_____

3. How do you spend your leisure time? _____

_____

CHAPTER 10

RELATING TOPICS AND
MAIN IDEA SENTENCES

* *
*

In Unit II you identified and selected topics in paragraphs and short passages. When you named the topic, you named the group to which all the details belonged. Now you are ready for the next step, expanding the topic of a paragraph into a main idea sentence. Consider the following.

EXAMPLE

A. Circus side shows
B. Side shows at the circus are filled with unusual attractions.

A lady with tattoos° all over her body parades around. Siamese twins° sing to large crowds. One brave man swallows a flaming sword. A man throwing knives at a lady frightens the crowd.

°pictures or designs permanently marked on the skin
°twins physically joined together from birth

QUESTIONS

1. Is A or B the better choice for an opening sentence in the paragraph?

   _____

2. Explain your reasons. _____

   _____

3. What does B tell you about A? _____

   _____

Choice B is the better opening sentence for the paragraph because it is a complete sentence, it names the topic, and it tells something general about the topic.

EXAMPLE

Side shows at the circus are filled with unusual attractions. A lady with tattoos all over her body parades around. Siamese twins sing to large crowds. One brave man swallows a flaming sword. A man throwing knives at a lady frightens the crowd.

1. What information does the highlighted sentence give you about the topic? _____

   _____

2. Do the details in the paragraph illustrate (A) Circus side shows or (B) the unusual attractions of circus side shows? _____

The highlighted sentence tells you that circus side shows are "filled with unusual attractions." It tells you something general about the topic "Circus side shows." The details are examples of the unusual attractions of circus side shows. They support the highlighted sentence. The highlighted sentence is called the **main idea sentence.**

> The **main idea sentence** of a paragraph is a statement that the author makes about the topic. The main idea sentence is also a general statement that the author makes about the details in the paragraph. The details support or develop the main idea sentence.

EXERCISE In each of the following exercises, the topic is in the left-hand column. One sentence in the paragraph at the right is the main idea sentence. It is the statement that the author makes about the topic. **Highlight** the main idea sentence in each paragraph.

Topic	Paragraph
1. Lively Discos 1. teenagers 2. 20's + 30's. 3. elderly people	Lively discos attract many people. Teenagers who love to dance spend hours there. People in their twenties and thirties, who enjoy the music and who like to dance, find discos the place to be. Even elderly people like discos.
2. Foreseeing the Future - see ahead.	Many people believe in predictions about the future. Some people read horoscopes° in the newspapers. Others go to fortune tellers. Others have their palms read or consult tarot cards. Still others interpret their dreams to predict the future.
3. Roller Coasters Different actions when we drive a roller coasters	I cannot understand why people go on roller coasters. Strapped into a tiny car, they begin by inching their way up a steep hill. At the top, the car stops for a second and they wait, suspended in midair. Suddenly, they plunge° down the steep tracks all the way to the bottom. They scream, cover their eyes, and hold on tightly. They are terrified. Why do they do it?

°forecasts about the future based on the position of the stars

°drop suddenly

4. Herb's Pet Lamb   Herb is very <u>proud</u> of his pet lamb. Next week, he is bringing his pet lamb to the local fair for the animal contest. He hopes that she will win first prize. Herb feeds her the best food, grooms her, and trains her every day. Many other pets will be in the competition, but only one will win.

EXERCISE   For each paragraph, write the topic on the line and highlight the main idea sentence. The first one is done for you.

Paragraph 1   **Coney Island is again becoming a major tourist attraction.** Once it was the model for most beachside amusement parks, but in the 1960s it lost its popularity. Recently, however, state and local governments have begun to finance its redevelopment. Soon crowds of New Yorkers and tourists will be enjoying Coney Island's rides, shows, beaches, and famous boardwalk again.

Topic: <u>Coney Island</u>

Paragraph 2   There are many exciting things to do at Las Vegas casinos. A crowd gathers to watch a high roller° at the dice table. An experienced blackjack player tries to beat the house° by remembering all the cards played. People spend hours pouring money into the one-armed bandits° in the hope that three-of-a-kind will appear. There are no clocks on the wall, and no one knows the time. They play all day and all night.

°a big gambler
°win
°slot machines

Topic: _____

Paragraph 3   Every spring our block association puts on a block party. The street is closed to traffic for the entire day. Neighbors prepare food, which they sell from their front stoops° or yards. They also display treasures from their basements that they hope to sell on the street. Children play stickball, have their faces painted by local artists, or pester° their parents for money to buy hot dogs, lemonade, and cookies. The money that our block association raises each year from this event is used to help beautify the block or to pay for other activities that the block association sponsors.°

°staircases in front of a house

°bother

°supports

Topic: _____

Paragraph 4   Marie Chen invited me to this year's Chinatown Festival. She says that there will be a 100-foot-long dragon winding° through the narrow streets. The Chen family will sell sparklers and fireworks at the front of their store. People will set them off at one o'clock. Then everyone will dance in the streets and happily celebrate this annual event.

°walking in a curved line

Topic: _____

PRACTICE Read each paragraph, write the topic of the paragraph, and highlight the main idea sentence.

Paragraph 1 County fairs appeal to the entire family. Children are attracted by the ferris wheels and merry-go-rounds. Dad and Grandpa are interested in seeing the livestock exhibits, while Mom and Grandma want to find out if their preserved fruits and vegetables have won a blue ribbon. Later, the entire family will enjoy themselves on the midway,° testing their sharp-shooting° skills or pitching pennies° in the games of chance.

° the main avenue of a carnival or fair
° shooting with the highest level of accuracy / °a game of tossing pennies

Topic: _____

Which of the following expresses the main idea sentence? Check the correct answer.

____ Parents enjoy county fairs.

____ County fairs are purely American events.

____ People of all ages have fun at county fairs.

Paragraph 2 Rodeos in the southwestern part of the United States draw people from all over the country. Tourists come to see modern displays of old-fashioned western skills. In the course of a week, people see steer wrestling,° calf roping,° wild horse riding, and sharp-shooting contests. Modern cowboys still wear ten-gallon hats, cowhide jackets with fringes,° handcrafted leather boots, and real silver spurs.° The spirit of the Old West lives on in the modern day rodeo.

° chasing and tying down a cow in record time / °chasing and tying down a baby cow in record time
° decorative borders
° sharp points on boots used to direct a horse

Topic: _____

Which of the following expresses the main idea? Check that answer.

____ Rodeo people wear expensive western outfits.

____ Rodeos are filled with western excitement.

____ Western towns have a yearly rodeo.

Paragraph 3 There is something for everyone at the circus. Under the big top° there is the greatest assortment of amusements anywhere in the world. The audience can watch a beautiful lady ride a big white horse, a sad clown tumble° in the sawdust,° daredevils° fly on the trapeze° or walk on high wires, and ferocious° lions dance with prancing° elephants. It is really hard to know where to look because all three rings are filled with daring and beautiful acts.

° a circus tent

° perform leaps and somersaults / °powderlike wood chips / °those who perform dangerous acts / °a high circus swing
° extremely wild; savage
° walking proudly on back legs

Topic: _____

Which of the following expresses the main idea? Check the answer.

____ There are attractions for everyone at the circus.

____ The circus has skilled animal acts.

____ Sad clowns perform under the big top.

Understanding Main Ideas

Good comprehension depends on understanding the main idea of a paragraph. This section concentrates on helping you to develop this skill. Read the following paragraph.

EXAMPLE

> The habit of going to the movies is making a big comeback today. For many years people stayed at home and watched television rather than go to the movies. However, new science fiction, war, romance, and spy thrillers have brought people back to the theaters. Once again, Friday and Saturday night audiences are standing on long lines, buying popcorn, and laughing or crying over Hollywood's creations.

QUESTIONS

1. What is the topic of this paragraph? _____

2. What general statement does the author make about the topic? _____

_____

3. What specific details in the paragraph are related to the main idea sentence? _____

_____

_____

The topic of this paragraph is "movies." The main idea sentence is "The habit of going to the movies is making a big comeback today." Each detail tells about the comeback: "people stayed at home for years"; "now we have science fiction, war, romance, and spy movies"; "people are standing on long lines, buying popcorn, and laughing or crying." These details support the main idea sentence.

> The **main idea sentence** is a general statement that the author makes about the topic. This general statement is developed by all the details in the paragraph. All the details support the main idea.

Use the following illustration to help you see the relationship of a main idea and its details. Think of the main idea as an umbrella that covers all the details in the paragraph. This is an easy check to see if you understand and can correctly identify the main idea.

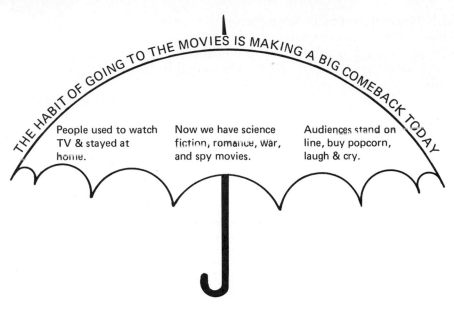

THE HABIT OF GOING TO THE MOVIES IS MAKING A BIG COMEBACK TODAY

People used to watch TV & stayed at home.

Now we have science fiction, romance, war, and spy movies.

Audiences stand on line, buy popcorn, laugh & cry.

EXERCISE Consider the sentences in each group. One of them is the main idea sentence. The other sentences support and develop it. Fill in the umbrella diagram by placing the main idea sentence at the top of the umbrella and the details underneath it.

A lady with tattoos all over her body parades around.
Siamese twins sing to large crowds.
Side shows at the circus are filled with unusual attractions.
One brave man swallows a flaming sword.
A man throwing knives at a lady frightens the crowd.

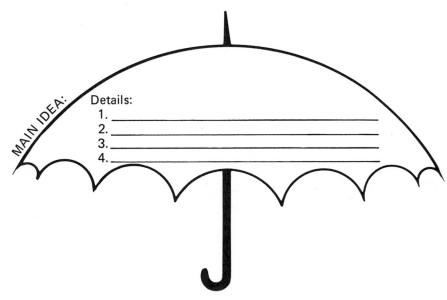

MAIN IDEA:

Details:
1. _____
2. _____
3. _____
4. _____

Relating Topics and Main Idea Sentences   **87**

The float will have "Lasting Peace" as its theme.
Thousands of flowers will cover the sides and the floor.
The peace dove will be made of a dozen white carnations.
The largest item will be two hands joined in friendship, made of carnations, roses, lilies, and daisies.
A Peace Float will be part of the California Rose Bowl Parade this year.

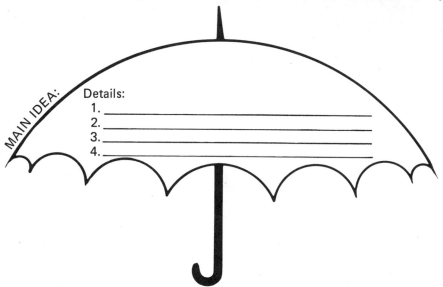

Nightly street parades start the festivities.
Thousands dress in colorful costumes and dance through the streets.
The New Orleans celebration of Mardi Gras is a week of festivities.
Tourists jam every hotel and restaurant in the city.
Jazz bands roam the streets, and people dance along with them.

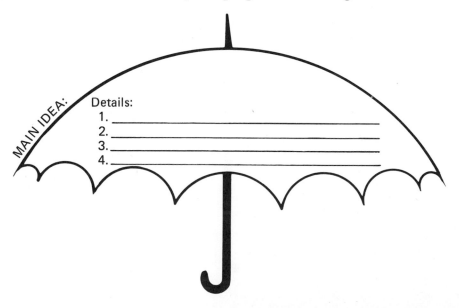

PRACTICE Highlight the main idea sentence in each paragraph.

Paragraph 1 Every year, the World Series provides people all over the world with a true sports spectacular.° Millions of fans watch the two best baseball teams in the United States compete in a best of seven° series. No matter what his or her favorite team is, everyone roots for° one of the teams in the series. Each game is televised in almost every country and offers people from other lands the opportunity to see the best players in action.

°an outstanding event
°four out of seven
°cheers

Paragraph 2 Many small circuses are joining bigger circuses. The small, family-owned circuses no longer find it profitable to travel across the country and play to local audiences. Many of the acts are joining larger organizations and are getting star billing and high salaries. They perform in major cities, attract large crowds of enthusiasts,° and often travel to other countries. The expense of bringing performers, animals, musicians, technicians, and workers to different lands is huge, and family circuses can't meet such expenses.

°supporters; fans

Recognizing the Location of the Main Idea in a Paragraph

QUESTIONS

1. In each of the practice paragraphs, you highlighted the main idea sentence. Where was the main idea sentence located?_____

_____

2. What purpose does each main idea sentence serve in that location?

_____

> When the main idea appears in the **first sentence** of a paragraph, it **introduces** the details in that paragraph.

EXERCISE   Highlight the main idea sentence in each of the following paragraphs. Then list the details that the main idea sentence introduces.

Paragraph 1   Technology is now a major part of the traditional carnival. Years ago carnivals had carousels and ferris wheels, but today they have many sophisticated° rides that throw and pull people in every direction as loud music plays. The few simple games of skill, so much a part of carnivals, have become complex, computerized, electronic games.

°based on advanced technology

The main idea sentence introduces the following details:

_____

_____

_____

Paragraph 2   Circus clowns are trained in special schools. There they learn how to apply makeup for sad or happy faces. They also learn tumbling, falling, juggling, and miming,° all basic to the clown's act. Old-timers help future clowns decide which baggy pants or flowered hat will best suit° their character. The course is difficult, and many will never make it.° Those who do go on to bring laughter to delighted audiences.

°silent imitating by acting out

°be appropriate
°succeed

The main idea sentence introduces the following details:

_____

_____

_____

_____

CHAPTER 11

USING THE DICTIONARY:
Guidewords

⁎

You learned many new words in Units I and II. Now you will learn how the dictionary helps you to pronounce and understand the meanings of new words. Read the following dialogue.

MARIA: Professor English is really a hard teacher. Just look at this assignment.

SULY: What's so hard about that? All you have to do is look up° the meanings of twenty new words.   °locate

MARIA: I started the assignment yesterday and I soon realized that it was taking me forever to find each word. After three hours, I gave up.

SULY: Why did it take you so long?

MARIA: I had to look through every page to find the word I wanted to define.

SULY: Didn't you use the guidewords at the top of each page?

MARIA: What are guidewords?

SULY: **Guidewords** are the two words at the top of every dictionary page. The guideword at the upper left is the first word on the page, and the guideword at the upper right is the last word on the page.

MARIA: I understand that, but how does it help me?

SULY: All the words on the dictionary pages are arranged **alphabetically.** The word that you are looking for will come between the two guidewords at the top.

MARIA: I have to define "complete." Here, use my dictionary.

SULY: Our first step is to skim through the dictionary until we come to the words that begin with "C." Next, we flip the pages until we come to a page with guidewords that are alphabetically close to "complete." Here they are. The closest guidewords are **compass —complex.**

MARIA: Let me see if I understand. You're saying that every word on that page will be alphabetically between **compass** and **complex.** That means my word "complete" should be on that page.

SULY: Right! Look for it. See, there it is—right before **complex**.

MARIA: This means that I don't have to read through every page with a "C" word to find the word I need. That will make the assignment much easier. I guess Professor English isn't so bad after all.

EXERCISE A sample page from a dictionary is on page 93. The guidewords are **slavey—slice.** Use this page to answer the following questions. Check each word that is found on the page.

____ slime	____ slipcover	____ sleigh
____ sloop	____ sleet	____ sleeve
____ slice	____ slick	____ sledge
____ slavey	____ slug	____ sling
____ slow	____ sleeper	____ slob

EXERCISE Here are the guidewords from another dictionary page: **emptily—enclose.** Put a check next to the words defined on that page.

____ endear	____ encourage	____ encore	____ emit
____ encase	____ enamel	____ enchant	____ emulate
____ enact	____ empower	____ endocrine	____ encounter
____ enable	____ endure	____ envelope	____ enclose

PRACTICE Here are several pairs of dictionary guidewords. Write a check next to each word on the right that can be found between the guidewords. The first one is done for you.

GUIDEWORDS

p. 10	**bossy—bounty**	✔ bouncer	____ boss	
		✔ bottle	____ borough	
		✔ bottom	✔ bother	
p. 226	**deep—defense**	____ defend	____ define	
		____ deejay	____ default	
		____ decompose	____ decode	
p. 347	**footless—form**	____ forceful	____ forbid	
		____ foreign	____ football	
		____ forbear	____ foothold	

(practice continues on p. 94)

slav·ey (slā′vē), *n., pl.* **-eys.** *Brit. Informal.* a female servant, esp. a maid of all work in a boardinghouse.
Slav·ic (slav′ik, slä′vik), *n.* **1.** a branch of the Indo-European family of languages, usually divided into East Slavic (Russian, Ukrainian, Byelorussian), West Slavic (Polish, Czech, Slovak, Sorbian), and South Slavic (Old Church Slavonic, Bulgarian, Serbo-Croatian, Slovene). *Abbr.:* Slav, Slav. —*adj.* **2.** of or pertaining to the Slavs or their languages. Also, **Slavonic.**
Slav·i·cist (slä′vi sist, slav′i-), *n.* a specialist in the study of the Slavic languages or literatures. Also, **Sla·vist** (slä′vist, slav′ist).
slav·ish (slā′vish), *adj.* **1.** of or befitting a slave: *slavish subjection.* **2.** being or resembling a slave; abjectly submissive. **3.** base; mean; ignoble: *slavish fears.* **4.** deliberately imitative; lacking originality. —**slav′ish·ly,** *adv.* —**slav′ish·ness,** *n.* —**Syn. 2.** groveling, sycophantic, fawning, cringing. See **servile.** —**Ant. 2.** independent. **3.** exalted.
Slav·ism (slä′viz əm, slav′iz-), *n.* something that is native to, characteristic of, or associated with the Slavs or Slavic. Also, **Slav·i·cism** (slä′vi siz′əm, slav′i-).
Slavo-, a combining form of **Slav:** *Slavophile.*
slav·oc·ra·cy (slā vok′rə sē), *n., pl.* **-cies. 1.** the rule or domination of slaveholders. **2.** a dominating body of slaveholders.
Sla·vo·ni·a (slə vō′nē ə), *n.* a former region in N Yugoslavia. Cf. **Croatia.**
Sla·vo·ni·an (slə vō′nē ən), *adj.* **1.** of or pertaining to Slavonia or its inhabitants. **2.** Slavic. —*n.* **3.** a native or inhabitant of Slavonia. **4.** a Slav.
Sla·von·ic (slə von′ik), *adj.* **1.** Slavonian. **2.** Slavic. —*n.* **3.** Slavic. [< NL *slavonic(us)* = ML *Slavon(ia)* SLAVONIA + *-icus* -IC] —**Sla·von′i·cal·ly,** *adv.*
Slav·o·phile (slä′və fīl′, -fil, slav′ə-), *n.* **1.** a person who greatly admires the Slavs and Slavic ways. —*adj.* **2.** admiring or favoring the Slavs and Slavic interests, aims, customs, etc. Also, **Slav·o·phil** (slä′və fil, slav′ə-). —**Slavoph·i·lism** (slə vof′ə liz′əm, slä′və fil iz′əm, slav′ə-), *n.*
Slav·o·phobe (slä′və fōb′, slav′ə-), *n.* a person who fears or hates the Slavs, their influence, or things Slavic. —**Slav′o·pho′bi·a,** *n.*
slaw (slô), *n.* coleslaw. [< D *sla,* short for *salade* SALAD]
slay (slā), *v.t.,* **slew, slain, slay·ing. 1.** to kill by violence. **2.** to destroy; extinguish. **3.** *Informal.* to affect or impress very strongly; overwhelm, esp. by means of amusement. **4.** *Obs.* to strike. [ME; OE *slēan;* c. D *slaan,* G *schlagen,* Icel *slā,* Goth *slahan* to strike, beat] —**slay′er,** *n.* —**Syn. 1.** murder, assassinate. **2.** annihilate, ruin.
sleave (slēv), *v.,* **sleaved, sleav·ing,** *n.* —*v.t.* **1.** to divide or separate into filaments, as silk. —*n.* **2.** anything matted or raveled. **3.** a filament of silk obtained by separating a thicker thread. **4.** a silk in the form of such filaments. [OE *slǣfan,* c. *slīfan* to split; see SLIVER]
slea·zy (slē′zē, slā′zē), *adj.,* **-zi·er, -zi·est. 1.** thin or poor in texture, as a fabric; flimsy: *a sleazy dress.* **2.** contemptibly low or unimportant. [?] —**slea′zi·ly,** *adv.* —**slea′zi·ness,** *n.*
sled (sled), *n., v.,* **sled·ded, sled·ding.** —*n.* **1.** a small vehicle consisting of a platform mounted on runners for sliding over snow or ice. **2.** a sledge. —*v.i.* **3.** to coast, ride, or be carried on a sled. —*v.t.* **4.** to carry on a sled. [ME *sledde* < MFlem or MLG; akin to G *schlitten,* Icel *slethi.* See SLIDE]
sled·der (sled′ər), *n.* **1.** a person who rides on or steers a sled. **2.** a horse or other animal for drawing a sled.
sled·ding (sled′ing), *n.* **1.** the state of the ground permitting use of a sled: *The snow made a good sledding.* **2.** the conditions under which any task is accomplished. **3.** the act of riding or carrying on a sled.
sledge[1] (slej), *n., v.,* **sledged, sledg·ing.** —*n.* **1.** a vehicle mounted on runners and often drawn by draft animals, used for traveling or for carrying loads. **2.** a sled. **3.** *Brit.* a sleigh. —*v.t., v.i.* **4.** to travel or carry by sledge. [< D (dial.) *sleedse* < *slede,* var. of *sledde* SLED]
sledge[2] (slej), *n., v.,* **sledged, sledg·ing.** —*n.* **1.** See **sledge hammer.** —*v.t., v.i.* **2.** to sledge-hammer. [ME *slegge,* OE *slecg;* c. D *slegge,* Icel *sleggja;* akin to SLAY]
sledge′ ham′mer, a large, heavy hammer wielded with both hands.
sledge-ham·mer (slej′ham′ər), *v.t., v.i.* **1.** to strike, hammer, or beat with or as with a sledge hammer. —*adj.* **2.** like a sledge hammer; powerful; ruthless.
sleek[1] (slēk), *adj.* **1.** smooth or glossy, as hair, an animal, etc. **2.** well-fed or well-groomed. **3.** smooth in manners, speech, etc.; suave. [var. of SLICK[1]] —**sleek′ness,** *n.*
sleek[2] (slēk), *v.t.* to make sleek; smooth; slick. Also, **sleek′en.** [var. of SLICK[2]]
sleek·it (slē′kit), *adj.* **1.** *Scot.* sleek; smooth. **2.** *Chiefly Scot.* sly; sneaky. [< ptp. of SLEEK[2]]
sleep (slēp), *v.,* **slept, sleep·ing,** *n.* —*v.i.* **1.** to take the repose or rest afforded by a suspension of the voluntary exercise of the bodily functions and the natural suspension, complete or partial, of consciousness. **2.** *Bot.* to assume, esp. at night, a state similar to the sleep of animals, marked by closing of petals, leaves, etc. **3.** to be dormant, quiescent, or inactive, as faculties. **4.** to allow one's alertness, vigilance, or attentiveness to lie dormant. **5.** to lie in death: *They are sleeping in their tombs.* —*v.t.* **6.** to take rest in (a specified kind of sleep). **7.** to accommodate for sleeping; have sleeping accommodations for: *This trailer sleeps three people.* **8.** to spend or pass in sleep (usually fol. by *away* or *out*): *to sleep the day away.* **9.** to get rid of (a headache, hangover, etc.) by sleeping (usually fol. by *off* or *away*). **10. sleep in,** (of domestic help) to sleep at the place of one's employment. —*n.* **11.** the state of a person who or animal or plant that sleeps. **12.** a period of sleeping: *a brief sleep.* **13.** dormancy or inactivity. **14.** the repose of death. [(n.) ME; OE *slēp* (Anglian), *slǣp, slāp;* c. D *slaap,* G *Schlaf,* Goth *slēps;* (v.) ME *slepe,* OE *slēpan, slǣpan; slāpan;* c. D *slapen,* G *schlafen,* Goth *slēpan*] —**Syn. 11.** rest, repose.
Sleep (slēp), *n.* **Marsh of.** See **Palus Somni.**
sleep·er (slē′pər), *n.* **1.** a person or thing that sleeps. **2.** a heavy horizontal timber for distributing loads. **3.** *Brit.* a railway tie. **4.** a sleeping car. **5.** bunting[3]. **6.** *Informal.* something that or someone who becomes or may become successful or important after a period of being obscured or unimportant. [ME]
sleep-in (slēp′in′), *adj.* (of domestic help) sleeping at the place of one's employment: *a sleep-in maid.*
sleep·ing (slē′ping), *n.* **1.** the condition of being asleep. —*adj.* **2.** asleep. **3.** of, noting, pertaining to, or having accommodations for sleeping: *a sleeping compartment.* **4.** used to sleep in or on: *a sleeping jacket.* **5.** used to induce or aid sleep or while asleep: *a sleeping mask.* [ME]
sleep′ing bag′, a large bag, usually of warmly padded material and having a zipper in front, in which a person sleeps, as when camping out of doors.
sleep′ing car′, a railroad car fitted with sleeping accommodations.
sleep′ing pill′, a pill, tablet, or capsule, usually prescribed by a physician, for inducing sleep. Also called **sleep′ing tab′let.**
sleep′ing porch′, a porch enclosed with glass or screening or a room with open sides or a row of windows used for sleeping in the open air.
sleep′ing sick′ness, *Pathol.* **1.** Also called **African sleeping sickness, African trypanosomiasis.** a generally fatal disease, common in parts of Africa, characterized by fever, wasting, and progressive lethargy: caused by a parasitic protozoan, *Trypanosoma gambiense* or *T. rhodesiense,* which is carried by a tsetse fly, *Glossina palpalis.* **2.** Also called **epidemic encephalitis, lethargic encephalitis, nona.** a virus disease affecting the brain, characterized by apathy, sleepiness, extreme muscular weakness, and impairment of vision.
sleep·less (slēp′lis), *adj.* **1.** without sleep: *a sleepless night.* **2.** watchful; alert: *sleepless devotion to duty.* **3.** always active: *the sleepless ocean.* [ME] —**sleep′less·ly,** *adv.*
sleep·walk·ing (slēp′wô′king), *n.* **1.** the act of walking while asleep; somnambulism. —*adj.* **2.** of or pertaining to the act of walking while asleep; somnambulistic. —**sleep′walk′er,** *n.*
sleep·y (slē′pē), *adj.,* **sleep·i·er, sleep·i·est. 1.** ready or inclined to sleep; drowsy. **2.** of or showing drowsiness. **3.** lethargic; inactive: *a sleepy village.* **4.** inducing sleep; soporific: *sleepy warmth.* [ME] —**sleep′i·ly,** *adv.* —**sleep′i·ness,** *n.* —**Syn. 1.** tired, somnolent, slumberous.
sleep·y·head (slē′pē hed′), *n.* a sleepy person.
sleet (slēt), *n.* **1.** a frozen coating formed on the ground by the fall of freezing rain. **2.** precipitation in the form of frozen raindrops. **3.** *Chiefly Brit.* the precipitation of snow and rain simultaneously. —*v.i.* **4.** to send down sleet. **5.** to fall as or like sleet. [ME *slete;* akin to LG *slote,* G *Schlossen* hail]
sleet·y (slē′tē), *adj.,* **sleet·i·er, sleet·i·est.** of or pertaining to sleet. —**sleet′i·ness,** *n.*
sleeve (slēv), *n., v.,* **sleeved, sleev·ing.** —*n.* **1.** the part of a garment that covers the arm. **2.** an envelope, usually of paper, for protecting a phonograph record. **3.** *Mach.* a tubular piece, as of metal, fitting over a rod or the like. **4. laugh up** or **in one's sleeve,** to be secretly amused or contemptuous. **5. up one's sleeve,** kept secretly ready or close at hand. —*v.t.* **6.** to furnish with sleeves. [ME *sleve,* OE *slēfe* (Anglian); akin to D *sloof* apron] —**sleeve′like′,** *adj.*
sleeve·less (slēv′lis), *adj.* without a sleeve or sleeves. [ME, OE *slieflēas*]
sleeve·let (slēv′lit), *n.* a fitted sleeve or cover worn on the forearm for warmth or to protect a shirt sleeve.
sleigh (slā), *n.* **1.** a light vehicle on runners, that is usually open and generally horse-drawn, used esp. for transporting persons over snow or ice. —*v.i.* **2.** to travel or ride in a sleigh. [< D *slee,* short for *slede* SLED] —**sleigh′er,** *n.*
sleight (slīt), *n.* skill; dexterity. [ME; early ME *slēgth* < Scand; cf. Icel *slǣgth.* See SLY, -TH[1]]
sleight′ of hand′, 1. skill in feats requiring quick and clever movements of the hands, esp. for entertainment or deception, as jugglery or palming; legerdemain. **2.** the performance of such feats.
slen·der (slen′dər), *adj.* **1.** having a circumference that is small in proportion to the height or length: *a slender post.* **2.** attractively thin and well-formed: *the slender girls who work as models.* **3.** small in size, amount, extent, etc.; meager: *a slender income.* **4.** having little value, force, or justification: *slender prospects.* [ME *slendre, sclendre* < ?] —**slen′der·ly,** *adv.* —**slen′der·ness,** *n.*
—**Syn. 2.** SLENDER, SLIGHT, SLIM imply a tendency toward thinness. As applied to the human body, SLENDER implies a generally attractive and pleasing thinness: *slender hands.* SLIGHT often adds the idea of frailness to that of thinness: *a slight, almost fragile, figure.* SLIM implies a lithe or delicate thinness: *a slim and athletic figure.* —**Ant. 2.** fat, stocky.
slen·der·ize (slen′də rīz′), *v.,* **-ized, -iz·ing.** —*v.t.* **1.** to make slender or more slender. **2.** to cause to appear slender. —*v.i.* **3.** to become slender.
slept (slept), *v.* pt. and pp. of **sleep.**
Sles·vig (sles′vikh), *n.* Danish name of **Schleswig.**
Sles·wick (sles′wik), *n.* Schleswig.
sleuth (slo͞oth), *n.* **1.** *U.S. Informal.* a detective. **2.** a bloodhound. —*v.t., v.i.* **3.** to track or trail, as a detective. [short for SLEUTHHOUND]
sleuth·hound (slo͞oth′hound′), *n.* a bloodhound. [ME *slōth* track, trail (< Scand; cf. Icel *slōth*) + HOUND[1]]
slew[1] (slo͞o), *v.* pt. of **slay.**
slew[2] (slo͞o), *v.t., v.i., n.* slue[1]. [?]
slew[3] (slo͞o), *n. U.S., Canadian.* slough[1] (def. 3).
slew[4] (slo͞o), *n. Informal.* a great number; lot: *a whole slew of people.* [< Ir *sluagh* multitude, army]
Slezs·ko (sles′kô), *n.* Czech name of **Silesia.**
slice (slīs), *n., v.,* **sliced, slic·ing.** —*n.* **1.** a thin, broad, flat piece cut from something: *a slice of bread.* **2.** a part; portion of any kind: *a slice of land.* **3.** any of various implements with a thin, broad blade or part; spatula. **4.** *Sports.* **a.** the path described by a ball, as in baseball or golf, that curves in a direction corresponding to the side from which it was struck. **b.** a ball describing such a path. —*v.t.* **5.** to cut into slices. **6.** to cut through or cleave with or as with a knife. **7.** to

p. 410	**haystack—headline**	____ haze	____ headlock
		____ head	____ heart
		____ hazzard	____ heat
p. 580	**mosquito—motor**	____ moss	____ mother
		____ mortgage	____ Mormon
		____ motel	____ mothball
p. 709	**relate—religion**	____ relief	____ rejoin
		____ remain	____ relate
		____ regard	____ relic
p. 800	**seal—seaweed**	____ seaside	____ sea
		____ seam	____ second
		____ sear	____ season
p. 876	**structure—stuff**	____ struck	____ student
		____ stung	____ strong
		____ style	____ stuff
p. 921	**tensile—terrain**	____ tend	____ tent
		____ tempt	____ terrify
		____ terminal	____ tense
p. 930	**tongue—topic**	____ topaz	____ toast
		____ tone	____ toyless
		____ topless	____ tooth
p. 1023	**weevil—welfare**	____ well	____ weather
		____ weep	____ wedge
		____ welcome	____ weight

PRACTICE Circle the word in the right-hand column that is **not** found on the same page as the guidewords. The first one is done for you.

GUIDEWORDS

1. **asphalt—assess**	1. aspirin (asset) assert
2. **bedroom—bigger**	2. beet bedspread bellow
3. **drive-in—dropout**	3. drop dresser driveway

4. **exhibit—expansion**   4. excuse   exotic   existence
5. **giveable—glass**   5. glance   given   ginger
6. **impacted—imperfect**   6. impact   impend   impassive
7. **master—match**   7. matter   mat   master-key
8. **outsell—over**   8. overcharge   outweigh   oven
9. **purge—push**   9. purr   pushy   purse
10. **short-term—showing**   10. shot   shortly   shovel

PRACTICE Using your own dictionary, look up these vocabulary words and write the guidewords for each one.

VOCABULARY WORD	GUIDEWORDS	
1. spectator	_____	_____
2. participant	_____	_____
3. infested	_____	_____
4. buccaneers	_____	_____
5. hologram	_____	_____

Reprinted by permission of Harry Greenberger.

PRACTICE READING

Untitled

The demolition derby is very popular in rural° parts of the United States. It is a contest between the drivers of battered° old jalopies.° These cars are no longer working very well, but their owners want to have some fun with them before they take them away to the junkyard.

°farm or country areas
°beat up / °old cars

°step heavily on the gas
pedal while the car is in
neutral / °splashes

Here is how the derby is run. First, the drivers take their cars onto a muddy field and line them up in two rows of about ten cars each, with the backs of the cars facing the center of the field. At a signal, the drivers gun their engines.° Mud flies everywhere. It splatters° the spectators who get too close. The cars crash back into each other.

The first crash usually knocks out half the cars. Those that can still move try to crash into other moving cars and knock them out. Soon the air is full of thick, choking smoke. The contest continues until only one car is still moving. The driver of that car is the winner, and the other cars are towed from the field.

°straps

This sport looks dangerous, but injuries are very rare. The mud prevents the cars from moving too fast. The cars carry very little gasoline in their tanks, and the drivers remove all glass from the car windows before the event. They also wear safety helmets and seat harnesses.° In fact, driving on a highway may be more dangerous than driving in a demolition derby!

VOCABULARY EXERCISE Using your dictionary to help you, supply the following information about each word.

GUIDEWORDS

1. demolition _____ _____
2. derby _____ _____
3. rural _____ _____
4. jalopies _____ _____
5. splatters _____ _____
6. harness _____ _____
7. credit _____ _____
8. between _____ _____
9. driver _____ _____
10. prevents _____ _____
11. gasoline _____ _____
12. remove _____ _____

LITERAL COMPREHENSION EXERCISE Answer the following questions True (T) or False (F) according to the story.

_____ 1. The drivers may be in danger from flying glass.

_____ 2. Spectators can be splattered with gasoline.

_____ 3. Usually, 50 per cent of the cars are out of the contest at the first crash.

_____ 4. Old cars are towed, and only new cars may compete.

_____ 5. Even while crashing into each other, drivers take safety precautions.

GENERAL COMPREHENSION EXERCISE Answer these questions.

1. What is the main idea of the second paragraph? _____

_____

2. What is the main idea of the third paragraph? _____

_____

3. What is a good title for the story? _____

_____

PRACTICE READING

Untitled

Is there such a thing as a typical American film? There are many features that mark a movie as American, but perhaps the most essential is the theme of the loner-hero. From the earliest days of silent films until the recent science fiction extravaganzas,° the American movie has concentrated on the role of one individual who spends his or her life combatting the forces of evil—and the good guy, the hero, usually wins.

°elaborate entertainments

In the western movie, which comes out of many legends of the American West, a typical figure is the lonesome cowboy. He wanders into a town and straightens out its troubles. Those troubles can be cattle rustlers or outlaws. Then the strong and independent hero rides off into the sunset alone. Americans like this image in their films because they are highly independent, and individualism° counts a great deal with them. An individual who is able to correct the evils of the world, or of a small town, is someone to admire.

°emphasizing the individual above society

Even the gangster movie, a very popular form of the typical American film, usually has a hero. Either he is a lawman out to catch the criminals or a gangster who suddenly sees the light° and tries to go straight.° During the violence-ridden period of Prohibition° in the 1920s, the gangster movie grew in popularity. These films kept the same tone as the western—the bad cannot triumph! One good person can save the innocent.

°understands the situation / °become honest
°the period when making and selling alcohol was forbidden by law

Recent science fiction films deal with the same themes. Against the forces of alien° powers, people will fight to protect their ideals. Here, too, the action centers around a single individual, but now he or she must save the world. The hero battles the unknown, trusting in inner capabilities° and in the power of good over evil. Fearless, the hero of a typical American movie does not hesitate to jump into the action. This dominant theme of the American movie is familiar to people around the world.

°coming from another world; strange
°abilities; powers

DICTIONARY EXERCISE Fill in the information requested for the following words. Use your dictionary.

GUIDEWORDS

1. typical _____ _____

2. extravaganza _____ _____

3. alien _____ _____

4. prohibition _____ _____

LITERAL COMPREHENSION EXERCISE Answer the following questions according to the story.

_____ 1. A distinctive feature of American films is
   a. the struggle between good and evil.
   b. the loner-hero.
   c. the cowboy.
   d. the gangster.

_____ 2. Americans like cowboy heroes because the heroes
   a. cause the troubles of the town.
   b. come from legends of the American West.
   c. battle alien powers.
   d. admire independence and strength.

_____ 3. The hero of the gangster film
   a. is a criminal.
   b. is usually a lawbreaker.
   c. wipes out troubles of the innocent.
   d. removes himself from the gang.

_____ 4. Science fiction films have heroes who
   a. protect their ideals.
   b. rely on help from powerful sources.
   c. gather the armies to fight evil powers.
   d. are fearful of entering the fight.

MAIN IDEA EXERCISE Highlight the main idea sentence in each paragraph of the passage. Then answer these questions.

1. Where is the main idea sentence of the first paragraph located? _____

_____

2. The second paragraph? _____

3. The third paragraph? _____

4. The fourth paragraph? _____

5. The best title for this passage is _____ .

CHAPTER 12

FINDING THE MAIN IDEA SENTENCE IN DIFFERENT LOCATIONS IN A PARAGRAPH

*_**

You have already practiced locating and highlighting the main idea when it occurred in the first sentence of a paragraph. This is the most common location of the main idea sentence, especially for the beginning writer. It is also a preferred location in textbook paragraphs where the first sentence introduces the details in the paragraph.

However, the main idea sentence may appear in other locations in a paragraph. Being able to recognize a main idea stated in another part of the paragraph is an important reading skill to develop. Some textbook authors vary the position of the main idea sentence, and readers have to be able to work with these variations. Consider the following.

EXAMPLE

For many years people stayed at home and watched television rather than go to the movies. The new science fiction, war, romance, and spy thrillers have brought people back to the theaters. Once again, Friday and Saturday night audiences are standing on long lines, buying popcorn, and laughing or crying over Hollywood's creations. The habit of going to the movies is making a big comeback today. (summary)

QUESTIONS

1. What is the main idea sentence of the paragraph? _____

_____

2. Where is the main idea sentence located in the paragraph? _____

_____

3. Does the main idea sentence have a special purpose in this location?

_____

4. Fill in the main idea sentence and related details from the sample paragraph in the diagram on the next page.

Locating the Main Idea Sentence in Different Parts in a Paragraph   **99**

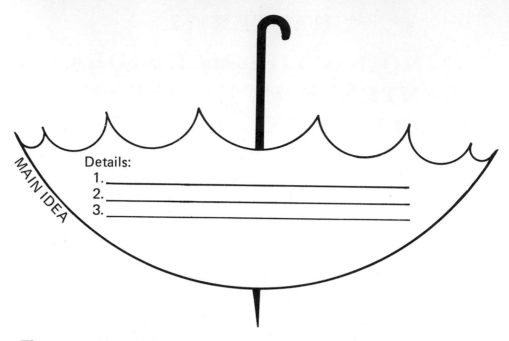

Details:
1. _____
2. _____
3. _____

MAIN IDEA

The main idea of the paragraph is "The habit of going to the movies is making a big comeback today." This idea is stated in the last sentence and serves to sum up the details in the paragraph.

When the main idea occurs in the **last sentence,** it **sums up** the details in a paragraph.

There is another possible location for the main idea sentence. Read this paragraph.

EXAMPLE

For many years people stayed at home and watched television rather than go to the movies. However, the new science fiction, war, romance, and spy thrillers have brought people back to the theaters. The habit of going to the movies is making a big comeback today. Once again, Friday and Saturday night audiences are standing on long lines, buying popcorn, and laughing or crying over Hollywood's creations.

QUESTIONS

1. What is the main idea sentence of this paragraph? _____

_____

2. Where is the main idea sentence located? _____

_____

3. What purpose does it serve in this location? _____

_____

4. Use the main idea sentence and related details to complete the diagram.

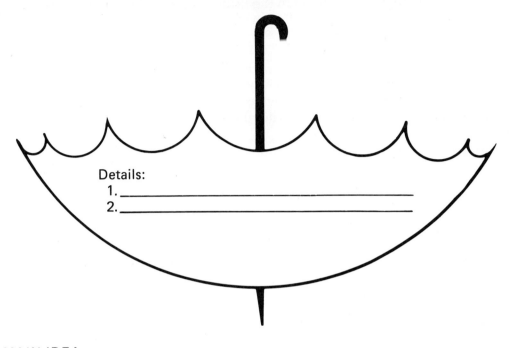

Details:
1. _____
2. _____

MAIN IDEA: _____

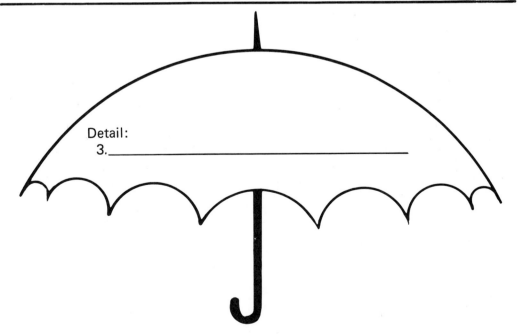

Detail:
3. _____

The main idea of the paragraph is "The habit of going to the movies is making a big comeback today." It occurs in the middle of the paragraph and serves as a link between the beginning and closing details.

> When the main idea occurs in the **middle** of the paragraph, it serves as a **bridge** between the details in the paragraph.

EXERCISE Read the following paragraphs and decide what the main idea sentence is. Then highlight it and draw the umbrella diagram showing the location. Finally, in the space provided, or on separate paper, fill in each umbrella with the main idea and details. The first one is done for you.

°fast pace and exciting

Paragraph 1 Teenagers who love to dance spend hours there. People in their twenties and thirties, who enjoy the music and who like to dance, find discos the place to be. Everyone likes the disco's up° atmosphere. **Lively discos attract many people.**

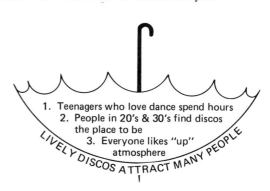
1. Teenagers who love dance spend hours
2. People in 20's & 30's find discos the place to be
3. Everyone likes "up" atmosphere

LIVELY DISCOS ATTRACT MANY PEOPLE

Paragraph 2 As the first settlers moved west across the country, they made up songs describing what they had seen and where they had been. They sang these simple tunes to their children who remembered them and added passages of their own to these songs. Through the generations, the songs of the mountain and plains folk spread throughout the country. As a result, Americans now have a treasury of folk songs describing the experiences of the earliest settlers in America.

°bend out of shape / °are being replaced by
°small tapes / ° large tapes

°machines controlling sound

°long-lasting quality

Paragraph 3 Plastic records that warp° or break are giving way to° cassettes° and 8-track° machines. Single-unit phonographs are being replaced by equipment with separate speakers, turntables, and amplifiers.° This equipment lasts longer and provides better sound. Modern technology has improved the quality and durability° of musical recordings. By turning on their radios and inserting blank tapes into cassette or 8-track systems, people can record directly into the stereo from AM or FM stations. These recordings will last a long time.

Paragraph 4 Once, only the people of Nashville, Tennessee enjoyed the local country and western sound coming from the Grand Ole Opry. In time, however, people came from neighboring cities and towns to join the crowds in the old hall. Eventually, radios broadcast the country and western sound. Within a few years, tunes began to appear in the Top Ten° all across the country, and disc jockeys° in major cities began to play them. The Opry grew along with the popularity of country and western music. On Saturday nights the hall was jammed with people from every part of the country. Television began to broadcast concerts from the hall. Now the Opry and country music are known to all America.

°the ten most popular tunes
°radio hosts who play popular records

PRACTICE Highlight the main idea sentence in each of the following paragraphs.

Paragraph 1 We dos-à-dos° and allemande-left,° all join hands and circle four hands round.° Square dancing and its foot-stomping° rhythms are as American as apple pie. At 8:00 we meet at Farmer Brown's barn. Fiddlers strike up the tune° promptly and lead everyone in group dances. People wear either bright shirts and dungarees or bright skirts and blouses. Everyone has a red or navy bandana° around his or her neck. Every weekend we look forward to square dancing.

°square dance steps
°stamping one's foot to the beat of the music
°begin playing
°scarf

Paragraph 2 Where is Motown? You can't find it on any map of the United States. It is not a geographical place. Rather, it is the feeling, the beat, and the sound of a musical form that has swept the country. The sound originated in Detroit. There, the record companies produce songs characterized by° a steady rhythmic beat, moody° lyrics telling of love, life, and people, and harmonies that can be sweet or strident.° The Motown sound is unique in the musical world.

°having the special quality of / °sad
°harsh

Paragraph 3   Henry and James are fiddlers. Every week they fill our music hall with their sweet fiddle music. Their fingers pluck across the strings. People clap to the country rhythm. Feet stomp to the beat. Henry plays a hillbilly° melody, and James' fingers pluck the strings in a quick and lively beat. Faster and faster they play the tunes of the hill people. Most of the music has no lyrics. Rather, people concentrate on listening to music as Henry and James fiddle the night away.

°from the mountains or backwoods

Paragraph 4   My friend Andy loves rock concerts. Every time a new group is in town, she is the first in line for tickets. She reads all the newspapers to check for the time and place of the next rock event. Andy says rock concerts are really free. She feels that they capture the spirit of our age because members of the audience can express themselves in their responses to the music and in the clothes that they wear. Rock concerts have a special magic of their own. They are as free and independent as the American spirit.

Paragraph 5   Popular American music has changed from the early big bands to smaller groups. In the 1920s and 1930s the radios and phonographs played the sounds of the big bands. Big bands were also popular in the 1940s, but during that decade smaller bands with prominent° lead singers found favor with° music lovers. Small rock and roll groups emerged in the 1950s. These small groups were soon replaced by larger rock bands, and lead singers again found the spotlight. Bands are still an important feature of popular American music. It is the size of the band and the role of the lead singer that keeps changing.

°well-known
°were well-liked by

Paragraph 6   Back in the 1950s and 1960s, the big sound in American music was a mellow° blend of voices and steady rhythms. In time, the California beach sound drifted across the country and was soon popular throughout the world. Groups like the Beach Boys and Jan and Dean created an easy summer sound complete with the roar of the surf. The carefree and smooth lyrics and the pleasing harmony were the background for the happy and youthful mood that swept the country. The surfing music of the 1950s created a freedom and sense of youthful living enjoyed by young and old alike.

°soft; gently pleasing

both 1 and last sentences (handwritten)

Paragraph 7   The typical themes of the Black American experience are found in rhythm and blues music. Some music critics feel that rhythm and blues expresses the soul and roots of American life. The lyrics of all the songs have a message, and it is an earthy, soulful one. The beat is usually slow and pulsing,° giving the music a moody quality. Rhythm and blues vocalists are easily distinguished from other singers. They moan° and wail° the lyrics of their songs that are about oppression, struggle, love, and rejection.

°beating regularly
°make a long sad sound / ° make a sad, crying sound

CHAPTER 13

USING THE DICTIONARY:
Diacritical Marks

* *
*

You have now learned how to find words quickly by using the dictionary guidewords. In addition to guidewords, each dictionary entry is marked with unusual symbols. In this chapter you will learn what those symbols are, and how they can help you to pronounce new words. Read this dialogue.

MARIA: Suly, I need your help again. Now that I've found the words on the correct pages, I don't know what some of the markings mean. They're very strange.

SULY: What markings are you talking about?

MARIA: After each word there are combinations of funny-looking letters and marks. Here are some:

MARIA: **bruth′ ər**   **hiz**   **an tēk′**   **kwôr′ tər**

What do these marks mean?

SULY: In our class, we studied this last week. Let me explain. Those marks are examples of pronunciation symbols called **diacritical marks.** They represent the sounds of English letters.

MARIA: I understand so far. But how am I supposed to know what the marks stand for?

SULY: Every dictionary has a **pronunciation key.** It is usually found at the bottom of every page. The key lists words you already know. There is also a large pronunciation key at the front of each dictionary. Along with each word in the key are **diacritical marks** that indicate the sounds of the vowel or consonant in the word.

MARIA: What page should I turn to in the dictionary?

SULY: It doesn't matter. The same key is repeated on each page. Sometimes the pronunciation key on each page is a shorter version of the front key, and, if you can't find what you need in a short key, look at the front key. Let's look at it now.

MARIA: Does that mean I can use any dictionary? I have a large heavy one at home, but I don't like to carry it. I have a small paperback version for school.

SULY: I suggest that you use the same dictionary for all your work.

Strange as it sounds, different dictionaries may have differences in their diacritical markings and in their pronunciation keys. Better check with your teacher and use just one dictionary.

MARIA: Let me see if I can figure out the words I gave you. The first one is "brother." The others are "his," "antique," and "quarter." That's not too hard.

°understand it

SULY: It's not difficult once you get the hang of it.° It just takes a little practice.

MARIA: Thanks a lot. Ī ō yōō ə fā′-vər.

PRONUNCIATION KEY

The symbol (′), as in **moth·er** (muŧh′ər), **blue′ dev′ils,** is used to mark primary stress; the syllable preceding it is pronounced with greater prominence than the other syllables in the word or phrase. The symbol (′), as in **grand·moth·er** (grand′muŧh′ər), **buzz′ bomb′,** is used to mark secondary stress; a syllable marked for secondary stress is pronounced with less prominence than one marked (′) but with more prominence than those bearing no stress mark at all.

a	act, bat, marry	i	if, big, mirror, furniture	p	pot, supper, stop	indicates the sound of
ā	aid, cape, way			r	read, hurry, near	a *in* alone
â(r)	air, dare, Mary	ī	ice, bite, pirate, deny			e *in* system
ä	alms, art, calm			s	see, passing, miss	i *in* easily
				sh	shoe, fashion, push	o *in* gallop
b	back, cabin, cab	j	just, badger, fudge			u *in* circus
ch	chief, butcher, beach	k	kept, token, make	t	ten, butter, bit	
				th	thin, ether, path	ə occurs in unaccented
d	do, rudder, bed	l	low, mellow, all	ŧh	that, either, smooth	syllables before **l** preceded by **t, d,** or **n,** or before **n** preceded by **t** or **d** to show syllabic quality, as in **cra·dle** (krād′əl) **red·den** (red′ən) **met·al** (met′əl) **men·tal** (men′t′əl) and in accented syllables between ī and r to show diphthongal quality, as in **fire** (fī°r) **hire** (hī°r)
e	ebb, set, merry	m	my, simmer, him	u	up, love	
ē	equal, seat, bee, mighty	n	now, sinner, on	û(r)	urge, burn, cur	
ēr	ear, mere	ñg	sing, Washington	v	voice, river, live	
				w	west, away	
f	fit, differ, puff	o	ox, box, wasp	y	yes, lawyer	
		ō	over, boat, no			
g	give, trigger, beg	ô	ought, ball, raw	z	zeal, lazy, those	
		oi	oil, joint, joy	zh	vision, mirage	
		ŏŏ	book, poor			
h	hit, behave, hear	ōō	ooze, fool, too	ə	occurs only in unaccented syllables and	
hw	white, nowhere	ou	out, loud, prow			

EXERCISE Use the pronunciation key given to help you pronounce these words. Say each word aloud. Then write the correct word on the line. The first one is done for you.

1. mes′ ən jər   messenger _____

2. ej   _____

3. krok′ ə dīl′　_____

4. in′ ə sənt　_____

5. miks　_____

6. spesh′ ə līz′　_____

7. sō′ shə līz′　_____

8. jaz　_____

9. rith′ əm　_____

10. hil′ bil′ ē　_____

EXERCISE　Read the following conversation aloud. Answer the questions. Use the pronounciation key to help you.

　Yoko: Doo yoo līk kun′-trē myoo′-zik?
Mi Yea: Ī hav nev′-ər hûrd it.
　Yoko: Kum too thə kon′-sûrt with mē.
Mi Yea: Hwen iz thə kon′-sûrt?
　Yoko: Tə-môr′-ō-nīt.

1. Where are the girls going? _____

2. What will they hear there? _____

PRACTICE　Use the pronunciation key to help you decide which of the choices at the right is the correct pronunciation in the sentence. The first one is done for you.

1. The number following five is _____. (sīz ⓢiks)

2. I will open my birthday _____. (pri-zent′ prez′-ənt)

3. Most trees will not grow in the _____. (dez′-ərt di-zûrt′)

4. A teacher works in a _____. (skul skool)

5. I like _____ in my coffee. (krīm krēm)

6. We will _____ to your party. (kōm kum)

7. Write your _____ on the paper. (mə-säzh′ mes′-ij)

8. Here is the _____ for three guitars. (ôr′-dər uth′-ər)

CHAPTER 14

LOCATING MAIN IDEAS
IN SHORT PASSAGES

* *
*

Usually you do not read single or isolated paragraphs. Rather, you read more full-length pieces such as newspaper stories, novels, and chapters in textbooks. Understanding what each paragraph is about helps increase your total comprehension of the story, novel, or chapter. The following short passages offer practice in understanding the paragraph.

> Remember that the **main idea** is the most general statement about the details in the paragraph. The main idea sentence may be located at the beginning, middle, or end of the paragraph. Therefore, **you must read the entire paragraph** before deciding what the main idea sentence is.

EXERCISE Read each passage and fill in the topic in the space provided. Then highlight the main idea sentence in each paragraph and answer the questions.

Passage 1 This weekend my family is going to enjoy all the rides at the church carnival. Sandy is excited about her chance to ride the giant ferris wheel. Aunt Senta is looking forward to the scary whip.° Alfredo and his girlfriend cannot wait to go through the House of Horrors. Little Cecelia will take at least five turns on the merry-go-round.

°a high-speed amusement park ride

Everyone will have a hot dog and soda. Cecelia was promised a special treat of cotton candy.° Maybe Mama and Papa will let us have fresh corn on the cob. Alfredo will surely spend money to buy his girlfriend the "Super Waffle Surprise." No doubt we will all eat too much at the carnival.

°a sugar candy that looks like cotton

Topic _____

VOCABULARY EXERCISE Answer each statement True (T) or False (F) according to the story.

____ The biggest ride is the whip.

____ Alfredo will get cotton candy.

____ The frightening ride is called the ferris wheel.

DICTIONARY EXERCISE Using your dictionary, locate these words and list the guidewords for each.

1. ferris wheel   _____   _____

2. cotton candy   _____   _____

3. whip   _____   _____

LITERAL COMPREHENSION EXERCISE Complete these sentences with information from the story.

1. There are _____ members of the family.

2. Cotton candy will be a special treat for _____.

3. _____ wants to go through the House of Horrors.

4. The family will probably eat a _____ amount of food.

5. The _____ carnival has rides and food.

GENERAL COMPREHENSION Answer each question according to the story.

____ 1. The best title for this passage is
    a. Carnivals Have Special Rides.
    b. The Family Dines Out.
    c. Going to a Carnival.
    d. Amusements.

____ 2. The two topics discussed in the paragraphs are
    a. families and carnivals.
    b. rides and candy.
    c. carnival rides and food.
    d. fairs and special treats.

3. The main idea sentence of paragraph 1 is _____ .

4. The main idea sentence of paragraph 2 is _____ .

Passage 2 What happens to a successful Broadway musical comedy? Producers decide to form road companies of the show and to have them play in major cities in the United States. New auditions° are held for singers, dancers, and lead actors. New scenery is built, new electrical equipment is ordered, and a new technical crew is hired. Road companies° duplicate the original production.   °tryouts   °traveling theater companies

    Road companies performing American musical comedies have been seen by millions of people over the years. Successful shows are translated into many languages. In fact, one musical may have as many as ten versions playing in the United States and abroad at any given time. People all over the world have enjoyed such favorites as *My Fair Lady, Oklahoma, Peter*

Pan, *Grease*, and *A Chorus Line*. These shows provide rich theatrical experiences for people in cities throughout the world.

Topic: _____

VOCABULARY AND DICTIONARY EXERCISE Using your dictionary, supply the information requested.

WORD	DIACRITICAL MARKS	ONE MEANING
1. Broadway	_____	_____
2. audition	_____	_____
3. road company	_____	_____
4. musical comedy	_____	_____

LITERAL COMPREHENSION EXERCISE Answer each statement with True (T) or False (F).

_____ 1. Ten musicals per year appear in other countries.

_____ 2. Road companies of all American musicals thrill people throughout the world.

_____ 3. *My Fair Lady* is an adaptation of a road company show.

°get a first job

°experimental theater /
°someone who works for
 another to learn a trade /
°summer theater production
°scenery
°prepared to act the role in
 place of
°the most important male
 actor

°the person who arranges
 dances for a performance
°a singer or dancer in a
 theatrical performance
°highly experimental
 theater
°the person who shows
 people to their seats in a
 theater
°a notice announcing
 tryouts
°be accepted for a show

Passage 3 Joe and I have been trying to break into° Broadway for three years. Joe is an excellent singer and dancer and has been in two off-Broadway° shows. Recently, he trained as an apprentice° in a summer stock° company. There he learned to paint a set,° sell tickets, and to handle stage lights. Last year, he finally got his chance in the chorus and understudied° the male lead.° Toward the end of the summer, he played the lead role. He got rave notices for his week's acting. These reviews were much better than the earlier ones he had received in the off-Broadway show he had appeared in. When he was starting out, he made many mistakes, but he has improved with experience.

I haven't been that lucky. I've worked as assistant choreographer° in a road company, chorus member° in one off-off-Broadway° show, and as a page° at Radio City Music Hall. I dance fairly well but have not had many chances to improve my skills. However, I practice singing every day and am getting stronger and better each week. Next week, Joe and I plan to answer another audition call° for a road company show. With some luck one of us should be able to make the troupe.°

Topic _____

VOCABULARY EXERCISE The defined words and phrases in this passage have special theatrical meanings. Use each in a sentence.

1. break into: _____

2. fabulous: _____

3. off-Broadway: _____

4. apprentice: _____

5. summer stock: _____

6. understudy: _____

7. choreographer: _____

8. off-off-Broadway: _____

9. page: _____

10. audition call: _____

DICTIONARY EXERCISE Rewrite these words using their diacritical marks. Use your dictionary to help.

troupe   fabulous   apprentice   choreographer   Broadway

_____   _____   _____   _____   _____

LITERAL COMPREHENSION EXERCISE Match the person with his or her professional experience.

1. Joe   ____ apprentice in summer stock

2. "I"   ____ assistant choreographer

                ____ understudy to male lead

                ____ page at Radio City Music Hall

                ____ two off-Broadway jobs

                ____ chorus member in an off-off-Broadway show

                ____ ticket seller

Passage 4 Our neighborhood theater group is putting on a new production this year that requires a good technical crew. The crew will consist of a stage manager, wardrobe mistress,° script° person, lighting and electrical technician, scenery designer, and a property manager.° Without each of these professionals, we would not be able to produce a show.

°the person responsible for the clothing used in a performance / °the written text of a play or movie
°the person responsible for all objects used in a performance

   We will also need a management staff. The producer will supervise all the managerial, technical, and acting decisions. The director will be completely in charge of all creative decisions and will work very closely with the actors and actresses. Directing the dialogue, placing the lights, sets, and people, as well as controlling the dancers, singers, and actors will be the functions of the director. In addition, there will be dozens of payroll personnel, advertising and ticket agents, and public relations people.

°all the actors in a
 performance

Last, but not least, will be the cast.° Auditions will be held for ten chorus members who can sing, dance, and act. At the tryouts people will talk about themselves and perform. Finally, everyone will go home and wait for a phone call. An actor who gets one part will understudy two or three other roles. There are many people who will play important parts in our local theater group's production.

Topic: _____

DICTIONARY EXERCISE Mark the vowel sounds and diacritical marks in these words. Use your dictionay to help. Then practice pronouncing the words.

1. manage _____   7. managerial _____

2. audit _____   8. auditions _____

3. technical _____   9. technician _____

4. produce _____   10. production _____

5. actor _____   11. actress _____

6. electric _____   12. electrical _____

LITERAL COMPREHENSION EXERCISE According to the story, which of the following answers best completes each sentence?

____ 1. Actors will audition for
    a. lead roles.
    b. understudy roles.
    c. the chorus.
    d. a and c.
    e. b and c.

____ 2. The management will consist of
    a. the scenery designer and property manager.
    b. the director and producer.
    c. the producer and wardrobe mistress.
    d. the script person, stage manager, and director.

____ 3. The largest portion of the staff will consist of
    a. managers.
    b. chorus members.
    c. technicians.
    d. agents.

_____ 4. A chorus member will
     a. play several roles at once.
     b. understudy several parts.
     c. act as the property manager.
     d. supervise the set design.

GENERAL COMPREHENSION EXERCISE Fill in the correct response.

_____ 1. The best title for the passage is
     a. Local Theater Groups.
     b. The Theater's Technical Staff.
     c. Auditioning for a Local Stage Production.
     d. Understudying Lead Roles.

2. The topic of paragraph 1 is _____.

3. The topic of paragraph 2 is _____.

4. The topic of paragraph 3 is _____.

5. List the main idea sentences for paragraphs 1, 2, and 3:

_____

_____

_____

CHAPTER 15

USING THE DICTIONARY:
Hearing Syllables

.

Now you are ready to learn more about the information in a dictionary. Read this dialogue.

MARIA: Suly, you've really helped me a lot. I have to ask you one more question.

SULY: What is that?

MARIA: You have explained what the diacritical marks mean, and you have shown me how to use guidewords, but there are other marks that are placed on words in the dictionary.

SULY: Show me the marks.

MARIA: Let me use a word from the last lesson: kwôr′-tər. What is the mark after the first "r"?

SULY: That mark shows which syllable is accented. We put stress or emphasis on certain syllables in words as we say them.

°progressing more quickly than I

MARIA: Wait a minute! You are way ahead of me.° What is a syllable?

SULY: Okay. Let me start with an explanation of syllables. Then we'll move into accent marks. Maria, I am going to write some words on this paper. I want you to say them aloud and write the number of **vowel sounds** you hear in each word.

secret ____   actor ____   celebrate ____   play ____
musical ____   carnival ____   concert ____   experience ____

MARIA: That was easy.

SULY: Now look at your answers and consider this.

> The number of vowels that are sounded in a word is the same as the number of **syllables** or parts of that word. Here are some examples.
>
> **play** = 1 vowel sound = 1 syllable
> **actor** = 2 vowel sounds = 2 syllables
> **musical** = 3 vowel sounds = 3 syllables

MARIA: You mean that every time there is a vowel sound, there is a syllable?

SULY: That's right. Here are some exercises for practice.

EXERCISE Say these words aloud. Listen for the vowel sounds in each word and write the number of syllables next to the word. The first one is done for you.

disco 2	annual ___	pantomime ___	life ___
create ___	creations ___	hillbilly ___	replace ___
steep ___	hotel ___	equal ___	pirate ___
circus ___	people ___	fabulous ___	understudy ___
parties ___	knives ___	caught ___	comedy ___

MARIA: That was simple. But I knew most of the words. What happens if I don't know the words?

SULY: There are some rules that will help you. They are not difficult, but they must be practiced. This is an important rule.

> When a single consonant (C) comes between two vowels (V) in a word, and the first vowel is long, then the word is usually divided before the consonant—**V̄-CV.** You can tell that a vowel is long if you say and hear the name of the letter. Here are some examples.
>
> **EXAMPLE**
>
> **lā-bor   rē-cent   mī-nor   tō-tal   mū-sic**

MARIA: Give me some words to practice.

EXERCISE Say each of these words aloud. The first vowel is pronounced as a long vowel sound in each word. You can apply the rule to these words. Divide each word into syllables. The first one is done for you.

agent ā-gent	open _____	motel _____
local _____	label _____	slogan _____
basic _____	hiker _____	notice _____
butane _____	bony _____	refill _____
stated _____	paper _____	vocal _____

MARIA: I can do those. Tell me, what are the other rules?

SULY:
> When a single consonant comes between two vowels in a word, and the first vowel is short, then the word is usually divided after the consonant—**V̆C-V.** Short vowel sounds do not sound like the name of the letter. Here are some examples.
>
> **EXAMPLE**
> **păn-el   mĕl-on   lĭv-er   hŏn-or   pŭn-ish**

MARIA: Let me practice this rule.

EXERCISE Say each of these words aloud. The first vowel is pronounced as a short vowel sound in each word. You can apply the new rule to these words. Divide each word into syllables. The first one is done for you.

travel   trăv-el   limit _____ dragon _____

study _____   never _____   medal _____

magic _____   punish _____   tragic _____

proper _____   cabin _____   wagon _____

second _____   honest _____   madam _____

Untitled

In the course of just thirty years, television has become the single most important form of entertainment in most American homes. While entertainment has been the focus up to the present, the real importance of television is only now being discovered.

In the future, television communications will serve many significant functions in the home. Already we have cassette tapes of programs, and we are able to use the home screen to play games such as electronic tennis and tic-tac-toe. Eventually, students might prefer to talk to an instructor on television through special attachments to their home sets, and this could mean the end of public schools as we know them.

Most of all, television will become a place for creative ideas. Instead of passively watching programs the way we do now, new developments will allow us to participate in shows and to feel and sense directly the emotions of the actors we watch. Also, there will be methods that will let us shape and create our own shows. We may even be able to press a button and have our own light show displayed on the screen. We will be able to think of an image and see that image flash on the screen in front of us. Different people in different places will be able to exchange ideas through television and even to interrupt and comment on shows for the benefit of performers in the television studio.

Television is a necessary part of our technological future. Now is the time for us to consider it as a responsibility, so that, when the new inventions make it more interesting to watch television, our own ideas and creative talents will be ready and waiting to make the technology of television more beneficial for all.

DICTIONARY EXERCISE Tell how many syllables each word has and mark each diacritically. Use your dictionary to help you.

Word	Number of Syllables	Diacritical Marks
1. television	_____	_____
2. direct	_____	_____
3. benefit	_____	_____
4. emotions	_____	_____
5. screen	_____	_____

LITERAL AND GENERAL COMPREHENSION EXERCISE Highlight the main idea sentence in each paragraph. Then answer the questions at the top of the next page.

_____ 1. In the future, television will provide more
     a. cassette tapes of programs.
     b. viewer participation in shows.
     c. televisions around the world.
     d. varied shows to watch.

_____ 2. The best title for this passage is
     a. Television and Our Technological Future.
     b. Creative Television Past and Present.
     c. Audience Participation in Future Shows.
     d. Television.

_____ 3. The best main idea for paragraph 3 is found
     a. in the middle of the paragraph.
     b. in the last sentence.
     c. in the first sentence.
     d. nowhere in the paragraph.

_____ 4. Viewer creativity will include
     a. sitting and watching a variety of shows.
     b. exchanging ideas with one's family.
     c. sending mental images onto the television screen.
     d. having studio performers participate in the shows.

WRITING PRACTICE Write four details in sentence form for each main idea sentence below.

Main Idea Sentence 1 Children can find outdoor activities at any time of the year.

In the winter, _____.

In the spring, _____.

In the summer, _____.

In the fall, _____.

Main Idea Sentence 2 I expect to spend my free time in different ways as I grow older.

When I am twenty-five, _____.

When I am forty, _____.

When I am sixty-five, _____.

When I am eighty, _____.

Main Idea Sentence 3 Before the year three thousand, our homes will have many new time-saving devices.

In the 1980s, ————————————————————————.

In the early 1990s, ————————————————————.

By 2000, ————————————————————————.

By 2025, ————————————————————.

Main Idea Sentence 4 In future years, cars will change radically.

Within five years, ————————————————————.

After ten years, ————————————————————.

In the next twenty years, ——————————————.

By the year 2050, ————————————————————.

Now select two of your main idea sentences and write a paragraph for each on separate paper. Be sure to indent the first sentence and to follow the margins. You may add sentences which describe each detail more thoroughly.

UNIT IV
WOULD YOU BUY
A USED CAR FROM
THESE AUTHORS?

Reprinted by permission of Harry Greenberger.

Advertising influences all forms of American communications, from television to children's books. In this unit you will learn about the nature of advertising and its effects on American life. The exercises in this unit are designed to develop your skills of note-taking and dividing words into syllables.

DISCUSSION

°a forceful impression

What commercials have made a great impact° on you in the last month? What makes you buy one brand instead of another? Do you remember advertisements when you shop? What kinds of advertisements appear in magazines in your country?

INITIAL READING

Advertising

We want *you* to try our product. Not only is it new, improved, and easy to use, but it also comes in a giant economy size that will save you money. Nine out of ten doctors recommend it, a famous Hollywood star uses it every day, and, if you buy it and try it, your love life will improve, and your neighbors will envy you. On the other hand, if you don't use our product, romance will fly out the window, and your neighbors will despise you. Even worse, you'll still have to listen to our commercials! So look for our brightly colored display in a store near you!

QUESTIONS

1. Could the paragraph above be used to advertise toothpaste, toilet paper, salad dressing, detergent, a sportscar, or all these items? _____

   _____

2. The paragraph uses many different advertising techniques. Which one do you find most effective? Which one do you find most offensive?

   _____

CHAPTER 16

RECOGNIZING THE RELATIONSHIP OF MAIN IDEAS AND DETAILS

* *
*

In the last unit you learned that the main idea sentence is the most general statement that is developed by the details in a paragraph. Using the umbrella design, you saw that a main idea sentence covers all the details and can appear anywhere in the paragraph.

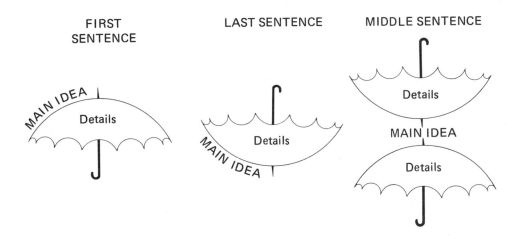

FIRST SENTENCE

LAST SENTENCE

MIDDLE SENTENCE

MAIN IDEA
Details

MAIN IDEA
Details

Details

MAIN IDEA

Details

Now, concentrate on the relationship of the details to the main idea. Understanding this relationship is the basis of good comprehension and of good note-taking skills. Consider this paragraph.

EXAMPLE

Estrella's problem began last week when she moved into a new apartment and was fixing it up. She went to get her mail and was surprised to find the box filled with ads and letters offering new services. More junk mail arrived in the next few days. By the end of the week, she was receiving coupons, restaurant ads, diaper service certificates, cleaning circulars,° and requests for money from local charities. Estrella became fed up° with all the junk mail she had received in her first week in the new apartment.

°advertisements that are given out
°disgusted

QUESTIONS

1. What is the main idea sentence of the paragraph? _____

_____

2. What are the details? _____

_____

_____

3. What purpose do the details serve? _____

The last sentence is the main idea: "Estrella became fed up with all the junk mail she had received in her first week in the new apartment." The supporting details are: "She went to get her mail and was surprised to find the box filled with ads and letters offering new services" and "By the end of the week, she was receiving coupons, restaurant ads, diaper service certificates, cleaning circulars, and requests for money from local charities."

The important details tell <u>why</u> Estrella was upset and <u>what</u> caused her to get upset. These details support and illustrate the main idea.

> **Details** relate to the main idea. They **illustrate** and **support** the main idea sentence in a paragraph.

EXERCISE Listed are several main idea sentences. Add three details to each main idea sentence. Remember that details must support or illustrate the main idea. The first one is done for you.

1. I enjoy watching skywriting for several reasons.

<u>P</u>lanes fly close to each other as they spell out words. _____

<u>M</u>essages stretch as far as one mile. _____

Sometimes the sky ads are <u>f</u>unny slogans. _____

2. Many television commercials are silly.

_____

_____

_____

3. People advertise products for many reasons.

_____

_____

_____

4. Magazines advertise many different kinds of products.

_____

_____

_____

5. Junk mail is a great nuisance.
                 a boder

_____

_____

_____

PRACTICE Add three supporting details to each main idea sentence.

1. Some commercials are annoying.

_____

_____

_____

2. Ads for pet foods actually appeal to people.

_____

_____

_____

3. There are only a few places where we don't see ads.

_____

_____

_____

EXERCISE In each of the following exercises, read the entire paragraph. Then highlight the main idea sentence and answer the question about the details.

Paragraph 1 Did you ever watch a child in front of a television set? Very interesting things can be observed. A child may be crawling on the floor, playing with his or her toys, or talking to himself or herself while the show is in progress. However, as soon as a commercial appears, the child stops what he or she is doing and faces the television set, intent on° the picture, motion, and sound coming from the screen. No matter what is said, the child stares at the set until the commercial has ended. Then the child returns to crawling, playing, and talking. The magnetic effect of commercials on children is amazing.

°watching with concentration

Recognizing the Relationship of Main Ideas and Details

_____ The details in this paragraph discuss which of the following?
   a. Examples of television's effects on children
   b. What happens to a child's behavior before, during, and after a television commercial
   c. Examples of a child's behavior

Paragraph 2   Reading the Sunday paper is like taking a walk through the largest department store imaginable. There are advertisements for apartments, cars, lost pets, department stores, and supermarkets. The largest number of ads on Sunday is for job opportunities. Hotels, motels, and airlines announce special package deals° in the Sunday paper as well. Theaters promote hit shows, and record stores display their latest discs.° Garden supply stores, health spas, sports arenas, and hobby clubs also advertise. There is no end to the list.

°special trips where prices
 include everything
°records

_____ The details in this paragraph discuss which of the following?
   a. Types of advertisements
   b. Things to buy in a big city
   c. Advertisements in the Sunday newspaper

Paragraph 3   On my first trip to the United States, I was quickly introduced to an unpleasant aspect of American advertising. Driving to my hotel I saw nothing but billboards, posters, and signs along the highway. Houses, trees, and ponds were completely blocked by giant ads for airlines, suntan lotions, cars, liquor, cigarettes, and many products and services. All along the highway, hundreds of ads almost completely blocked lovely grassy areas. The term pollution should be expanded to include highway advertisements.

_____ The details in this paragraph discuss which of the following?
   a. Sights along the country's highways
   b. Ways to advertise on the roads
   c. Highway advertising pollution

PRACTICE   Read each paragraph and highlight the main idea sentence. In the space next to each paragraph write the number of details that support or illustrate the main idea.

Paragraph 1 _____ The best way to find a moving company is to look in the Yellow Pages. All kinds of businesses advertise their services in the Telephone Company's Yellow Page book. People use this book to find the names and telephone numbers of local companies. The Yellow Pages offers the names of companies, but it does not list rates. People must call the companies for rates and hourly minimums.

Paragraph 2 _____   Even if I forget my newspaper or book, I always have something to read on the way to work. Every day, Alfred, Raphael, and I ride the bus to the City Hall area. I have learned that "f i kn rd ths ad i kn gt a vry gd jb." We know when City Hall was built, and where we can look for employment opportunities. Alfred once called the hot line° to see if someone would answer. I know where to adopt a pet, and Raphael can tell you where to get a high school diploma. We have learned a lot from reading advertisements on buses.

°a special telephone number for immediate help or advice

Paragraph 3 _____ Watching a television movie is really like watching twenty commercials with a movie sandwiched in between. When I sit down to watch the show and am really enjoying the story, suddenly the movie stops. There is a commercial interruption. That is the time for me to walk straight out of the living room and head for the refrigerator. I prepare a snack and come back just in time for the start of the movie. I hope that the sponsors° aren't counting on me to buy their products. I don't even know what they are selling.

°those paying for advertising time

Paragraph 4 _____ There is a great deal to be said for radio advertising. Television advertisements show the viewer everything. However, when people listen to radio advertisement jingles,° talking commercials, or dialogue advertisements, they must imagine a great deal. They must picture people arguing about a product, or they must imagine kids in the backyard yelling for something cool to drink. Faraway places have to take shape before their eyes. There is much more for people to think about when they have to picture scenes themselves. Radio advertisements make the listener work hard.

°songs promoting products

CHAPTER 17
UNDERSTANDING SYLLABLES

* *
*

Being able to divide words into syllables [sound] will help you to pronounce new and difficult words. Read the following dialogue.

MARIA: I've been having difficulty pronouncing new words, Suly. Can you help me?

SULY: Yes! Professor English taught me a wonderful method that helps me when I read new words.

MARIA: What did he say?

SULY: He said we can divide known and unknown words into syllables or word parts.

MARIA: What do you mean?

SULY: Listen to me say these words:

better   mention   dancer   jogger

How many parts do you hear in each word?

MARIA: Two.

SULY: That's right. Each word has two parts or syllables. It's easy to hear them.

MARIA: Wait a minute! How does that help me if I can't say the word? It's easy when you say words you know, but not at all easy when the word is new.

SULY: Here are some clues, Maria, to help you split new words into syllables. When they're split according to these rules, they're easier to pronounce.

Dividing Words Into Syllables: VC-CV

vowel - consonant

When a word has two vowel sounds separated by two consonants, **VC-CV**, such as "better," "dancer," or "jogger," you usually divide the word between the two consonants.

EXAMPLE

    VC CV   VC CV   VC CV

    bet / ter   dan / cer   jog / ger

EXERCISE All the words following have two vowel sounds separated by two consonants. Divide each word into syllables by drawing a line between the syllables. Then say each word.

1. oc/cur
2. spon/sor
3. ser/vant
4. pic/ture
5. con/test

6. at/tend
7. ef/fect (n) affect (v)
8. pol/lute
9. mem/ber
10. or/der

11. sec/tion
12. cir/cus
13. let/ter
14. ser/vice
15. sug/gest

PRACTICE Look at the words in this list. The words have two vowel sounds separated by two consonants. Divide the words into syllables. Say each word aloud.

1. gim/mick
2. prob/lem
3. pic/nic
4. mag/net
5. com/merce
6. fes/tive
7. sug/gest
8. main/tain
9. num/ber
10. af/fect

11. pub/lic
12. at/tract
13. in/ter/rupt
14. con/scious
15. pub/lish
16. sup/port
17. par/ties
18. mar/ket
19. gar/den
20. ex/pand

Dividing Words Into Syllables: Consonant Blends

Some consonants appear together in a word and are pronounced as **blends.** Being able to pronounce blends in new words is an important reading tool. The following consonant combinations often are pronounced as blended sounds and stay together when the word is divided into syllables.

bl cl fl gl pl sl br fr dr pr tr
sc sk sl sm sn sp sw st scr spl str

Other combinations are pronounced as one sound and stay together when the word is divided into syllables:

ch   gh   ph   sh   th   ck

EXAMPLE

con/**str**uct im/**pr**ess pa**ck**/age te**ch**/nique

EXERCISE Divide the following words into syllables.

1. ex/press
2. in/struct
3. de/flate
4. bro/ther
5. dis/charge
6. be/friend
7. re/ply
8. mer/chant
9. bro/chure
10. pur/chase
11. trans/fer
12. an/swer
13. re/flex
14. fran/chise
15. hun/dreds
16. dis/grace

child   long   short
mate   mat

PRACTICE READING

Untitled

America is a society in which children have watched approximately 18,000 television commercials by the time that they have reached their middle teens. My friend Jolie learned this fact a few weeks ago and decided to do something about it. She thinks that the number of commercials that children see can influence the way in which they view the world. That is, Jolie believes that children who watch so many ads will grow up to believe that the most important thing in life is to buy, buy, buy! This, says Jolie, is wrong. A little child cannot understand advertisements for what they are and so believes totally in what he or she hears.

I have been thinking about what Jolie has told me. I suppose that she is right. I know that it is easy to manipulate° the minds of children because they don't see things logically,° as adults do. And I am upset myself at how the advertisers can control a child's outlook on the world. I think I should join Jolie in her efforts to change advertising tactics° when it comes to advertisements for children. I really have a responsibility to make sure that future generations are given every chance to develop their minds without the interference of mass media.°

Of course, there is another side to the issue. After all, parents ought to take responsibility for what their children watch and how much television they see. I know that many parents just want their children to be quiet, and so they let them watch as much television as they want. But, in the long run, the methods of advertisers have enormous power because we are a society of consumers. I only hope that some day there can be a solution to this problem. Children need *our* guidance, not the guidance of advertisers.

°handle or use something to one's advantage
°reasonably; sensibly

°plans; methods; strategies

°communication areas such as television, newspapers, radio, and magazines

VOCABULARY EXERCISE Use one of the words defined in the passage to complete each sentence.

1. Adults think more _____ than small children.

2. _____ have a great influence on children's minds.

3. Advertisers try to _____ the minds of children with clever commercials.

4. Advertisers use various _____ to sell their products.

SYLLABICATION EXERCISE Pronounce each of the following words aloud. Then divide these words into syllables. Use your dictionary to check your answers.

1. A/me/ri/ca
2. a/ver/age
3. de/cid/ed
4. com/mer/cials
5. ad/ver/tis/ing
6. me/di/a
7. con/trol

8. ma/nip/u/late
9. tac/tics
10. re/spon/si/bil/i/ty
11. tel/e/vise
12. sol/u/tion
13. fu/ture
14. watched

LITERAL COMPREHENSION EXERCISE Answer the following statements True (T) or False (F) according to the information in the passage.

_____ 1. There are 18,000 commercials produced each year.

_____ 2. Jolie believes that television advertising has a bad influence on children.

_____ 3. The writer of this passage agrees with Jolie's opinion of television advertising.

_____ 4. All parents want their children to watch television.

_____ 5. Children should be influenced by advertising, not by parents.

MAIN IDEAS EXERCISE Reread the passage and highlight the main idea of each paragraph in one color.

Would You Buy a Used Car from these Authors?

CHAPTER (18)

HIGHLIGHTING MAIN IDEAS AND DETAILS:
Note-Taking

* *

You have been highlighting main ideas in previous exercises. Look at this short paragraph.

EXAMPLE

Billboards and posters are examples of highway advertising. Another type of highway advertisement is the brightly lit neon° sign. In some places paintings are done on walls or on the sides of buildings or barns. **There are many ways to advertise products on major roadways.**

°a gas used in electric signs

QUESTIONS

1. Can you see the main idea sentence quickly? _____

2. What helps you to see it? _____

3. Can you see the details quickly? _____

4. Explain. _____

The main idea sentence stands out because it is highlighted. You can see it quickly. The details are not as easily identified. You can make the details just as easy to see by highlighting them as well. However, you must use a <u>different color</u> highlighting marker to show the difference between the main idea and the details.

Highlighting the **main idea in one color** and **the details in another color** is the beginning of note-taking. You can quickly see the main idea and its related details. Highlighting is helpful when it is time to review your notes for a quiz.

It is not necessary to highlight the entire detail sentence. If you did that, you might highlight the entire passage. An easy way to avoid that is by turning the main idea into a question starting with **what, who, why,** or **how.** The important details will answer that question.

Main Idea Sentence: There are many ways to advertise products on major roadways.

Question: **What** are the different ways to advertise products on major roadways?

Answer: **billboards, posters, neon signs,** and **paintings**

EXERCISE Here are main idea sentences and their related details. In each sentence, the question has been started for you. First, complete the question and then highlight the part of each detail that answers that question. The first one is done for you.

MAIN IDEA	DETAILS
1. A product package contains two parts. Question: <u>What are the two parts in a product package?</u>	a. A product package includes the **container for the product.** b. There is also the **box that the container comes in.**
2. The shape of a package is important for sales. Question: <u>Why is</u>	a. People like packages that can be handled easily. b. Interesting shapes attract the attention of consumers.
3. Manufacturers pay a great deal of attention to product names. Question: <u>Why do</u>	a. A good product name is remembered easily. b. A product should have a catchy name that will attract the consumer's attention.
4. Designers spend a lot of time choosing package colors. Question: <u>Why do</u>	a. Bright colors suggest a bright product. b. Pale colors can have a soothing effect on the consumer.
5. Some colors clearly suggest elegance. Question: <u>What</u>	a. Colors such as brown, gold, and purple suggest richness. b. Silver and navy also suggest luxury.

6. Some packaging clearly emphasizes bright colors.

Question: <u>What do</u> _____

_____

    a. Bright colors such as red, yellow, and aqua suggest youth and liveliness.

    b. Bright green and orange suggest an active life.

7. Packaging a product requires many people's talents.

Question: <u>Why does</u> _____

_____

    a. Many people are involved in package design.

    b. Many people are involved in package production.

8. The way a package is displayed is vital to good sales.

Question: <u>Why is</u> _____

_____

    a. People are attracted by well-designed product displays.

    b. Good displays single out the product for sale.

9. Packages must be test-marketed° before they are put into production.

Question: <u>Why must</u> _____

_____

    a. Consumer opinions of the packaging help make final decisions about the package.

    b. The package may need to be redesigned.

°test public reaction to the package

10. Packages sometimes take years to develop.

Question: <u>Why do</u> _____

_____

    a. Packages must be designed and test-marketed.

    b. They may be reworked and marketed again.

    c. The package must be produced, shipped, and displayed.

EXERCISE Now practice highlighting main ideas and details in paragraphs. Highlight the main idea sentence in one color. Then turn the main idea sentence into a question and highlight the relevant parts of the details in another color. The first paragraph is done for you.

Paragraph 1 Every day puzzled shoppers stand in front of dozens of brands of detergent° in the market, trying to decide which one to buy. What are they looking at? It could be the **size** or **shape of the box.** It may be the **colors** used or the **names** selected for each product. Perhaps **something about the product rings a bell.**° They may remember the **slogan**° or **commercial** used for the product on television. Maybe they **subconsciously**° **remember the commercial.** The **ingredients** in most of the detergents **are the same,** and the **prices are fairly equal. Many factors influence shoppers in the choices that they make.**

°a strong soap

°brings to mind / °a word or phrase used in advertising
°without realizing or being aware

Paragraph 2 Last night I noticed a special kind of advertising technique called the testimonial. I watched a sponsor try to sell his product by having a famous person endorse° it. Sponsors may also use actors, actresses, football players, or senators who praise the wonderful product that they have been paid to advertise. I realized that consumers are not really buying the product because it is the best on the market. Rather, they are buying "Socko" cereal because a famous person is selling it.

°give approval to

Paragraph 3 Advertisers use many interesting techniques to promote their products. One of the most common is the transfer,° or association,° method. Consider a men's cologne,° for example. The commercial that advertises it may tell you very little about the cologne. Instead, your attention is focused on all the women who are chasing after the lucky man wearing the cologne. The product is not what is being sold. You, the consumer, are being sold! The message is simply this: If you buy the product, you will be irresistible to women. Think about it!

°an advertising technique
°a men's perfume

Paragraph 4 Last night Theresa was watching a television program and saw a cosmetics commercial. The ad promised her beautiful skin, a radiant° complexion, and a healthy glow. This morning Theresa went to the drugstore and spent $42.00 on all the products she saw advertised last night. She bought face cream, skin lotion, eye cream, a special soap, and makeup remover. She now has everything that the actress in the advertisement told her to buy. Theresa bought the products, the commercial, and the dream of being beautiful.

°glowing; shining

Paragraph 5 My friend Ivan graduated from a business school this week and beginning in July will be working in the advertising department of a large corporation. He was told that his job will be to write copy° for magazine and newspaper advertisements. He will be thinking up clever ways to sell the newest deodorants. His advertising copy must make the reader want to buy the deodorant, remember the deodorant's brand name, and quickly identify the product in a store. Ivan must come up with witty° slogans that will sell the deodorant. Ivan's copywriting talents will be more a test of his creativity° than of his writing ability.

°written material for an advertisement

°clever or amusing

°originality; imagination

Paragraph 6 Professor English assigned Rosalind and me the task of writing a beautiful people° commercial. In class, we learned that some advertisements show a beautiful person using a product. Sometimes the product has no connection with the person or with beauty. For example, a handsome movie star sells auto filters or a socialite° talks about potato chips. Rosalind and I made up a commercial in which a famous singer tells about spark plugs for a car. Rosalind and I wrote a beautiful people advertisement that used a famous person to sell an everyday product.

°wealthy, elegant people

°someone well-known among the rich

Paragraph 7 Nowadays, more sponsors are using ordinary looking people to sell products. People who are fat, old, ugly, bald, or just plain looking are becoming the hottest° stars of commercials. Maybe viewers are getting tired of watching beautifully-dressed housewives waxing their kitchen floors with Wisko. Somehow, people have trouble believing that every male is slim, thirty-five, good looking, and sexy. In the future, we will be seeing more ordinary people selling products.

°most popular

Paragraph 8 My schoolmates Guy and Lorenzo will be starting acting school next fall. They have both appeared on television and have had small parts in the movies. However, Guy and Lorenzo are giving all that up. In September, they will begin studying commercial acting, and they have a good reason for wanting to make commercials. If they hit it right,° they will appear in many commercials. The salaries can be excellent. Usually, they will be paid every time that a commercial is shown. This means that, in six months, they will still be receiving residuals° from the commercials. If they succeed, they will make a lot of money.

°find success

°money paid to someone from the sale or performance of his work

Paragraph 9 Years ago, actors like Bert Lahr made television history when they decided to make commercials. Bert Lahr, a wonderful comedian, perhaps best known as the cowardly° lion in *The Wizard of Oz,* made his commercial debut selling potato chips. Since then, many actors have followed his lead, because getting into the business of making commercials is very profitable for well-known stars. John Wayne received top dollar° for the commercials he made. Nowadays, many stars are selling all sorts of products and services on television.

°fearful; without courage

°the highest pay or salary

CHAPTER 19

DIVIDING WORDS
INTO SYLLABLES:
V-CV or VC-V
⁎⁎

MARIA: I think I'm beginning to understand how to break up words into syllables. Is there anything else I should know about syllables?

SULY: Yes. If you can identify long and short vowel sounds, you will be able to separate many new words into syllables.

MARIA: What do you mean? I already know the sounds of vowels.

SULY: Listen to these words.

protein   label   erase

Is the first vowel sound in each word long or short?

MARIA: That's easy. The first vowels all have a long sound.

SULY: Right. In these words the vowel sound is long. This means that you can divide the word after the vowel sound. Professor English said that knowing how to divide words into syllables will help us to pronounce new words.

> When a single consonant comes between two vowels and the first vowel is long, divide the word before the consonant: **V̄-CV**.

MARIA: Let me try that rule with the three words that you used.

prō/tein   lā/bel   ē/qual

EXERCISE Divide the following words into syllables.

1. de/tail
2. re/gal
3. pri/ces
4. re/mind
5. a/gent
6. fi/nal
7. pre/view
8. ba/sic
9. pro/ceed
10. slo/gan
11. de/ter
12. fla/vor
13. mo/tion
14. po/tent

Would you Buy a Used Car from these Authors?

SULY: Now listen to these words:

man|age   fin|ish   met|al

Is the first vowel sound in each word long or short?

MARIA: Short.

SULY: Here is how Professor English said to divide these words into syllables. If we follow this guide, we will be able to read many new and difficult words.

> When a single consonant comes between two vowels and the first vowel is short, you divide the word after the consonant: **V̆C-V.**

MARIA: That means that I can divide the words you said to me like this:

măn / age   fĭn / ish   mĕt / al

EXERCISE Divide the following words into syllables.

1. t r a v|e l
2. m e d|a l
3. n e|v e r
4. l i|m i t
5. t a|l e n t
6. l e|v e l
7. p r o|m i s e
8. p r o|p e r
9. p a|t e n t
10. s e|c o n d
11. h a|b i t
12. p u|n i s h
13. m o|d e r n
14. d a m|a g e

PRACTICE Say each of the following words aloud. Write the vowel sound that you hear in the first syllable. Then divide the word into syllables. The first two are done for you.

	VOWEL SOUND	SYLLABICATION
1. ba|sis	long a	bā-sis
2. med|ic	short e	mĕd-ic
3. fi|nance		
4. dram|a		
5. pro|fit		
6. gro|cer		
7. clin|ic		
8. ma|jor		
9. no|vel		

10. deliver _____   _____

11. program _____   _____

12. direct   *direct* _____   _____

13. retail _____   _____

14. cosmetic _____   _____

15. local _____   _____

Would You Buy a Used Car from these Authors?

Dividing Words Into Syllables: -LE

MARIA: I thought that I understood how to break up words into syllables. Now we are studying words that end in **-le** like fable and jingle, and I'm confused.

SULY: I know **-le** words are difficult, but here is a clue to figure that out. Say these words out loud:

sable   angle   purple   table

What is similar about them?

MARIA: They all end in **-le.**

SULY: Say them aloud again. Do you hear the end syllables in sable and angle?

MARIA: Yes, in each one I hear a consonant, and the **-le** at the end sounds like **əl.**

When a word ends in **-le** and has a consonant before it, the word is usually divided before that consonant.

EXAMPLE

tăn / glĕ   sĭm / plĕ   ā / blĕ   Bī / blĕ

EXERCISE Divide each of the words into syllables. Say the words out loud.

1. as/sem/ble
2. ca/ble
3. hum/ble
4. sti/fle
5. mid/dle

6. can/dle
7. fum/ble
8. strug/gle
9. peo/ple
10. han/dle

PRACTICE Here are some longer words. Divide them into syllables.

1. a/vai/la/ble
2. ex/am/ple
3. un/cle
4. res/pon/si/ble
5. rec/tan/gle

6. drink/a/ble
7. val/u/a/ble
8. le/gi/ble
9. per/ish/a/ble
10. prin/ci/ple

PRACTICE Using syllabication guidelines, divide the following words into syllables. Say each word aloud first.

1. cir/cu/lar
2. as/so/ci/ate
3. cat/chy
4. so/lu/tion

5. sta/tion
6. com/pa/ny
7. heal/thy
8. ex/pen/sive

9. me/re/l y
10. sta/ble
11. cos/me/tic
12. ac/tu/all y
13. fluf/fy
14. com/pu/ter
15. in/for/ma/tion
16. ro/yal/ties
17. tes/ti/mo/ny
18. pro/gram
19. pre/sent

20. e/quip/ment
21. wit/ty
22. tech/ni/que
23. sug/gest
24. cal/cu/late
25. va/lue
26. cor/po/ra/tion
27. de/ter/gent
28. ex/pe/ri/men/ting
29. pro/spect
30. com/mon/ly

Would You Buy a Used Car from these Authors?

CHAPTER 20

HIGHLIGHTING MAIN IDEAS
AND DETAILS
IN LONGER SELECTIONS

⁎

Now you can practice highlighting main ideas and details in longer selections. Remember that, in these passages, each paragraph has a main idea and related details. Highlight each **main idea in one color** and the **details in another color.** Then answer the questions at the end of the passage.

Passage 1 Every time we turn on our radio, we hear jingles.° These are catchy° tunes and lyrics used to sell almost any product imaginable. It is not easy to sell some products, but good jingles are a surefire° way of promoting sales.

°songs promoting products
°easily remembered
°guaranteed

What makes a really good jingle? First is the tune. It must be hummable.° Like any record hit, people must be able to remember the melody. Sometimes people even walk down the street humming the tune of a commercial. Next, the words must be easily understood and must catch people's attention. Finally, the jingle must be aired° frequently so that people recognize it and associate it with the product.

°easy to hum

°played on the radio or television

There are many good examples of jingles. They include "The Pepsi Generation," MacDonald's "You Deserve a Break Today," Coke's "I'd Like to Teach the World to Sing," and Chevrolet's "See the U.S.A." commercials. These are just a few on a long list of hit commercials. They all follow the rules: good tunes, catchy lyrics, and frequent showing. Can you remember any other jingles? Are there others that follow the rules?

SYLLABICATION EXERCISE Using the syllabication guides presented in this unit, divide the following words into syllables.

al/most	fi/nal/ly	com/mer/cial
real/ly	hum/ming	pro/mot/ing
re/cord	fre/quent/ly	catch/y
a/ble	Chev/ro/let	prod/uct
re/mem/ber	ex/am/ple	lyr/ics
un/der/stood	pos/si/ble	i/ma/gin/able
mel/o/dy	jin/gle	

COMPREHENSION EXERCISE Answer the following questions by deciding if each is True (T) or False (F).

_____ 1. Tune, melody, and lyrics are the three basics of hit commercials.

_____ 2. The most important ingredient of a hit commercial is the tune.

_____ 3. Chevrolet's big hit was "You Deserve a Break Today."

_____ 4. Good lyrics will catch people's attention.

_____ 5. A surefire way of promoting sales is by using television.

_____ 6. The best title for this passage is "Jingles Sell Products."

°an elegant bird

Passage 2   There is a Hall of Fame in America that has a cow, a bear, a dog, and a peacock° among its members. Does that sound strange? Well, it is not strange to people who are aware of the large impact that the advertising industry has on the American consumer. All these animal characters were awarded Hall of Fame status because of their success in selling products.

Many of the advertising Hall of Famers are well known. Among the animals are NBC's peacock (television), Exxon's tiger (gasoline), RCA Victor's listening dog (phonograph records), Borden's Elsie the Cow (dairy products) and Elmer the Bull (glue), the Forest Service's Smokey the Bear (fire prevention in forests), MGM's Leo the Lion (motion pictures), General Cigar and Tobacco's White Owl (cigars), Kellogg's Tony the Tiger (breakfast cereal), and Star-Kist Food's Morris the Cat (cat food). Other characters associated with special products include Procter & Gamble's Mr. Clean (heavy-duty detergent), Green Giant's Jolly Green Giant (vegetables), Standard Brand's Miss Blue Bonnet (margarine), GE's Mr. McGoo (light bulbs), Bristol Meyers' Speedy Alka Seltzer (pain reliever), Pillsbury's Doughboy (flour), Dutch Boy's Dutch Boy (paints), Smith Brothers' Smith Brothers (cough drops), and Perdue Farms' Frank Perdue (chickens).

Each of these names should bring to mind a character or a product. Each one can be recognized instantly. Seeing Elsie the Cow makes almost everyone think of milk and dairy products. Smokey the Bear reminds people to prevent forest fires. Every time people see one of these symbols, they are seeing the results of well-planned and well-executed° advertising campaigns.°

°carried out
°plans for selling a
 product

DICTIONARY EXERCISE   Give the number of vowel sounds pronounced in each of the following words. Write the diacritical marks for each word. Use your dictionary to help. The first one is done for you.

WORD	NUMBER OF VOWELS PRONOUNCED	DIACRITICAL MARKS
1. American	4	ə mer′ i kən
2. fame		
3. cow		

Would You Buy a Used Car from these Authors?

4. bear   _____ / _____   _____

5. strange   _____ / _____   _____

6. Dutch Boy _____ / _____   _____

7. paint   _____ / _____   _____

8. aunt   _____ / _____   _____

9. product   _____ / _____   _____

10. dough   _____ / _____   _____

SYLLABICATION EXERCISE Give the number of vowels pronounced in each of the following words. How many syllables does each word contain? Divide each word into syllables. The first one is done for you.

Word	Number of Vowels Pronounced	Number of Syllables	Word Divided
1. symbol	2	2	sym-bol
2. Smokey	2	2	
3. status	2	2	
4. Elsie	2	2	
5. characters	3	3	
6. advertise	3	3	
7. picture	2	2	
8. Tony	2	2	
9. Tiger	2	2	
10. product	2	2	
11. consumer	3	3	
12. awarded	2	2	
13. recording	3	3	
14. special	2	2	
15. campaign	2	2	
16. forest	2	2	
17. execute	2	2	
18. result	2	2	
19. Morris	2	2	
20. Bonnet	2	2	
21. industry	3	3	

22. impact _____2_____ _____2_____ _____

23. Whipple _____2_____ _____2_____ _____

24. popularity _____5_____ _____5_____ _____

25. because _____2_____ _____2_____ _____

LITERAL COMPREHENSION EXERCISE   Match the symbol with the product.

_7_ peacock   1. milk

_6_ dog   2. paint

_1_ cow   3. Alka Seltzer

_8_ bear   4. cough drops

_5_ lion   5. MGM

_2_ Dutch Boy   6. RCA

_4_ Smith Brothers   7. NBC

_3_ Speedy   8. forest safety

LITERAL COMPREHENSION PRACTICE   Select the best answer according to the story.

_C_ 1. A lion, a bear, and a tiger are all members of the
     a. Baseball Hall of Fame.
     b. Football Hall of Fame.
     c. Advertising Hall of Fame.

____ 2. The characters mentioned in the passage have all achieved
     a. instant recognition.
     b. popularity in selling products.
     c. Hall of Fame status.
     d. all of the above.

____ 3. Some characters may be associated with
     a. a particular product.
     b. an industry.
     c. a company.
     d. all of the above.

_B_ 4. Elsie and Smokey are symbols for
     a. forest safety and paints.
     b. dairy products and forest safety.
     c. cough drops and bananas.
     d. records and television.

Would You Buy a Used Car from these Authors?

GENERAL COMPREHENSION EXERCISE Choose the best answer according to the story.

_____ 1. The best title for this selection is
   a. The American Hall of Fame.
   b. Cartoon Characters.
   c. The Advertising Hall of Fame.
   d. Elsie the Cow and Smokey the Bear.

2. Go back to the selection and reread the highlighted main idea sentence and details in the second paragraph. All twenty of the details are examples of _____.

Passage 3 Advertising follows the seasons.° In winter, advertisers try to warm up° their audiences. In December and January, advertisers often place their products near a crackling fire. This appeals to all of us, especially when we are trying to keep warm in sub-zero weather. Other advertisers may place their product in a tropical setting. Because many people would like to be in a warm climate in winter, they are attentive to such advertising. Apparently, a setting can often influence consumers to buy a product.

Summer advertising is designed to make us feel cool. A tall glass filled with ice can increase the appeal of a simple glass of water. When it is ninety degrees outside, cool white cream applied to a sunburn promises relief for red-hot skin. Advertisements offering escape from the blistering heat of summer appeal to us all.

°advertise according to winter, spring, summer, and fall
°put the audience in a good mood

SYLLABICATION EXERCISE Divide each word into syllables.

1. a d/v e r/t i/s e r
2. a p/p e a l
3. i n/f l u e n/c e
4. w e a/t h e r
5. c l i/m a t e

6. D e/c e m/b e r
7. c o n/t r a s t
8. w i n/t e r
9. t r o/p i c
10. s u m/m e r

LITERAL COMPREHENSION EXERCISE Match the season with the advertising approach.

_2_ warm up the audience   1. summer

_1_ use of cream on hot skin   2. winter

_2_ use of fire

_2_ use of snowy mountains

_1_ use of ice in a frosty glass

_1_ cool the audience

_1_ use of palm trees

GENERAL COMPREHENSION EXERCISE

1. In the second paragraph, the details are examples of _____
   _____.

2. The best title for this passage is _____.

Passage 4 Sylvester and I are watching television advertisements because we need information for a class research project. We have to discuss realism and fantasy in television advertising, and so we are looking for examples of distortions° and falsehoods° in television commercials. The question we are asking is, "Is the commercial true to life,° or does it offer an unreal picture of the product?"

°twisted facts / ° lies
°real; genuine

Sylvester is keeping track of° the distortions, and he already has quite a long list. He says that all housewives seem to live in lovely homes, dress beautifully, and love their household chores. They smile and boast about floor waxes and proudly display their dirty laundry, dusty tabletops, and filthy ovens. In addition, he has never seen men doing housework. Sylvester thinks that this view of family life is filled with distortions.

°following carefully

I am keeping track of the people who appear in the advertisements. I have found handsome men courting the All-American Girl, and they are always recommending brand X toothpaste or brand Y cologne. I see teenagers and children surrounded by their friends, having wonderful times at parties and at school, and they are usually enjoying large harmonious° family gatherings. I think that these advertisements are also filled with fantasy.

°pleasant; sociable

Sylvester and I have concluded that much of American life is pictured unrealistically in commercials. Teenagers do not always have fun at parties, and very few people love doing chores. People do have problems, but few of these are ever shown in commercials. Instead, we watch Cinderella discover a miracle floor wax, finish the kitchen chores, and waltz off to the ball. Our heads are filled with these fantasies, and they also suggest that, for any problem, brand Z will provide the instant cure. Sylvester and I will have very few facts and a lot of fantasy to write about in our research reports.

SYLLABICATION EXERICSE Divide these words into syllables.

1. re/search/ing
2. ver/sus
3. dis/tor/tions
4. lo/ve/ly
5. beau/ti/ful/ly
6. dir/ty
7. fil/thy
8. co/log/ne

9. tee/na/gers
10. un/u/sual/ly
11. unrealistically
12. peo/ple
13. dis/co/ver
14. mi/ra/cle
15. kit/chen
16. con/clude

Would You Buy a Used Car from these Authors?

Which of the following words are properly divided into syllables? Check them. Then correct the rest in the space provided.

_3_ 1. fan-ta-size _____

_2_ 2. vers-ion _____

_3_ 3. con-ti-nue _____

_2_ 4. dis-tort _____

_4_ 5. har-moni-ous _____

_2_ 6. con-cer-n _____

_2_ 7. re-search _____

_2_ 8. pro-blem _____

_2_ 9. sur-round _____

_2_ 10. laund-ry _____

VOCABULARY EXERCISE Match these words with their meanings. Use the passage or your dictionary to help.

____ fantasy   1. a scent

____ miracle   2. beautiful

_5_ continuously   3. something romantic or unreal

_7_ distortion   4. a lie

____ falsehood   5. happening all the time

____ court   6. not based on the facts

____ cologne   7. a twisted fact

_8_ harmonious   8. pleasant, sociable

____ unrealistic   9. date or see a person

____ glamorous   10. marvelous

LITERAL COMPREHENSION EXERCISE Based on the story, choose the best answer to complete the statement.

_b_ 1. Sylvester is keeping track of
    a. advertisements showing brand X.
    b. advertising fantasies and distortions.
    c. advertisements showing housewives.
    d. both a and c.

Highlighting Main Ideas and Details in Longer Selections   **149**

B 2. Housewives in advertisements are
  a. disgusted with laundry.
  b. happy with their chores.
  c. courted by men using cologne.
  d. none of the above.

A 3. The best title for this passage is
  a. Our Research Project.
  b. Keeping Track of Television Advertising.
  c. Distortions in Television Advertising.
  d. Beautiful People on T.V.

D 4. The author found unrealistic advertisements picturing
  a. dirty laundry.
  b. city dwellers.
  c. suburban housewives.
  d. happy teenagers.

B 5. People's real problems are
  a. the basis for all advertising.
  b. distorted by commercials.
  c. never shown in commercials.
  d. told honestly in commercials.

GENERAL COMPREHENSION EXERCISE According to the story, answer the following statements True (T) or False (F).

F 1. Advertisers offer instant cures for any problem.

F 2. American teenagers are shown as popular characters.

T 3. The average homemaker has problems similar to those shown on television.

F 4. Harmonious family gatherings are true-to-life television creations.

T 5. Advertisers offer a balance of realism and fantasy in television commercials.

MAIN IDEAS AND DETAILS EXERCISE On the line, write the main idea sentence for paragraph 2 of passage 4. Below it, list the details supporting the main idea sentence. Next, write the main idea sentence for paragraph 3, and below it write the supporting details.

Would You Buy a Used Car from these Authors?

Paragraph 2

MAIN IDEA SENTENCE _____

_____

DETAILS _____

_____

_____

Paragraph 3

MAIN IDEA SENTENCE _____

_____

DETAILS _____

_____

_____

CHAPTER 21

DIVIDING WORDS
INTO SYLLABLES:
Verbs Ending in -ED

✳✳

MARIA: Now I'm puzzled about pronouncing words that end with **-ed.** I hope that you can help me.

SULY: Sure, I'll help you with those endings. The **-ed** form of the verb is a little difficult to learn because it can be pronounced in three ways.

MARIA: What are the three ways to pronounce words ending with the **-ed** form of the verb.

SULY: Here they are:

> **I.** When **-ed** is added to **verbs** ending in t or d, it is pronounced as **əd** or **id** and is a separate syllable.
>
> **EXAMPLE**
>
>   dread / **ed** = əd or id   shout / **ed** = əd or id

EXERCISE Pronounce each of these words aloud. Then divide each word into syllables.

1. res/pon/ded
2. bran/ded
3. mar/ket/ed
4. clo/se/ted
5. foun/ded
6. at/tem/p/ted
7. star/ted
8. re/tes/ted
9. nee/ded
10. bud/ge/ted

> **II.** When **ed** is added to some verbs, it is pronounced like the letter **t** as in "stopp**ed**" and is not a separate syllable.
>
> **EXAMPLE**
>
>   pass**ed** = t   walk**ed** = t

EXERCISE Pronounce each of these words aloud. Do you hear the final "*t*" sound in each word? Now divide each word that can be divided into syllables.

1. t y p e d
2. d i s/c u s s e d
3. r e/m a r k e d
4. p r i/c e d
5. s c r a p/p e d

6. s h o c k e d
7. r e/p l a c e d
8. e s/t a/b l i s h e d
9. c h a s e d
10. e n/d o r s e d

III. When **-ed** or **-d** is added to other verbs, it is pronounced as the letter **d** as in "said" and is not a separate syllable.

EXAMPLE

    travel**ed** = d   star**ed** = d

EXERCISE Pronounce each word aloud. Do you hear the final "d" sound in each word? Divide each word that can be divided into syllables.

1. p r e/p a r e d
2. t u r n e d
3. c h a r g e d
4. e m/p l o y e d
5. t e/l e/p h o n e d

6. f i l e d
7. a p/p e a r e d
8. s l o w e d
9. i n/f o r m e d
10. f a r e d

PRACTICE Pronounce each of these words aloud. Then divide each word into syllables. The first one is done for you.

1. reviewed	re/viewed	11. compensated	_____
2. happened	_____	12. photographed	_____
3. remained	_____	13. gathered	_____
4. distorted	_____	14. unpacked	_____
5. developed	_____	15. delivered	_____
6. reproduced	_____	16. estimated	_____
7. discolored	_____	17. influenced	_____
8. compared	_____	18. proposed	_____
9. demonstrated	_____	19. accounted	_____
10. entered	_____	20. invented	_____

Untitled

°outdoor advertisements
°road signs giving directions

On my arrival in America, the one thing I noticed more than anything else was the tremendous amount of advertising that went on, —on the radio, on television, on billboards° and signposts,° and in magazines. In the last three years, I have become accustomed to this fact in American life, for I believe that it is a creative and necessary part of an industrial society. I, too, want to improve my life-style and to buy better products, so I look to advertising to show me how to do it.

Deciding what to believe in advertising, however, isn't easy. It seems to me that a person must purchase things with a lot of care. As a consumer, I want to get the best for my money, but I really have to understand the techniques of advertising. Otherwise, manufacturers will be able to sell me anything, no matter what its quality may be.

°aware

°imperfections

More and more people are becoming conscious,° like me, of the ways in which advertising can affect them. The creative aspects of commercials, for instance, often cover up defects° or problems in products. I have learned this well, since I have made purchases and lost money because the items were of poor quality.

The future of advertising most likely will involve a much greater degree of public participation. I intend to become involved in consumer groups that want to protect people from misleading advertising. But I also want to see Americans keep their high standard of living in the process. In the future, if consumers like me really care about the quality of something as well as the quantity, maybe advertisers will begin to care more about what they are trying to sell.

VOCABULARY EXERCISE Write the number of the closest meaning of each vocabulary word in the space provided.

Words	Definitions
_7_ billboards	1. imperfections
_5_ consumer	2. methods, procedures
_6_ conscious	3. views
_4_ aspects	4. deceiving
_1_ defects	5. buyer, user
_3_ misleading	6. aware
_2_ techniques	7. outdoor advertisements

SYLLABICATION EXERCISE Pronounce the following words aloud. Then divide these words into syllables. Check your answers in your dictionary.

1. arrival _____
2. tremendous _____
3. necessary _____
4. industrial _____
5. purchased _____
6. society _____

7. aspects _____
8. defects _____
9. participated _____
10. quality _____
11. techniques _____
12. conscious _____

COMPREHENSION EXERCISE Use the information in the passage to help you decide which answer best completes each statement. Write the letter on the line.

_a_ 1. The writer of this passage
    a. has always lived in America.
    b. arrived in America three years ago.
    c. visited America three years ago.

_c_ 2. Advertisements are not found on
    a. billboards.
    b. television and signposts.
    c. textbooks.

_a_ 3. Misleading advertisements can
    a. cover up product defects.
    b. produce a better life-style.
    c. decrease public participation.

_c_ 4. American advertising is
    a. misleading.
    b. easy to understand.
    c. creative and necessary.

MAIN IDEAS AND DETAILS EXERCISE Reread the passage, highlighting the main idea of each paragraph in one color and the details of each paragraph in a second color.

Dividing Words into Syllables: **155**

WRITING EXERCISE Write a main idea sentence in the space provided based on the topics given.

1. Problems in children's advertising: _____
   ___ *They just follow doesn't good or bad* ___

2. Humor in television advertisements: _____
   ___ *Sometime stupid* ___

3. Salaries paid in advertising: _____
   ___ *Make employe feel get a good job* ___

4. Government regulation of products: _____
   _____

5. The informed consumer: _____
   ___ *Sometime it not true* ___

Write another possible main idea sentence based on the same topics.

1. _____
2. _____
3. _____
4. _____
5. _____

Select two of your main idea sentences, and on separate paper develop each into a paragraph.

WRITING PRACTICE On a separate sheet of paper, write a description of one of the following.

1. The messiest (or neatest room) in my house is _____.
2. My school cafeteria is very neat (very dirty).
3. The clown put on the makeup for a silly (sad) face.

Would You Buy a Used Car from these Authors?

UNIT V
GROWING UP IN SPITE
OF IT ALL

Reprinted by permission of Queensborough Community College.

In modern society, television and the educational system often compete for the minds of children. Some claim that our youth are as much influenced by television as they are by the schools that they attend. In this section, you will read about some of the various influences that shape the minds of young people in the United States. In addition, you will practice taking notes and learn about prefixes.

DISCUSSION How do television, magazines, and newspapers influence children? How does American education differ from education in other countries?

INITIAL READING

Untitled

Children in the United States are exposed to many influences other than that of their families. Television is the most significant of these influences, because the habit of watching television usually begins before children start attending school. And, by the time that the average child finishes high school, he or she will have spent 18,000 hours in front of a television set as opposed to 12,000 hours in a classroom.

Parents are concerned about these figures. They are also concerned about the lack of quality in television programs for children. The degree of violence in many of these shows also worries them. Even if it is unreal—a cartoon cat beating up a cartoon mouse with a baseball bat— this violence may have a negative effect on the young minds exposed to it. Studies indicate that, when children are exposed to violence, they may become aggressive or insecure.

Parents are also concerned about the commercials that their children see on television. Many parents would like to see fewer commercials during programs for children. And some parents feel that these shows should not have any commercials at all because young minds are not mature enough to deal with the claims made by advertisers.

Educational television has no commercials and has programs for children that many parents approve of. The most famous of these is "Sesame Street," which tries to give preschool children a head start in learning the alphabet and numbers. It also tries to teach children useful things about the world in which they live.

Even though most parents and educators give "Sesame Street" and shows like it high marks for quality, some critics argue that all television, whether educational or not, is harmful to children. These critics feel that the habit of watching hours of television every day turns children into bored and passive consumers° of their world rather than encouraging them to become active explorers of it.

°people who purchase products without judging them

We still do not know enough about the effects of watching television to be able to say whether or not it is good for children. Until we do, perhaps it would be wise to put a warning on television sets such as the one on cigarette packages: "Caution: Watching Too Much Television May Be Harmful to Your Child's Developing Mind."

QUESTIONS

1. What do you think about the quality of programs shown on television?

   _____

   _____

2. Do people watch too much television? Explain. _____

   _____

3. In what ways do children benefit or suffer from television? _____

   _____

CHAPTER 22

TAKING NOTES:
Highlighting and Outlining

* *
*

In Unit IV you practiced highlighting main idea sentences and details in paragraphs and short selections. You learned to highlight the main idea sentence in one color and the important details in a second color. Now consider this paragraph.

EXAMPLE **Many daytime television commercials aim specifically at turning young viewers into consumers.** **Free gifts are offered to youngsters** who send in one or two box tops of a certain product. **Attractive fantasy experiences are suggested** through professional ads. Moreover, **advertisers** often **do not reveal a product's hidden ingredients or possible dangers.** Parents have to find that out. Instead they **emphasize the fun that a child can have by owning the product.**

QUESTIONS

1. What is the main idea of this paragraph? _____

2. What are the important details that support or illustrate the main idea?

   _____

   _____

   _____

   _____

3. Were you able to see the main idea sentence and the related details quickly? ____

4. Explain your answer to question 3. _____

   _____

The main idea of this paragraph is found in the first sentence. The related details are "Free gifts are offered to youngsters"; "Attractive fantasy experiences are suggested"; "Advertisers often do not reveal a product's hidden ingredients or dangers"; and "Advertisers emphasize the fun that one can have with the product."

Andrei and Natalia have highlighted the paragraph. Both of them did it correctly, as shown. Now, they want to write the facts in their notebooks. They will be having a quiz on this work and will want to have the facts ready for study. Here are Andrei's notes on the left and Natalia's notes on the right. Read them.

ANDREI'S NOTES	NATALIA'S NOTES
Daytime television commercials sell goods to young viewers. Free gifts are offered for boxtops. Attractive fantasy experiences are suggested by ads. Advertisers don't often reveal a product's hidden ingredients or possible dangers. Emphasis is on the fun of consuming or owning a product.	A. Daytime television commercials sell goods to young viewers. 1. Free gifts are offered for boxtops. 2. Attractive fantasy experiences are suggested by ads. 3. Advertisers don't often reveal hidden ingredients or dangers. 4. Emphasis is on the fun of consuming or owning a product.

QUESTIONS

1. From whose notes would you rather study? _____

2. Why? _____

Did you answer "Natalia's notes"? Her notes will make studying much easier. Now answer these questions.

3. Do Andrei's notes and Natalia's notes contain the same information?

_____

4. Do both sets of notes have the correct facts from the highlighted paragraph? _____

Written notes and highlighted notes have the **same** information.

But wait! If both sets of notes have the correct information, why are Natalia's notes better? Answering these questions may help you decide.

5. Can you see at a glance the main idea sentence and related details in

Andrei's notes? ____ in Natalia's notes? ____

6. Can you name three ways that Natalia's notes **help** you see the main idea sentence and the related details?

_____

_____

_____

> In **written notes,** such as **outlines,** the main idea sentence is often separated from the important details in three ways:
> 1. A capital letter, such as A, B, or C, precedes the main idea.
> 2. The details are in a numbered list.
> 3. The detail list is indented.

Now you can see why you chose Natalia's notes. You probably said that Natalia's notes were "easier to see" or that they were "better organized." That was no accident. Natalia took the information and carefully **organized** it for future study.

EXERCISE The paragraphs on the left have been highlighted. Using the highlighted information, complete the outline on the right.

HIGHLIGHTED PARAGRAPH   PARAGRAPH OUTLINE

1. **My mother knows that Hiram, my little brother, loves cartoons, and she allows him extra viewing time on Saturday mornings.** For example, because he enjoys **"Bugs Bunny,"** she tells him when the cartoon is on the air.° She also makes sure he watches **"Road Runner"** and **"Popeye,"** two of Hiram's other favorites. Most important, she remembers his favorite program is **"Sesame Street"** and turns on the channel at the correct time so that **he never misses a show.**

°playing on the radio or television

A. _____

_____

1. _____

_____

2. _____

_____

3. _____

_____

4. _____

_____

5. _____

_____

6. _____

_____

2. **Parent and educational groups are continually evaluating children's educational programs.** They **research the educational effects of cartoon shows** and also **study the effects of violence on children.** Moreover, they **watch and evaluate commercials** aimed at young audiences in order to **determine their effects on children.** These groups **send reports to the presidents of television networks°** and **hope the reports will help in future programming decisions.**

A. _____

_____

1. _____

_____

2. _____

_____

3. _____

°chains of television broadcasting stations

_____

4. _____

_____

5. _____

_____

PRACTICE Highlight each of the following paragraphs. Then complete the outline for each of the highlighted paragraphs.

1. Are children affected by violence shown on television? Studies are being conducted in which researchers look for relationships between youthful crime patterns and television violence. Researchers cite a recent juvenile° case as support for their view that television is harmful. A youth was charged with murder, and his defense lawyer argued that the boy was only imitating an incident from a popular television series. This is only one of many cases. Fortunately, others have not had such tragic consequences, but who knows what may happen in the future?

A. _____

_____

1. _Relations_ _____

_____

2. _TV is harmful_ _____

°referring to children; not yet adult

_____

3. _____

_____

2. Uncle Avram has been a loyal fan of public television for years. Every year during the fund-raising telethon,° he has been called, and each year he has donated money to support public television. He says that he wants to help bring theater, dance, symphonic, and movie offerings to a wider audience. He wants to be a part of a non-com-

A. _____

_____

1. _he has been called_ _____

°a television program for fund-raising

2. _wants to be a part of a non-commercial_

_____

°a risky undertaking or job

mercial television venture.° He especially likes the nightly lectures and
panel discussions. Uncle Avram is one
of millions of people who help support
public broadcasting in America.

3. _He especially likes_

4. _Uncle Avram is one_
of millions people who
5. _help support ---_

6. _____

°program time on
television

3. Since television sponsors pay for
airtime° and program production
costs, they want to control the content
of a show, and they exercise their control throughout all of the stages of production. First, they review prospect-
ive° shows and decide which ones will
draw° large audiences. After choosing
a show, the sponsors pay for a specific
number of commercials. Once the
show is on the air, the sponsors check
its ratings° to see how many people are
viewing the show. If the number is
small a continued investment may not
be worth their time. Finally, the sponsors decide whether or not to continue
paying for the show.

°expected in the future;
probable
°attract

°ranks or positions as
compared with other
programs

A. _Sponsors want to_
control the content
1. _Review and choose_

2. _Pay_

3. _check_

4. _Decide_

5. _____

4. Fantasy and violence are common
elements in many television shows
and movies. These factors have negative effects on some children. For example, recently, a nine-year old who
had just seen "Superman" tried to fly
from his roof and suffered two broken
legs. In addition, two six-year-olds
were recently hospitalized for gunshot
wounds after acting out their favorite
detective show using their fathers'
loaded guns. Steps must be taken to
develop a more thorough understanding of the effects of televised fantasy
and violence on children's behavior.

A. _____

1. _Negative effects on some_
children

2. _____

3. _____

4. _____

5. _____

B.

CHAPTER 23

RECOGNIZING PREFIXES:
Negatives

* *

This section will introduce you to the meanings of some common prefixes. Many English words have prefixes. You will be able to understand the meanings of more words when you know what prefixes are and how they add to the meanings of words. Read this dialogue.

SULY: Do you remember what Professor English told us about prefixes?

MARIA: Yes. A **prefix** is a word part that is added to the beginning of a basic word or root.

SULY: That's right. But did you know that prefixes add something to the meaning of words without changing the meaning of the base word, and that some prefixes have more than one meaning?

MARIA: Why is that?

SULY: Well, for example, the prefix **in-** has several meanings, such as "not" or "inside." But let's concentrate on the negative meaning "not." If you add the negative prefix **in-** to the word sufficient, the word becomes **insufficient.** Now the word means something that is **not** sufficient or **not** enough.

MARIA: Are there other negative prefixes that add to the meanings of words?

SULY: There are many **prefixes** that add a negative meaning to a base word. Here are several:

non- dis- un- mal- mis- anti- im- in- ir- il-

EXAMPLE

inexpensive = **not** expensive;
unoccupied = **not** occupied.

MARIA: I know those examples, Suly. But you gave me a long list of negative prefixes. How do I know which one goes with which word?

SULY: I'm afraid that there are usually no set rules for knowing which negative prefix belongs with a word. I can tell you that the spoken language has influenced the negative prefix you use. For example, it is difficult to say "inlogical," and so the form of it has be-

Recognizing Prefixes   **165**

come "illogical." The prefix **in-** has become **il-** before words starting with the letter "l."

MARIA: That's the same as in "illegal" and "illegitimate."

SULY: Also, you can't say "inregular." You must say "irregular." The prefix **in-** has become **ir-** in words beginning with the letter "r."

MARIA: I see! I must say "irrelevant" or "irresponsible."

EXERCISE Rewrite each base word and prefix. Then write the meaning of the new word. The first one is done for you.

WORD	+	PREFIX	=	NEW WORD	MEANING
1. scheduled	+	un		unscheduled	not scheduled
2. regular	+	ir		irregular	
3. approve	+	dis		disapprove	
4. perfect	+	im		imperfect	
5. legitimate	+	il		illegitimate	
6. movable	+	im		immovable	
7. effective	+	in		ineffective	
8. employed	+	un		unemployed	
9. understood	+	mis		misunderstand	
10. agree	+	dis		disagree	

PRACTICE Circle the correct word in each sentence. Use your dictionary to check the ones you don't know.

1. The children's reactions are (ilpredictable   unpredictable).
2. Do you think that the television industry is always (misresponsible   irresponsible)?
3. Children are often (unwilling   antiwilling) to turn off the television and read a book.
4. Crime programs often make (mallegal   illegal) activities seem exciting.
5. Children seem to enjoy watching the bad guys (disobey   unobey) the law.
6. Where are the (nonviolent   disviolent) programs?
7. They find public television programs (irresistible   unresistible).
8. Public television offers (unstop   nonstop) programs with no commercial interruptions.
9. Other stations find it (ilpractical   impractical) to produce programs without advertising.
10. Loss of advertising is (disprofitable   unprofitable) for the stations.

Photo by Hugh Rogers Photography, N.Y. Reprinted by permission of Queensborough Community College.

Which Books Would You Choose?

°not civilized; wild

If you were going to spend the rest of your life in a savage° wilderness and could only take five books with you, which five would you choose? Remember, these books may be the only books that you would be able to read for the rest of your life. This was a question that faced many of the early settlers who came to live in America, for there were no books, printing presses, or universities here. All reading materials had to be imported from Europe.

°false beliefs

The early colonists had few illusions° about the hardships that awaited them. Tales had reached them about the long, cruel winters, the wild animals, and the lack of companionship. Deeply religious and serious people, they prepared for the difficulties ahead through their books. Whether they were French, Spanish, or English colonists, they would have taken the *Bible* and other books for religious instruction. Some would have brought along books of poetry. Because it was necessary to educate children in the New World, all the colonists would have brought along instructional books to teach the children reading, writing, and arithmetic.

If you were going to spend the rest of your life on the moon and could only take five books with you, which five would you choose? Remember, these books may be the only books that you would be able to read for the rest of your life! The one book that we might still select is the *Bible*. But millions of books have been published since 1620, and so our other choices would be much more difficult!

VOCABULARY EXERCISE Add one of the following prefixes to each of the words at the right. The new word must match the definition at the left. Prefixes: **re-, im-, un-**.

DEFINITION	PREFIX + BASE WORD
1. not ready	_____un_ prepared
2. absolute	_____un_ questionable
3. not practical	_____im_ practical
4. not important	_____un_ important
5. work again	_____re_ work

LITERAL COMPREHENSION EXERCISE Answer the following statements True (T) or False (F).

_____ 1. Early settlers found few books when they arrived in America.

_____ 2. Colonists selected books in preparation for the difficult times ahead.

_____ 3. Colonists brought the *Bible* with them.

_____ 4. Children brought along their favorite storybooks.

_____ 5. Today, people going on adventurous journeys might choose the very same books as the early settlers did.

GENERAL COMPREHENSION EXERCISE Complete each of the following.

Early settlers _____

Today's adventurers _____

Book selections _____

1. brought a few treasured books with them.

2. were made carefully because of the hardships ahead.

3. have millions of books to choose from.

OUTLINE EXERCISE Reread the passage and highlight the main idea sentence and details in each paragraph. Then write an outline of the first paragraph in this space.

CHAPTER 24

TAKING NOTES:
Single Paragraph Outlines

***

You have practiced outlining highlighted main idea sentences and related details in a single paragraph. Now, you are ready to apply these skills of highlighting and outlining to paragraphs. The following review of guidelines will help you take good notes:

1. Highlighted and outlined notes show the same main idea sentences and related details.
2. Highlighted paragraphs show the main idea sentence in one color; outlined paragraphs show the main idea sentence with a capital letter placed at the margin.
3. Highlighted paragraphs show the details in a second color; outlined paragraphs show a list of numbered details that is indented.

EXERCISE Highlight the paragraph on the left, and then outline it on the right.

PARAGRAPH TO HIGHLIGHT	OUTLINE

1. Educational television programs for children are now considered valuable basic teaching tools by parents and teachers alike. As a result of the exposure of young children to such shows, more pupils are starting school equipped with elementary reading and arithmetic skills. For example, four- and five-year olds easily recognize the letters of the alphabet and identify numbers. In addition, the performers appearing on children's educational programs provide young children with examples of cooperative behavior. Young children are exposed to this behavior and practice it in school and at home.

A. _____
_____

1. _____
_____

2. _____
_____

3. _____
_____

4. _____
_____

5. _____
_____

2. Children of all ages need to feel accepted by their peer groups.° It is not uncommon for people to act in a special way in order to make a group accept and like them. For example, if the in crowd° wears straight-leg or bell-bottom° jeans, youngsters who want to be "in" will dress in those styles. Or if rude behavior is the style of one group, a child who wants to belong to the group may speak rudely. And if it's "in" to go steady at age ten, then some ten-year-olds will begin to have steady dates. The need to belong may have both positive and negative effects.

A. _____
   _____
1. _____
   _____
2. _____
   _____
3. _____
   _____
4. _____
   _____
5. _____
   _____

°people equal in age

°people who are at the center of what is popular socially
°flared pant cuffs

3. Private and public schools are very different. First, private school classes are smaller than public school classes. For example, while it is unusual to find more than twenty children in a classroom in a private school, it's rare to find fewer than thirty in a public school classroom. Second, the parents of private school children are usually more affluent° than the parents of public school children. They have to be, since the cost of educating a child in a private school can range from $2,000 to $4,000 a year. Third, private schools offer many enrichment° classes, but public schools, with their tight budgets, can offer only the basic classes.

°wealthy

°improvement made by adding a variety of skills

4. The principal represents many things to elementary school children. For example, the principal is the voice who speaks to them from the loudspeaker, makes speeches in the auditorium, and disciplines° those who misbehave. For others, the principal may be a kind ear to listen and a soft lap to sit on when problems arise. For most children, the principal is the last person to wave good-bye before they start for home at 3:00.

°punishes; teaches obedience

°spread out

5. I visited a classroom where children weren't sitting at desks. Instead, they were sprawled° all over the floor in the room and out in the hallway. Some were working in small groups while others were working alone. The teacher wasn't sitting at her desk either. She was walking around the room stopping with each group of students. What I was observing was an open classroom° where the teacher works with individual students or with small groups of students while the rest of the class works on independent or group projects.

°a class with unstructured learning

°improve steadily; grow

6. If a teacher is sensitive to a child's needs, the child can thrive.° If, on the other hand, the teacher is not aware of a child's emotional and intellectual needs, problems can arise. For example, a child may misbehave to get attention from the teacher. Another may stop doing work or start doing sloppy work. These children may be responding to what they think is a lack of concern on the teacher's part. It is clear that a teacher's attitudes, both positive and negative, influence the child.

[handwritten margin note: A. TEACHER's attitudes positives and negative. 1) child misbehave a) stop doing work b) doing sloppy work]

PRACTICE Outline each of the following paragraphs (you may highlight each one first if you wish).

PARAGRAPH TO HIGHLIGHT	OUTLINE

1. Educational opportunities are now open to very young children. Starting the youngster's formal education at age two was once considered unorthodox,° but recently educators have begun to reevaluate° earlier theories of child rearing.° The current theory is that children learn every day and in every situation. Whether in day-care centers, prekindergarten groups, nursery groups, at home, or in a playground, youngsters are being exposed to the complex world around them.

°not customary; not generally accepted or traditional
°reexamine
°raising or bringing up children

Educators and parents are now incorporating° these early experiences into structured learning situations.

2. Some children spend most of their waking hours in instructional settings. Carlotta goes to school from nine to six, seven days a week. She attends public school from nine to three daily. On Monday, Tuesday, and Thursday, she receives ballet instruction at 4:00. Carlotta and her younger sister play musical instruments, and each girl has a lesson every Wednesday at 3:30. Both girls attend swim class on Saturday mornings, and each has a diving class the same afternoon. The entire family attends religious school on Sunday mornings. Recently, Carlotta complained that she has no time for her friends. She is very worried that she is becoming overschooled and unpopular.

3. Most children function better when they know what is expected of them. For example, eight-year-old Gilbert has been misbehaving recently. He never cleans his room and often cries when he cannot find his favorite toy. Gilbert's mother has decided that he must learn to act responsibly. He cannot continue mistreating his possessions. Now, Gilbert must permit his mother to inspect his room daily. If he misplaces a toy, he must do without it. It is amazing how quickly Gilbert has learned to become more orderly and how concerned he has become about his appearance and possessions.

4. Shyness in youngsters can be overcome when the problem is handled intelligently and sensitively. Verna has been learning all sorts of new things since she entered nursery school. At first she was a shy four-year-old who had difficulty playing with so many new youngsters. Soon Verna joined a

°including

A. Observing an open classroom
1. Children were not sitting at desks
2. child were
3 Some were working in small groups
4. The teacher was walking around stopping with each group of students.

small playgroup and began making
friends. Her circle of friends° grew and
she lost her shyness. In fact, she was
recently invited to twelve birthday parties. Verna has become more outgoing
since she started school last year.

CHAPTER 25

RECOGNIZING PREFIXES:
Frequently Used Prefixes

⁎

There are many prefixes in the English language. In the following exercises you will learn some of those most frequently used. They will help you to understand new and difficult words. First, read this dialogue.

SULY: We've done a lot with prefixes, Maria, but I think we should practice with some more.

MARIA: Fine. I'd like to know what they mean, so I can figure out the meanings of more new words.

SULY: Let's look at the most common prefixes that we see in the words we use every day.

Two useful prefixes are **pre-** and **post-**. Consider these words:

EXAMPLE

preview	**post**graduate
pretape	**post**date
predate	**post**script

The word "preview" means to view something before. The word "pre-tape" means to tape something before. And the word "predate" means to put an earlier date on something such as a check.

The prefix **pre-** means before.

The word "postgraduate" means continued education after graduation from college. The word "postdate" means to put a later date on something. The word "postscript" means something written after you have finished writing your letter.

The prefix **post-** means after or later.

EXERCISE Using the dictionary to help, write the meaning of each of the following words:

1. predict _____

2. prerequisite _____

3. prejudice _____

4. postmortem _____

5. postpone _____

PRACTICE   Using the dictionary, write the meaning of each of the following words.

1. preface _____

2. postwar _____

3. preschool _____

4. postpaid _____

5. postnatal _____

PRACTICE   Choose two of the words in the exercise or practice, and use each in a sentence.

1. _____

2. _____

Another prefix is **re-**. Do you know the meaning of these words?

EXAMPLE

   review   **re**enter   **re**structure

   The word "review" means to look at something again. The word "reenter" means to go back into a room or to enter it again. The word "restructure" means to structure something again.

The prefix **re-** means again or to go back.

EXERCISE   Using the dictionary to help, define each of these words.

1. resume _____

2. recall _____

3. rewrite _____

4. rejoin _____

5. reproduce _____

PRACTICE Using the dictionary, define each of these words.

1. recurring _____

2. remind _____

3. repeat _____

4. reteach _____

5. readjustment _____

PRACTICE Choose two of the words in the exercise or practice, and use each in a sentence.

1. _____

2. _____

Other important prefixes are **ex**- and **e**-. Are you familiar with these words?

EXAMPLE

    expel   **e**migrate   **ex**clude   **e**ject

The words "expel" and "eject" mean to throw out. The word "emigrate" means to move out of a country, and the word "exclude" means to shut out others.

The prefixes **ex-** and **e-** mean out.

EXERCISE Using the dictionary to help, define each of these words.

1. exterior _____

2. erase _____

3. excommunicate _____

4. evacuate _____

5. exit _____

PRACTICE Using the dictionary, define each of these words.

1. exclaim _____

2. exception _____

3. erupt _____

4. erosion _____

5. exhale _____

Another useful prefix is **inter-**. Read these words aloud.

EXAMPLE

interaction   **inter**fere   **inter**view

The word "interaction" means action between two parties or things. To "interfere" is to come between two people or things. The word "interview" means a meeting or discussion between two people.

The prefix **inter-** means between.

EXERCISE Using the dictionary to help, define these words.

1. intermingle — mix together _____

2. interruption _____

3. interracial _____

4. intervene _____

5. interfaith _____

PRACTICE Using the dictionary to help, define these words.

1. interlock _____

2. intercourse _____

3. intersession _____

4. interpret _____

5. interchangeable _____

PRACTICE Choose two of the words in the exercise or practice, and use each in a sentence.

1. _____

2. _____

Still another prefix is **trans-**. What do these words mean?

EXAMPLE

transport   **trans**fer

The word "transport" means to carry from one place to another. The word "transfer" means to bring from one place across to another.

> The prefix **trans-** means across.

EXERCISE Using the dictionary to help, define these words.

1. transplant _____

2. transatlantic _____

3. transparent _____

4. transcribe _____

5. transportation _____

PRACTICE Using the dictionary, define these words.

1. transmit _____

2. transcontinental _____

3. transform _____

4. translate _____

5. transgress _____

PRACTICE Choose two of the words in the exercise or practice, and use each in a sentence.

1. _____

2. _____

CHAPTER 26

TAKING NOTES:
Outlining Several Paragraphs

*_**

You have now had a lot of practice outlining single paragraphs. It is important to understand this skill because it is the basis for further work in note-taking. Read the paragraphs and look carefully at the notes.

PARAGRAPHS	OUTLINE

Sarah started college this week, and she was amazed at all the rules she had to follow. Sarah **couldn't get a parking permit** because she was **only a freshman.** She **couldn't wear dungarees to any of her classes.** Also, she was **required to sign out every time she left the dormitory.**°
 	
 Sarah was also amazed at all the routines she had to follow. Several of her **classes were scheduled at 12:00 noon.** Since the **dormitory kitchen was only open from 12:00 to 2:00, she often missed lunch.** She was only **allowed to spend five minutes on the house phone.** Sarah will spend the entire term trying to adjust to these routines.
	A. Sarah had to follow many rules.
	   1. She couldn't get a parking permit because she was a freshman.
	   2. She couldn't wear dungarees to classes.
	   3. She was required to sign out every time she left the dorm.
	 B. Sarah had to follow routines.
	   1. Her classes were at 12:00.
	   2. The kitchen was open from 12:00 to 2:00, and so she missed lunch.
	   3. She was allowed five minutes on the phone.

°college housing facility

QUESTIONS

1. Are these paragraphs highlighted the same as paragraphs in previous chapters? ____

2. Do these outlined paragraphs look the same as those you outlined before? ____

3. Explain answer 2. _____

_____

You probably saw that the highlighted paragraphs follow the same form as in previous chapters. The outline, however, differs. The only difference between this outline and previous ones appears in the second paragraph. It is labeled "B".

> It is customary to label the main idea sentence of each paragraph in a selection. You can do this by using the **letters of the alphabet**.

EXERCISE Outline the following short passages and answer the questions.

How Ana gets a scholarship.

PASSAGE	OUTLINE

1. Just two months ago, Ana, a teenager, was preparing for an important exam. Winners would receive scholarships and be able to study in the United States. Ana knew her grades were excellent, but she realized that she must do well on the exams in order to qualify for the $3,000 stipend.° Although Ana had worried about the interview portion of the exam, she came through with flying colors.° She spoke to the American interviewers about her family background and discussed her educational plans with them. Her hard work paid off, for she was one of twenty awarded a four-year scholarship earlier this month.

°a regular allowance

°did extremely well

Now Ana can't believe that she is sitting in a business management class at the University of California at Los Angeles. Although she has had seven years of English language classes, Ana is having difficulty with the text and lectures because there are so many new words and technical° definitions to remember. Ana is finding it difficult to understand the professor. Now she must work twice as hard to maintain her high grades.

°specialized

VOCABULARY EXERCISE Divide the following words into syllables.

1. technical _____

2. portion _____

3. scholarship _____

4. interviewers _____

5. difficulty   _____

LITERAL COMPREHENSION EXERCISE Answer the following questions according to the information in the passage.

____ 1. Ana realizes that
    a. her grades are poor.
    b. she must do well on the exam.
    c. she is sitting in a business management class.
    d. she must work twice as hard to get good grades.

____ 2. Ana has been studying English for
    a. seven years.
    b. two months.
    c. all her life.
    d. the last two years.

____ 3. Ana experiences difficulty with
    a. texts.
    b. technical definitions.
    c. the professor's lectures.
    d. all of the above.

____ 4. Ana tells the interviewers about
    a. her flying colors.
    b. her family.
    c. her difficulty in understanding new words.
    d. her worries about the interview.

GENERAL COMPREHENSION EXERCISE Choose the best answer according to the passage.

____ 1. The best main idea for the first paragraph is
    a. Ana has many experiences taking the interview exam.
    b. Ana prepares for the interview exam.
    c. Ana comes through with flying colors.
    d. Ana takes exams.

____ 2. The best main idea for the second paragraph is
    a. Ana is taking business courses at U.C.L.A.
    b. Ana must work hard to get good grades in her courses.
    c. Ana experiences difficulty in understanding lectures.
    d. Ana is in a business management class at the University of California.

The best **topic** for the entire selection is _how much grade scholarship_ .

2. A sympathetic environment can help a newcomer overcome many obstacles. When Dimitrios first started college in the United States, he was worried about meeting new people. He had always had many friends back home, but now he was entering a new school in a new country. Dimitrios thought, "Will I have new friends?" and "Will my new friends think I talk strangely?"

As soon as Dimitrios began attending classes, his questions were answered. Both students and professors were friendly to him. Guidance counselors met him and asked him to attend a special orientation° class for foreign students. In this class Dimitrios met other international students, and they discussed mutual° concerns, such as getting medical help, checking student visa cards, joining clubs, and getting good grades in classes. With the help of counselors and students, Dimitrios joined student organizations, found out where to get medical checkups, and started using the school's language laboratory. Dimitrios is learning to cope with his new surroundings and with the heavy workload at college.

°a formal introduction to a new situation

°common

VOCABULARY EXERCISE   Use each of the following words in a sentence.

1. mutual: _____

2. orientation: _____

LITERAL COMPREHENSION EXERCISE   Answer the following statements True (T) or False (F) according to information in the story.

___ 1. Dimitrios is worried about his friends back home.

___ 2. Students in the orientation class discuss ways of getting scholarships.

_____ 3. Dimitrios soon learns how to use the school's language lab.

_____ 4. Students and counselors help Dimitrios adjust to school life.

GENERAL COMPREHENSION EXERCISE Choose the best answer according to the information in the story.

_____ 1. The best main idea for the first paragraph is
   a. Dimitrios starts college in the United States.
   b. Dimitrios is worried about making new friends.
   c. He has many friends back home.
   d. Making new friends is very difficult.

_____ 2. The best main idea for the second paragraph is
   a. Students and counselors help Dimitrios adjust to his new life.
   b. Dimitrios attends special classes offered at the college.
   c. Orientation classes are attended by all students.
   d. Learning to cope with college is difficult.

The best **title** for the entire passage is _The First time for a foreign student go to the college._

PRACTICE Outline the following groups of passages and answer the questions.

PASSAGE	OUTLINE

°ability to view something factually; without prejudice

°adds / °closes tightly

Completing teacher evaluations requires maturity and objectivity.° Every semester we are given the opportunity to evaluate our instructors. We are supposed to judge their lectures, interest in student problems, methods of assigning work, and general ability to conduct a class. Then, when the instructor has left the room, we must write our evaluations on the forms provided. We are not supposed to exchange views or discuss our responses. After everyone has completed the forms, one student collects and tallies° the responses and then seals° them in an envelope.

It is very difficult to evaluate another person's performance objectively. For example, Senta recently wrote irresponsible remarks about her instructor because she was failing the course. Her friend Sam wrote a marvelous description of the same instructor because he was receiving an A in the course. Both Senta and Sam were not fairly evaluating the instructor. They were influenced by the grades they were earning and were biased° in their judgments.

°prejudiced; influenced, usually unfairly

Another irresponsible form of evaluation occurred when James rated his instructor excellent because the instructor is "easy." He gives few tests and only assigns one paper during the entire term. His lectures are often filled with jokes and endless stories about his family. On the other hand, James rated Professor Jones poor because he assigns text work daily, gives pretest previews and posttest reviews, and packs his lectures with information.

Senta, Sam, and James have not thought about their instructors' teaching abilities. They have written unfair evaluations and have not given thought to their ratings. They have not made fair judgments, but instead have been swayed° by personality and have equated° little work with excellence in teaching.

°influenced
°compared equally

VOCABULARY EXERCISE Circle the prefix in each word, and define the word.

1. preview _____ before the
2. irresponsible _____ not responsible
3. pretest _____ before the test
4. posttest _____ after the test
5. unfair _____ not fair

SYLLABICATION EXERCISE Divide the following words into syllables.

1. student _____
2. remarks _____
3. reviews _____

4. supposed _____

5. person _____

6. problems _____

7. described _____

8. lectures _____

9. responded _____

10. assigns _____

LITERAL COMPREHENSION EXERCISE   Choose the best answer according to the story.

_____ 1. Students should evaluate their instructors
   a. by discussing opinions with classmates.
   b. by rating the instructors' interest in students' problems, their lectures, and work.
   c. by discussing opinions with instructors.
   d. by rating instructors' humorous remarks.

_____ 2. Teacher evaluations should be written in
   a. an objective way.
   b. an irresponsible way.
   c. a biased way.
   d. an irrational way.

_____ 3. Irresponsible evaluations consist of
   a. biased answers.
   b. fairly written answers.
   c. information based on teacher performance.
   d. well thought-out judgments.

_____ 4. Senta and Sam are both influenced by
   a. the instructor's teaching ability.
   b. the professor's humorous stories.
   c. the grades that they are earning.
   d. the long assignments given.

_____ 5. James is influenced by
   a. the quality of the lectures.
   b. his own performance.
   c. the instructor's personality.
   d. answers a and c.

MAIN IDEAS AND DETAILS EXERCISE Choose the best answer according to the information in the passage.

_____ 1. The best main idea for paragraph 1 is
  a. Instructor evaluations are conducted according to set procedures.
  ✓ b. There are guidelines to follow when judging an instructor's lectures.
  c. Evaluations are conducted yearly.
  ✓d. Teachers should always be prepared.

_____ 2. The best main idea for paragraph 2 is
  a. Senta and Sam write marvelous descriptions of their teachers.
  b. Unfair evaluations are common.
  c. Teacher evaluations are difficult.
  ✓d. It is difficult to evaluate teachers objectively.

_____ 3. The best main idea for paragraph 3 is
  a. James has easy teachers.
  b. James evaluates teachers in an irresponsible manner.
  c. Professor Jones often assigns too much text work.
  d. Irresponsible student evaluations are rare.

_____ 4. The best main idea for paragraph 4 is
  ✓a. Sometimes students do not rate their teachers fairly.
  b. Senta, Sam, and James are often swayed by a teacher's personality.
  c. Excellence in teaching is evaluated in different ways.
  d. none of the above.

_____ 5. The best title for this passage is
  a. Teacher Evaluations.
  ✓ b. How to Be Objective.
  c. Evaluations.
  d. Easy vs. Tough Teachers.

CHAPTER 27

RECOGNIZING PREFIXES:
Quantity

* *

MARIA: Professor English sometimes uses words that I don't understand. Yesterday, he announced a bi-weekly quiz on prefixes, and I don't know what he means by bi-weekly

SULY: A bi-weekly quiz means that Professor English will be giving a test once every two weeks. The prefix **bi-** means two.

MARIA: I see. He also said he'll be testing us on the pronunciation of multisyllabic words. What does that mean?

SULY: **Multi-** is a prefix that means many, so multisyllabic words are words with more than one syllable.

MARIA: Are there any other prefixes that give us the number of things?

SULY: Yes, there are several other prefixes that indicate quantity.

MARIA: What are they?

SULY: Several useful ones are **mono-, poly-, semi-,** and **uni-.**

MARIA: I'll never remember all those.

SULY: Here are some examples with those prefixes. Remember that each prefix represents either a general quantity or a specific number.

uni- means one	**bi-** means two	**multi-** means many
mono- means one	**semi-** means half	**poly-** means many

EXERCISE Using the dictionary to help, define each of these words.

1. bifocal _having two focal lengths_
2. bicentennial _relating to a 200th anniversary - 2 centuries_
3. bilingual _containing or expressed in two languages_
4. binomial _a biological species name consisting of two terms_
5. bilateral _having two sides - 2 countries_
6. monocle _monocular having one eye_
7. monotone _a single unvaried musical tone_
8. monogram _a sign of identity use, formed initial_
9. multiply _to increase in numbers_

10. multisyllabic _→ more than one syllable._
11. multiple choice _→ many choice._
12. polyglot _Speaking or writing several languages_
13. semiannual _every half year_
14. semicircle _half circle_
15. semimonthly _every 2 weeks_
16. semiskilled _half skilled → not complet skill_
17. uniform _look the same_
18. unilateral _one sided_

PRACTICE Look over the prefixes that you have learned in this unit. Then use your knowledge of prefixes to help you define each of the underlined words.

1. Some children attend <u>prekindergarten</u> classes.

   <u>prekindergarten</u> means _____

2. At the beginning of the school year children are <u>pretested</u> and later they are <u>retested</u>.

   <u>pretested</u> means _____

   <u>retested</u> means _____

3. It is difficult to <u>translate</u> certain words from one language to another.

   <u>translate</u> means _____

4. Many words have <u>multiple</u> meanings.

   <u>multiple</u> means _____

5. Many children come from <u>interracial</u> or <u>interfaith</u> homes.

   <u>interracial</u> means _____

   <u>interfaith</u> means _____

6. Learning <u>multiplication</u> can be fun.

   <u>multiplication</u> means _____

7. <u>Interaction</u> with others is necessary for students who have recently <u>emigrated</u> from their homelands.

   <u>interaction</u> means _____

   <u>emigrated</u> means _____

8. <u>Bilingual</u> programs are offered in many schools.

   <u>bilingual</u> means _____

9. Schools try to motivate <u>uninterested</u> children with <u>irresistible</u> programs.

   <u>uninterested</u> means _____

   <u>irresistible</u> means _____

10. There are <u>interage</u> classes in some schools.

    <u>interage</u> means _____

11. In France, some students wear <u>uniforms</u> to school.

    <u>uniform</u> means _____

12. <u>Prerequisite</u> courses are the basis for entrance into some programs.

    <u>prerequisite</u> means _____

13. A discussion of <u>misconceptions</u> about American life-styles will be held in school today.

    <u>misconceptions</u> means _____

14. <u>Maladjusted</u> students often seek counseling.

    <u>maladjusted</u> means _____

15. <u>Preregistration</u> is necessary in some schools.

    <u>preregistration</u> means _____

Courtesy of Queensborough Community College.

Untitled

Americans have always been ambivalent° in their attitudes toward education. On the one hand, free and universal public education was seen as necessary in a democracy, for how else would citizens learn how to govern themselves in a responsible way? On the other hand, America was always a country that offered financial opportunities for which education was not needed: on the road from rags to riches,° schooling—beyond the basics of reading, writing, and arithmetic—was an unnecessary detour.°

°having mixed feelings

°from poverty to great wealth
°interruption

Even today, it is still possible for people to achieve financial success without much education, but the number of situations in which this is possible is decreasing. In today's more complex world, the opportunities for financial success are closely related to the need for education, especially higher education.

Our society is rapidly becoming one whose chief product is information, and dealing with this information requires more and more specialized education. In other words, we grow up learning more and more about fewer and fewer subjects.

In the future, this trend is likely to continue. Tomorrow's world will be even more complex than today's world, and, to manage this complexity, even more specialized education will be needed.

PREFIXES EXERCISE The underlined prefixes were added to words from the selection. Write each word in a sentence.

1. <u>mis</u>govern: _____

2. <u>im</u>possible: _____

3. <u>dis</u>continue: _____

4. <u>non</u>specialized: _____

5. <u>ir</u>responsible: _____

LITERAL COMPREHENSION EXERCISE Using the information in the story, complete the following sentences.

1. Americans' attitudes toward education have always been _____

   _____.

2. Today people can still achieve _____ without much education.

3. In the future, more _____ education will be needed.

GENERAL COMPREHENSION EXERCISE Select the best answer according to the information in the passage.

____ 1. The topic of the essay is
    a. education.
    b. Americans' attitudes.
    c. American education.
    d. higher education.

____ 2. The best title for this selection is
    a. The Future of the American Educational System.
    b. The History of American Education.
    c. Attitudes toward American Education.
    d. The Need for Specialized Education.

____ 3. Today, financial success is closely related to the need for
    a. higher education.
    b. public education.
    c. responsible citizens.
    d. learning the basics.

OUTLINE EXERCISE Reread the passage and highlight the main idea and details in each paragraph. Then write an outline of the passage on separate paper.

WRITING EXERCISE Write a brief paragraph on a separate sheet of paper describing your best or worst experience with the American educational system.

WRITING PRACTICE Write a main idea sentence for each of the topics listed below.

TOPIC	MAIN IDEA SENTENCE
Teachers	Teachers are the good persons for students follow or explain something they know to the students
Classrooms	in free are better than High School.
Non-credit courses	Yoga is a non credit course
Getting an A	How you get an A?
Getting an F	Try to learn more for getting a grade better than F.

Select one of the main idea sentences and develop it into a paragraph on separate paper.

UNIT VI
IF I HAD IT TO DO
ALL OVER AGAIN . . .

Courtesy of Harry Greenberger.

In recent years, traditional attitudes toward dating and marriage have changed radically. In this unit, you will learn about some of those changes. Also, you will continue to develop note-taking and vocabulary skills.

DISCUSSION Do you view marriage differently from the way that your parents did? Do you think that marriage is here to stay?

INITIAL READING

Untitled

Andrea and Nicholas decided to take a course in early American customs and manners because they wanted to know how the first Americans lived their daily lives. They were very surprised to learn how different the rules of dating were in colonial times.° Young people were watched very closely, and they were not allowed to meet each other unless a chaperone° was present! There were no discos and no theaters, and even dancing was viewed with displeasure, especially in New England.

°relating to the 1700s when America consisted of thirteen colonies
°someone who escorts unmarried couples on dates

One custom, however, puzzled them both. It was called "bundling." On winter nights houses were very cold, for there was no central heating. On those nights, parents allowed young men and women to meet and talk to each other in a special cloth sack that was sewn down the middle. Lying down as though it were a sleeping bag, each one could get into the cloth sack, and then the boy and girl could be warm while they spoke to each other. They would be left alone. But, once the warm weather returned, the custom of bundling stopped, and the young people had to rely on chaperones again!

Andrea thought the custom was a lovely one, so she made a sack for Nicholas and herself. She sewed a seam down the middle, so that there were separate pockets for them both. Usually, she and Nicholas stayed out at local nightclubs until the small hours of the morning,° but, when she showed him the bundling sack, he agreed that it might be nice just to spend a winter evening talking to each other according to the old custom of bundling.

°2 A.M. to 5 A.M.

There was a problem the first evening that they tried it. Andrea's mother came into the living room and saw them having a conversation in the double cloth sack on the floor. She raised the roof!° After that, they were not allowed to bundle at all. Once again, Andrea was puzzled. When she stayed out very late at night alone with Nicholas, her mother didn't say a word, but when she decided just to talk to Nicholas and get to know him better through conversation instead of dancing, her mother became upset! It was clear that customs had changed over the years, but Andrea found out that parents hadn't.

°became very angry

QUESTIONS

1. What special customs in courtship or marriage do people in other countries follow? _____

   _____

2. What major differences between American dating and dating in other countries have you noticed? _____

   _____

3. Are there differences between American dating customs and dating customs from your parents' native countries? What are they? _____

   _____

CHAPTER 28

OUTLINING:
Titled Paragraphs in a Selection

.

You have practiced outlining related paragraphs and are now ready to learn to outline a titled selection. Consider this short passage. Highlight the main idea and details. Then use that information to complete the outline.

EXAMPLE   OUTLINE

TITLE: DATING ETIQUETTE IN THE 1930s AND 1940s

I. TITLE: _____

_____

°accepted rules for social behavior

Dating etiquette° in the 1930s and 1940s was very structured. The rules for acceptable dating behavior were firmly established. Boys and girls usually began dating in high school. Of course, they needed their parents' approval. Many teenagers were even chaperoned. After the boy met his date's parents and talked with them for a little while, the young couple usually left for a movie, soda, and snack which the boy paid for. The young people observed strict curfews° and said their goodnights at the front door.

°set times for coming home from a date

  A. _____

    1. _____

    2. _____

    3. _____

    4. _____

    5. _____

    6. _____

    7. _____

    8. _____

    9. _____

QUESTIONS

1. Is this highlighting different from the highlighting you have practiced? ____
2. Is the outline different from the outlines you have done? ____
3. What information from the selection belongs on the first blank space of

   the outline? _____

The highlighting is similar to the highlighting that you have practiced before. The outline is the same except for the addition of the title "Dating Etiquette in the 1930s and 1940s."

The **title of the paragraph** is the general topic of that paragraph. To show the importance of the title, place the **title at the margin** and **label it with a Roman numeral.** Then **indent the labeled main idea** and further **indent the numbered details** to show the relationship of each to the other.

EXAMPLE

I. Dating Etiquette in the 1930s and 1940s
  A. Dating etiquette in the 1930s and 1940s was very strict.
    1. The rules were established.
    2. Boys and girls began dating in high school.
    3. They needed approval of their parents.
    4. Many were chaperoned.
    5. The boy met and talked with the girl's parents.
    6. The couple left for a movie, snack, or soda.
    7. The boy paid.
    8. They observed strict curfews.
    9. They said goodnight at the front door.

QUESTIONS

1. Where is the title placed in this outline? _____

   Why? _____

2. Where is the main idea placed? _____

   Why? _____

3. Where are the details placed? _____

   Why? _____

As you write the following outlines, remember these guidelines. They will help you develop clear and consistent notes.

Indenting helps you to distinguish titles, main ideas, and details.
Roman numerals (such as I, II) signal a title.
Capital letters (such as A, B) signal main ideas.
Numbers (such as 1, 2) signal details.

EXERCISE Highlight each selection. Then outline the selection using a Roman numeral to signal the title, a capital letter to signal the main idea, and numbers to signal the details. The first two are started for you.

SELECTION	OUTLINE

1. DUTCH TREATS

°entertainment for which each person pays for himself or herself

Dutch treats° are often the answer to a limited budget. Charlie wanted to take Cathy to the movies, but he did not have enough money. So he decided to ask her to go Dutch treat. Cathy accepted, and they both paid for their own movie tickets, hamburgers at the soda shop, and bus fares. Going Dutch allowed Charlie and Cathy to enjoy a pleasant afternoon together.

I. DUTCH TREATS

A. Dutch treats are _____

1. _____

2. _____

3. _____

4. _____

5. _____

2. GOING STEADY

°dating one person only

Going steady° is very popular among high school students. Marcus and Carmina have been going steady for six months. They go to school together, share lunches, meet at the hamburger shop after school and attend all school and neighborhood activities together. Marcus and Carmina date no other people and are always seen together.

I. GOING STEADY

A. Going steady is very _____

1. _____

2. _____

3. _____

4. _____

5. _____

6. _____

7. _____

3. TELEPHONE DATING

Sometimes Ken and Marsha tie up° the phone for hours. They talk about school, friends, movies, and each other. They only stop talking when their parents demand that they get off the line.° Marsha lives in a nearby town, and so Ken often dates her over the phone. They have both run up° tremendous telephone bills. Telephone dating is the answer to Ken and Marsha's transportation problems.

°keep busy or unavailable

°hang up the telephone

°accumulated

4. DOUBLE-DATING

Double-dating° has always appealed to certain young people. For example, Gerald is the type of person who has difficulty asking girls out, and he often cannot think of much to say on a date. Double-dating now solves many of his problems. Instead of being alone with his date, he can talk to her in a group. He finds it much easier to communicate with several friends and actually looks forward to dates now.

°two couples going out together

5. BLIND DATES

Pierre's blind dates don't always turn out well. He had arranged a blind date for Jean and was eagerly awaiting word of Jean's reactions. Jean was Pierre's best friend, and Pierre wanted everything to go well. Jean finally called, politely thanked Pierre, and hung up. Pierre immediately knew that the blind date had not gone very well.

PRACTICE Outline these titled paragraphs.

1. COURTING WITH FLOWERS

°dating

°an assortment

Years ago, on many social occasions, men gave flowers to women. Flowers were a welcome gift on a date, birthday, anniversary, or even on any day of the year. A young man courting° a woman usually brought her a small bouquet° of flowers. Today, flowers symbolize only the most special occasions.

2. EXPENSIVE DATES

°a light meal

Dating is often very expensive. Today, even the simplest date can cost over $20.00. A couple on a date may go to the movies and have a snack° afterwards. Movies now cost $3.00–$5.00 per person, and a snack can easily cost more than $10.00. Because of today's rising prices, many couples choose to stay home and watch television instead of spending so much money on movies.

3. SHOPPING FOR THE SENIOR PROM

°a shawl

Ilyana and Judy are going with Max and Arthur to the Senior Prom, and need new clothes. Each girl needs a new dress, shoes, a handbag, and a wrap,° and so they are spending the entire weekend shopping for these items. Ilyana has $70.00 to spend, and Judy has $90.00. They will probably buy their dresses first and then their shoes and pocketbooks. If they spend all their money on these items, they know they can borrow wraps from their mothers. They are doing their shopping together so they can help each other choose the best outfits.

If I Had It to Do All Over Again . . .

CHAPTER 29

RECOGNIZING SUFFIXES

⋅

Understanding how suffixes affect base word meanings can help you develop your vocabulary skills. Read this dialogue.

MARIA: Professor English just told the class to add suffixes to this week's vocabulary list. I can't do the assignment because I have no idea what a suffix is.

SULY: Don't worry, I can tell you what a suffix is.

MARIA: Oh, great! What is it?

SULY: A **suffix** is a word part that is added to the end of a base word. Sometimes it changes the use of the word in the sentence. For example, if you add the suffix **-able** to the verb **accept,** you have made the word **acceptable.** It is used differently in the sentence. It now becomes a new part of speech, and it changes its position in the sentence. For example, you can use **accept** in this sentence: "I **accept** the present." And you can use the word **acceptable** in this sentence: "The present is **acceptable.**"

MARIA: I think I understand it. Now, can you tell me about other suffixes to add to *accept*?

SULY: Yes, accept + **-ed** = accept**ed,** accept + **-ing** = accept**ing,** and accept + **-s** = accept**s.**

MARIA: I see. I guess there are many other suffixes I should learn.

Verb Endings: -en, -ize, -ify

Some suffixes can change the part of speech of a base word. Read the following sentences.

EXAMPLE

1A. Here is a **short** passage.
1B. **Shorten** the passage from ten lines to five.

QUESTIONS

1. In 1A is "short" a noun, a verb, or an adjective? _____

2. In 1B is "shorten" a noun, a verb, or an adjective? _____

In 1A "short" is an adjective, and in 1B "shorten" is a verb.

Some **suffixes** added to base words **change the part of speech** of those words.

EXAMPLE

PART OF SPEECH	WORD	+	SUFFIX	=	NEW WORD	PART OF SPEECH
Adjective	vocal	+	**-ize**	=	vocal**ize**	Verb
Adjective	short	+	**-en**	=	short**en**	Verb
Adjective	false	+	**-ify**	=	fals**ify**	Verb

The suffixes **-ize, -en,** and **-ify** all mean **to make,** and change base words to verbs.

Sometimes it is necessary to make spelling changes in the base word before adding a suffix. For example, the **silent e** in "false" is dropped before adding the suffix **-ify.** A word ending in **y** is spelled differently when a **suffix beginning with a vowel** is added. Often, it is necessary to use your dictionary to check on the correct spelling and the suffix to use.

EXERCISE First underline the suffix in each word. Then write the definition of each of the following words. Use the meanings of the suffixes to help you.

1. liven _____live_____
2. capitalize _____
3. solidify _____
4. symbolize _____
5. simplify _____simple_____
6. loosen _____loose_____
7. broaden _____broad_____
8. familiarize _____familiar_____

PRACTICE Add the correct suffix from the chart to complete each of the base words. Then write the meaning of each word with its suffix ending. Use your dictionary if you need help. The first one is done for you.

1. vital: _vitalize - to make alive_
2. tough: _toughen_
3. character: _characterize_
4. social: _socialize_
5. soft: _soften_
6. stable: _stabilize   stablize_
7. haste: _hasten_
8. strength: _strengthen_
9. memory: _memorize_
10. central: _centralize_

Verb Endings: -ed, -ing

Some suffixes can be added to verbs. Consider these words.

EXAMPLE

attract   attract**ed**   attract**ing**
state   state**d**   stat**ing**

QUESTIONS

1. What two basic words are given? _____

2. What suffixes are added to the words? _____

> The suffix **-ed** can be added to the simple form of a regular verb to create either the **past tense or past participle form.** When the simple form ends in **e,** only **-d** is added.
>
> The suffix **-ing** can be added to the simple form of a verb to create the **"ing" form of the verb or present participle form.** When the simple form ends with a **silent e,** that **e** is dropped before adding **-ing.**

EXERCISE Add the suffixes **-ed** and **-ing** to the simple form of each of the following verbs.

1. travel   _____   _____

2. pack   _____   _____

3. share   _____   _____

4. follow   _____   _____

5. enjoy   _____   _____

6. attend   _____   _____

7. tie   _____   _____

8. allow   _____   _____

9. proclaim   _____   _____

10. expand   _____   _____

WRITING PRACTICE From the list in the previous exercise, select five words ending in **-ed** and five words ending in **-ing** and use each one in a separate sentence.

1. _____

2. _____

If I Had It to Do All Over Again . . .

3. _____

4. _____

5. _____

6. _____

7. _____

8. _____

9. _____

10. _____

Verb Endings: -s -es

Now consider these sample sentences.

EXAMPLE

    2A. The boy runs quickly.
    2B. Two children run down the street.
    2C. The girl wishes for a car.
    2D. Many people wish for a job.

QUESTIONS

1. Which two sentences have singular subjects? _____

2. Which two sentences have plural subjects? _____

3. What are the verb endings for singular subjects? _____

4. Is there a verb ending for plural subjects? _____

Sentences 2A and 2C have singular subjects; sentences 2B and 2D have plural subjects. Singular subjects have the suffix **-s** or **-es** added to the third-person singular verb form. Plural subjects have no suffix ending added to the verb form.

> When a verb form ends with the suffixes **-s** or **-es,** the third-person singular is being expressed. The suffix **-es** is added to verbs ending in **ch, sh, ss,** and **x** to express the third-person singular.

EXERCISE Write the suffix **-s** or **-es** after each of the following verbs to express the third-person singular form.

1. mix ____   4. fix ____   7. nourish ____ 10. punch ____

2. wish ____ 5. catch ____   8. pass ____   11. communicate ____

3. join ____ 6. celebrate ____ 9. wait ____   12. rush ____

PRACTICE Correct each sentence by adding the suffix **-s** or **-es** to any verbs that should be expressed in the third-person singular.

1. The groom rush to the wedding ceremony.

2. All the relatives celebrate the holidays together.

3. The child join the party for her sister.

4. The superintendent of a building fix anything that need repairing.

5. The bridesmaid catch the flowers that the bride throws over the crowd.

WRITING PRACTICE Correct the following sentences by adding an **-s** or **-es** ending to the verb or by crossing it out if the subject of the sentence is plural. The first has been done for you.

1. His bosses knows~~s~~ how to sell advertisements.
2. Many of our advertisers seeks his help.
3. She understand the importance of advertising nationally.
4. Her product need more public exposure.
5. Successful advertising campaigns begins with a good idea.
6. Many breakfast cereals uses television advertising to reach children.
7. A new product deserve new advertising techniques.
8. Some advertisers attempts to be offensive.
9. They feels that they catches the attention of the public this way.
10. Everyone sell his own product vigorously.

Noun Endings: -s, -es, -ies

MARIA: I failed a test on suffixes yesterday.

SULY: Why? I thought we had all those rules straight.

MARIA: When I tried to show the plural of party, I added an **-s,** but Professor English said I had spelled "partys" wrong, and I don't know how to spell it correctly.

SULY: I'm really sorry, Maria. I forgot to tell you about plural nouns and some spelling changes that occur with nouns that end in **y.**

MARIA: You mean that some words change their spelling when suffixes are added?

SULY: Yes. Most plural nouns end in **-s** or **-es.** However, nouns that end in **y** change their spelling when the suffix is added. The **y changes to an i** before the **-es** suffix. Some words that don't follow this rule are "keys," "monkeys," "valleys," and "donkeys."

MARIA: Oh, I should have written "parties" instead of "partys." What a silly mistake.

SULY: Not at all. I should have told you about that. Here are some words to practice. Just remember to change the **y to an i** before you add the suffix **-es** to make a noun plural.

> When the suffixes **-s, -es,** and **-ies** are added to singular nouns, the nouns become plural nouns. The plural suffix **-es** is added to nouns ending in "**ch,**" "**sh,**" "**ss,**" or "**x.**" The plural suffix **-ies** is added to nouns ending in **y.** However, the **y** is dropped before the suffix **-ies** is added. Some exceptions are "monkeys," "valleys," "attorneys," "keys," "alleys," "donkeys," and "turkeys."

EXERCISE Change these nouns into their plural forms by adding the suffix **-s, -es,** or **-ies.**

1. family _families_
2. chair _chairs_
3. baby _babies_
4. friend _friends_
5. city _cities_

6. class _classes_
7. thirty _thirties_
8. box _boxes_
9. eighty _eighties_
10. candy _candies_

11. spy _spies_
12. match _matches_
13. paper _papers_
14. lady _ladies_
15. glass _glasses_

PRACTICE Correct each sentence by adding the suffixes **-s, -es,** or **-ies** to any underlined noun that should be plural.

1. There are many <u>fly</u> in the room. _flies_

2. I want six cheese <u>pastry</u> from the bakery. _pastries_

3. I have a collection of all of Beethoven's <u>symphony</u>. _symphonies_

4. Can you hum the seven <u>melody</u> I have here? ___melodies___

5. Both <u>sex</u> should be treated equally on the job. ___sexes___

PRACTICE Correct each sentence by adding the suffixes **-s** or **-es** to any noun that should be plural.

1. You can't have two dates at the same time.

2. How many chaperones will be at the party?

3. We need two cases of soda, five bags of potato chips, and three gallons of ice cream.

4. The party decoration will include many flowers, several baskets, a few balloons, and one poster.

5. All the members of the high school graduating class bought two class pictures.

WRITING PRACTICE Select five words from the previous exercise and for each one write two sentences. Use the singular form of the word in the first sentence and the plural form of the word in the second sentence.

1. _____

   _____

2. _____

   _____

3. _____

   _____

4. _____

   _____

5. _____

   _____

PRACTICE READING

Untitled

My name is Christopher. My family came to America before I was born. In two weeks I am going to be married, and my fiancée Samantha and I expect to be very happy. We do not plan to have a honeymoon because we want to spend two weeks setting up our own new business as real estate agents.

My mother, who is very traditional, says that our plans are absurd.° She thinks that we should just spend the two weeks on a holiday in the Caribbean. In her day, and in the old country, young people didn't start businesses together. Instead, the man went out to work, and the wife stayed home to raise a family.

Both Samantha and I want children, in a while, and together we plan to raise them. Needless to say, our plans and my mother's views don't agree. I suppose it's hard for my mother and father to understand our point of view. They are used to another way of setting up a marriage and a life.

Another thing that bothers my parents is the fact that Samantha and I are going to be spending seven days a week on our business until it is run-

°not sensible

If I Had It to Do All Over Again . . .

ning smoothly. As my mother has pointed out to us, such a schedule will leave us little time for socializing or for a night on the town.° A young couple should enjoy themselves and get to know each other under less hectic° circumstances, my mother says.

°going out to celebrate in a big way
°intensely active; overly busy

Actually, Samantha and I know each other pretty well. We are both dedicated to our goals, and neither of us minds giving up weekends for a while. We are young and enthusiastic.

VOCABULARY EXERCISE Check each sentence in which the underlined word is used correctly.

____ 1. It is <u>absurd</u> to think that young couples will be happy.

____ 2. The best aspect of <u>socializing</u> is meeting no one.

____ 3. Working a twelve-hour day can be called <u>hectic</u>.

____ 4. The fans' <u>enthusiasm</u> helped the players on the field.

____ 5. The bride and groom usually pledge to <u>dedicate</u> their lives to one another.

LITERAL COMPREHENSION EXERCISE Select the answer that best completes the statement.

____ 1. Christopher and Samantha will not honeymoon because
    a. they expect to be happy.
    b. they know each other pretty well.
    c. they will spend seven days a week running a business.
    d. they want to start setting up their real estate business.

____ 2. "Young people don't start businesses," says
    a. Christopher's mother.
    b. Christopher's parents.
    c. Christopher.
    d. none of the above

____ 3. Christopher's mother and father are
    a. against the young couple's marriage.
    b. used to the old-country customs.
    c. expecting to be very happy.
    d. becoming more adjusted to American marriages.

____ 4. Christopher and Samantha feel that they
    a. must socialize at least one night a week.
    b. must start their business running smoothly.
    c. are not sacrificing any aspect of marriage.
    d. will soon be able to know each other better.

GENERAL COMPREHENSION EXERCISE Complete the following statements.

_____ 1. The best title for this passage is
   a. Samantha and Christopher's Marriage.
   b. Building a Modern American Marriage.
   c. Old World Views on Marriage.
   d. Starting a New Business.

_____ 2. When Samantha and Christopher discuss their plans, they
   a. run into three major objections from Christopher's mother.
   b. are in absolute agreement.
   c. are each fully committed to the business.
   d. all of the above

CHAPTER 30

OUTLINING MULTIPLE PARAGRAPHS AS A SELECTION

* *
*

In the beginning of this unit, you outlined a short titled passage. In that outline, you signaled the title by using a Roman numeral, the main idea by using a capital letter, and the details by using numbers.

Here is the passage that you have already outlined. More information has been added to it. Outline this selection in the space provided.

EXAMPLE

DATING ETIQUETTE THEN AND NOW	OUTLINE

Dating etiquette in the 1930s and 1940s was very structured. The rules for acceptable dating behavior were firmly established. Boys and girls usually began dating in high school. Of course, they needed their parents' approval. Many teenagers were even chaperoned. After the boy met his date's parents and talked with them for a little while, the young couple usually left for a movie, and a soda and snack, which the boy paid for. The young people observed strict curfews and said their goodnights at the front door.

The situation is quite different nowadays. Dating is far more casual. Children begin dating in junior high school, and many youngsters have steady girlfriends or boyfriends. The younger couples may be escorted by their parents, but as soon as they are in high school, couples rebel at the idea of being chaperoned. Dutch treat dating is acceptable, and because of the teens' limited finances, it occurs quite frequently. Girls call boys and ask for dates. They even pay for dates. Cur-

I. _____

  A. _____

    _____

    1. _____

      _____

    2. _____

      _____

    3. _____

      _____

    4. _____

      _____

    5. _____

      _____

    6. _____

      _____

    7. _____

      _____

    8. _____

      _____

fews are enforced only in a few households. Today, teenagers exercise more
independence in all aspects of dating.

9. _____

_____

B. _____

_____

1. _____

_____

2. _____

_____

3. _____

_____

4. _____

_____

5. _____

_____

6. _____

_____

7. _____

_____

8. _____

_____

9. _____

_____

QUESTIONS

1. Do the outlines for paragraphs A and B differ from any that you have
   practiced? _____

2. How has the title of the selection changed? _____

_____

3. Why was the title changed? _____

   Paragraphs A and B are outlined in the same manner as were previous
examples. The title for this selection is expanded to include the information
in both paragraphs. Because the main idea of the first paragraph concerns

dating etiquette years ago and the main idea of the second paragraph concerns dating etiquette now, the title must cover both main ideas.

In the following exercises you will have an opportunity to practice outlining two-paragraph passages. Be sure to include a title that covers the main ideas of both paragraphs.

EXERCISE Read and outline the following selections. Then add a title to the passage and place that title in the outline.

1. _____

Are today's teenagers freer than teenagers of twenty years ago? The answer is clearly yes. Today's teens are more informed about sex and openly discuss it with their parents, their friends, and sometimes even with people they don't know well. Sexual relations before marriage are common among today's teens. Years ago, on the other hand, young people rarely discussed sex with anyone. If a young couple had sexual relations, they tried to keep their secret from everyone.

The reasons for these changes are fairly clear. One reason may be that today's teenagers find sexual references everywhere. On every newsstand, sex-oriented magazines and novels are displayed prominently.° This was unheard of years ago. Today, movies display more sex on the screen than ever before. It's no wonder today's teens have different views from their counterparts° of twenty years ago.

I. _____

  A. _____

    _____

    1. _____

    _____

    2. _____

    _____

    3. _____

    _____

    4. _____

    _____

    5. _____

    _____

  B. _____ °easily seen

    _____

    1. _____

    _____ °equals in age

    2. _____

    _____

    3. _____

    _____

2. _____

Friends or contemporaries° are a great influence on the actions, thoughts, and words of young people. This influence, known as peer pressure, is quite common among children. Why are children so easily af-

I. _____ °people of the same age

fected by what their peers do, think, or say?

Most of us, children included, feel a strong need to be liked by others. We seek acceptance and friendship. In order to gain them, we act like our friends and listen to their advice, whether or not it is helpful. Some of us even begin to think like our friends, sometimes at the expense of our own beliefs and values. An example that comes to mind is the young person who gets involved with drugs because his peer group is experimenting with them. Parents may try to exert pressure to keep him away from drugs, but frequently peer pressure is too great. This conflict between being your own person° and, at the same time, responding to the pressures of a group remains a problem for young people.

°being independent

PRACTICE Read and outline the following passage.

OUTLINE

In some societies it is the custom for parents to arrange the marriages of their children. The father and mother of the bride will meet with the father and mother of the groom, and if both families are pleased with each other, an agreement will be made. Often the bride and groom will not be asked for their opinion in this matter, and sometimes they do not even meet each other until the day of the wedding. In some countries, men advertise for mail-order brides in the local paper.

Most Americans find the idea of arranged marriages difficult to understand or accept. They believe that two people should marry for love, after a period of dating or courtship. During that period, the prospective marriage partners are supposed to learn enough about each other to decide whether or not they will be able to build a suc-

[handwritten, in the Outline area:]
I   ARRANGED MARRIAGES.
A - PARENT. arrange the marriage.
   1 - FATHER AND MOTHER of bride will meet. Fand M of groom.
   2 -

If I Had It to Do All Over Again . . .

cessful marriage. Today in America, it is common for people to live together as a way of preparing for marriage. The idea of an arranged marriage seems very old-fashioned indeed.

But aren't all marriages arranged in one way or another? In the United States marriages are seldom formally° arranged, but quite a lot of informal arranging goes on before two people become husband and wife. People who get married are introduced to each other by friends. These friends have already decided that the two people are right for each other and arrange for them to meet. In the United States this kind of arrangement is very common. Because friends have such great influence, their approval of a dating or mating partner is very important.

°according to customs or rules

Families also exert open and subtle pressures on their children to influence their choices of marriage partners. Parents often arrange dates for their own children. One parent often tells a friend about her beautiful daughter or handsome son. Also, parents can meet the perfect marriage prospect for their son or daughter through business relationships. Since parents often assist their children financially, they feel that they have the right to help the bride and groom select where they will live, what type of furniture they will purchase, and what their life-style will be like.

To a large extent, social class determines the choice of a marriage partner in the United States. Marriages are usually arranged between people of similar religious, ethnic, and financial backgrounds. Despite what we see in the movies, the son of a bank president rarely marries or even meets a coal miner's daughter. Americans may not accept or understand arranged marriages, but marriages in the United States are arranged nevertheless.

CHAPTER 31

RECOGNIZING SUFFIXES:
Adjective Endings

.

MARIA: Every time I think that I know all the suffixes, I discover new words that I never knew existed. Will I ever be able to understand how a word's function in the sentence changes if I don't know the suffixes?

SULY: Don't worry, Maria. I'll give you some more help in understanding suffixes. Let me tell you about some of the common types.

MARIA: What are they?

SULY: Well, there are several suffixes that are used with words that describe things or people. Listen to these words:

comic**al**   comfor**table**   doubt**ful**   itc**hy**   diges**tive**

All these words are adjectives. They describe something or someone.

MARIA: I see. All of these suffixes are used with words to make them **describe** something or someone. I can almost picture something "itchy" or "comical."

SULY: Let's work on these together. I have to practice these suffixes too.

Read the following sentences.

EXAMPLE

1A. Mary went on vacation to Hawaii because she needed a rest.
1B. Mary enjoyed a restful vacation.

2A. Paul likes the taste of sasparilla.
2B. Paul finds sasparilla a tasty beverage.

QUESTIONS

1. What part of speech is the word "rest" in 1A? _____

   What part of speech is the word "taste" in 2A? _____

2. What part of speech is the word "restful" in 1B? _____

   What part of speech is the word "tasty" in 2B? _____

3. What does the suffix **-ful** add to the meaning of "rest?" _____

What does the suffix **-y** add to the meaning of "taste?" _____

In 1A and 2A the underlined words are **nouns.** In 1B and 2B, the underlined words are **adjectives.** The suffixes **-ful** and **-y** change the part of speech of the base words to a new part of speech, in this case from nouns to adjectives.

Here are the meanings of some frequently used adjective suffixes. Note that when a base word ends in the letter **e,** the e is usually dropped before adding a suffix that begins with a vowel.

BASE WORD AND SUFFIX	SUFFIX MEANING	WORD MEANING
enjoy**able**	able to be	able to be enjoyed
flex**ible**	able to be	able to be flexed or bent
univers**al**	relating to	relating to the universe
salt**y**	tends to be, like	tends to be full of salt, like salt
act**ive**	tends to (be)	tends to be involved, tends to act
rest**ful**	full of	full of rest

SAMPLE SENTENCES:

1. Randi had an <u>enjoyable</u> time at every party she attended.
2. Scott's work schedule is <u>flexible</u>, so he gets a lot of free time.
3. English is a <u>universal</u> language.
4. The roast is too <u>salty</u> for my taste.
5. The couple had an <u>active</u> social life in their town.
6. They spent a <u>restful</u> weekend at a quiet beach.

EXERCISE Using your dictionary to help you, choose one of the adjective suffixes from the right-hand column to complete each of the underlined words. Then write the definition of the word. The first one is done for you.

1. attract<u>ive</u> flowers means: <u>flowers that tend to attract</u>   (-ive, able)

2. support ___ parents are: _____ *supportive*   (-ful, -ive)

3. beauti ___ friends are: _____ *beautiful*   (-al, -ful)

4. a sleep ___ person is: _____ *sleepy*   (-able, -y)

5. an enjoy ___ discussion is: _____ *enjoyable*   (-ible, -able)

6. an option ___ decision is: _____ *optional*   (-ful, -al)

7. a disagree ___ date is: _____ *disagreeable*   (-able, -ible)

8. a transmitt ___ disease is: _____ *transmittable*   (-ful, -able)

Recognizing Suffixes   221

9. an accept ____ plan is: _____ *acceptable* (-y, -able)
10. an act ____ child means: _____ *active* (-ful, -ive)

PRACTICE Circle the correct adjective in each sentence.

1. The girl wore an (expensive   expenseful) dress to the party.
2. Ernest's ideas were (creatable   creative) and (inventive   inventful).
3. Eva's parents were (thankable   thankful) when her date brought her home early.
4. It was (easeful   easy) to talk with my friends.
5. Kwang was (hopeful   hopefully) that everyone would attend his party.
6. Plastic plates and cups are (reuseful   reusable).
7. Snack foods containing artificial coloring are not (healthal   healthful).
8. Adele was (forceful   forcible) in her request for (additional   additionable) chaperones for the prom.
9. Gus (continuably   continually) called his girlfriend.
10. It is (impossable   impossible) to talk with a (mouthful   mouthable) of food.

CHAPTER 32

OUTLINING:
Short Selections

✢✳✢

You have practiced outlining groups of titled paragraphs.

> In textbooks, titles for grouped paragraphs are called **subtitles.** Subtitles divide a chapter into major subjects.

Read the following portion of a chapter. It has a subtitle and paragraphs, and is followed by another subtitle and paragraphs. Then complete the outline.

EXAMPLE

I. THE NEEDS OF SINGLE PEOPLE

Because single people usually live alone, they tend to rely on a network of friends for their social and emotional needs. Without the responsibilities of raising families, single people have more freedom to pursue leisure-time activities such as discussion groups or sports. Their most serious discussions tend to occur more frequently with friends rather than with family members.

Because single people live alone, their financial security depends on their own efforts. As a result, career goals become extremely important to them. Their single status gives them the opportunity to pursue career goals based solely on their own needs.

II. THE NEEDS OF MARRIED PEOPLE

Because married couples have each other to rely on, they tend not to depend on an extensive network of friends for

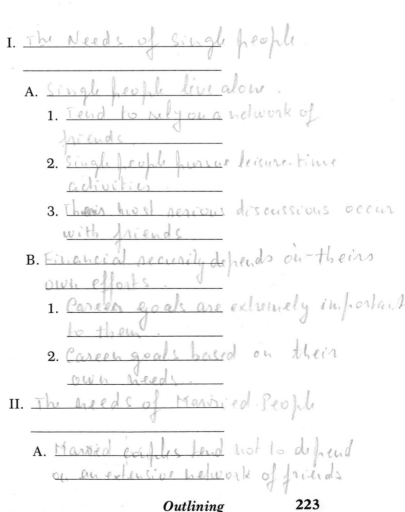

I. The Needs of single people

A. Single people live alone.
　1. Tend to rely on a network of friends
　2. Single people pursue leisure-time activities
　3. Their most serious discussions occur with friends
B. Financial security depends on theirs own efforts
　1. Career goals are extremely important to them
　2. Career goals based on their own needs.

II. The needs of Married People

A. Married couples tend not to depend on an extensive network of friends their social and emotional needs. Responsibilities to each other and possibly toward their children, create demands that often leave little time for many leisure activities. Usually the most important discussions take place within the family unit.

For married couples, the responsibility of financial security is often shared. Career goals affect not just one person, but rather an entire family. It is difficult for them to relocate or readjust career choices because an entire family is affected.

1. Responsibilities to each other and their children
2. They spend little time for many leisure activities
3. Most important discussion take place within the family unit

B. Financial security is often shared
1. Career goals affect an entire family.
2. It is difficult to readjust career choices

QUESTIONS

1. Why are there two Roman numerals in this selection? _____

_____

2. How does this outline differ from any you have done before? _____

_____

The two Roman numerals signal the subtitles from the chapter. As in previous outlines, the Roman numeral at the margin clearly shows the major subtitled subject, and the capital letters clearly show the main idea of each paragraph. The listed numbers are indented even farther to show the details.

EXERCISE Outline the following selection and answer the questions that follow.

Outline
_____

I. PRESSURES TO GET MARRIED

Young people are often pressured to marry by their families and friends. Rose and Bill talk about the frustrations and disagreements Rose has had with her family. She has told Bill about how her family continually asks her why she isn't married. Her family has been putting pressure on° Rose to

°influencing; insisting

find a husband, and this makes Rose angry.

Bill understands how Rose feels. He has also been upset about how his friends react to his single life. His women friends usually find him dates, even if he doesn't want them. They introduce him to new people as the eligible bachelor.°

°a man available for marriage

Sometimes Rose and Bill feel they might be better off financially if they each found a marriage partner. They know that two people living together and earning two salaries can afford more than a single person can. They also know about the income tax advantages married couples enjoy. However, for the moment, each of them is committed to remaining single.

II. Pressures Not to Get Married

Young people feel many pressures not to get married. Rose has a very good job at the bank, and there is a possibility of a promotion in the near future. A promotion means a higher salary and more responsibility. She questions whether she can combine success in business with marriage. Both demand a great amount of time and work.

Bill, too, is hesitant° about getting married because of his active social life. He has many friends and is out with one of them almost every night. How can he ever settle down and stay home with one person? Will he lose his friends?

°uncertain; undecided

At this point Rose and Bill are each trying to settle the question of whether to get married. Both Rose and Bill know they will reach a decision without being pressured.

VOCABULARY EXERCISE Add one of the following suffixes to the words listed to complete the sentence. Be aware of any necessary spelling changes. Noun suffixes are **-s**, **-es**, and **-ies**; verb suffixes are **-s**, **-es**, **-ed**, and **-ing**; adjective suffixes are **-ible** and **-able.**

1. (frustration) There are many _____ a single person faces.

2. (understand) Bill never _____ why his friends think he must marry.

3. (partner) Both _____ in a marriage must respect one another.

4. (question) Some relatives have _____ motives when they offer advice.

5. (disagreement) Both married and single couples often have _____

   _____.

6. (advantage) Married and single life-styles offer many _____

   _____.

7. (pressure) Don't be _____ into getting engaged.

8. (couple) Unmarried _____ have many adjustments to make.

9. (response) Singles often hold _____ positions at work.

10. (salary) Two _____ are often better than one.

11. (make) Rose is _____ bread this morning.

12. (feel) Bill _____ like the extra man at parties.

13. (pressure) Singles experience many _____ to get married.

14. (marry) _____ couples have adjustments to make.

15. (understand) It is _____ that you have doubts about marriage.

LITERAL COMPREHENSION EXERCISE Choose the best answer according to the story.

____ 1. Rose is frustrated by her family's
   a. constant pressure about marriage.
   b. unwillingness to accept Bill into the family.
   c. ignorance of her career potential.
   d. all of the above

_____ 2. Bill understands
   a. his friends' attitudes.
   b. the feeling of being pressured.
   c. that a single person does better financially.
   d. that he is better off settling down with one person.

_____ 3. Both Rose and Bill
   a. will probably live together.
   b. will come to a decision together.
   c. are trying to decide whether or not to get married.
   d. are ignoring their friends' advice.

_____ 4. Married couples usually enjoy
   a. more luxuries.
   b. better salaried positions.
   c. better tax advantages.
   d. both a and b

_____ 5. Bill and Rose both feel the pressures placed upon them by
   a. close relatives.
   b. friends who find them dates.
   c. employers who want to hire only married persons.
   d. people who are close to them.

GENERAL COMPREHENSION EXERCISE Answer these questions based on the information in the story.

_____ 1. Bill and Rose are
   a. considering marriage to each other.
   b. in their teens.
   c. living the ideal single life.
   d. experiencing difficulties.

_____ 2. The pressures against getting married are
   a. greater than the pressures to marry.
   b. less than the pressures to marry.
   c. influencing both Bill and Rose fairly equally.
   d. influencing Bill more than Rose.

PRACTICE Outline the following selection and answer the questions that follow.

OUTLINE

I. WHO BELONGS TO THE SINGLES' SCENE?

The singles' scene° is made up of all types of people. For example, my

°activities of and places where single people meet

Outlining   227

cousin Lydia is a part of it. She is in her early twenties, has never been married, and lives in the city. Lydia dates many men, goes out with groups of friends, or spends an evening alone at a movie or at a show. She often visits the local singles' places, such as the corner bar and the local disco.

Sven, on the other hand, is in his late twenties. He lives in a suburb of the city. He was married for two years, but has been divorced for a year. Many of his single friends are also divorced or separated. They are all members of the singles' scene.

II. WHAT IS THE SINGLES' SCENE?

The singles' scene is made up of single people and the places which attract them. Both Sven and Lydia enjoy the singles' social scene. They have no permanent ties and are free to date or socialize with friends. They enjoy their mobility.° On a moment's notice, each can pack a bag and head for the nearest resort. Lydia enjoys meeting and dating many men. Sven also loves the excitement of socializing with people at parties and traveling whenever and wherever he likes.

°freedom to move about

The singles' scene is also made up of places where singles gather. Lydia and Sven's crowd of friends socialize in their neighborhood restaurants and discos. They know they can always find a familiar face in these places. Singles frequently attend lectures, the theater, and movies together. Such events also provide an opportunity for socializing. In addition, the crowd spends vacations at resorts known to attract a singles' crowd.

VOCABULARY EXERCISE Divide the following words into syllables.

married   divorced   separated

If I Had It to Do All Over Again . . .

SUFFIXES EXERCISE Add the noun suffix **-s** to each base word. Write a sentence using the new word.

SENTENCE

1. love _____: _____
2. single _____: _____
3. date _____: _____
4. lecture ____: _____
5. divorce ____: _____

Now add the verb suffix **-ed** or **-d** to each of these verbs and write each one in a sentence.

SENTENCE

1. love _____: _____
2. single _____: _____
3. date _____: _____
4. lecture ____: _____
5. marry _____: _____
6. divorce ____: _____
7. separate ___: _____

LITERAL COMPREHENSION EXERCISE Answer the following questions according to the story.

_____ 1. Lydia, a member of the singles' scene,
    a. lives in the suburbs.
    b. visits her parents.
    c. is in her twenties.
    d. is divorced.

_____ 2. Sven
    a. has never been married.
    b. has only friends who are married.
    c. has friends who have been married and divorced.
    d. has little opportunity for travel.

_____ 3. Both Sven and Lydia
    a. are free to date and socialize with friends.
    b. pack bags and head for the nearest resort.
    c. love the excitement of socializing.
    d. all of the above

_____ 4. Singles gather at
   a. lectures, theaters, and movies.
   b. resorts and restaurants.
   c. pizza parlors and universities.
   d. both a and b

_____ 5. Sven and Lydia's friends
   a. enjoy both urban and suburban life.
   b. are mostly widowed or divorced.
   c. prefer lectures and movies to resorts.
   d. only socialize with singles.

GENERAL COMPREHENSION EXERCISE Use information in the story
to answer each of these questions.

_____ 1. Lydia and Sven are
   a. eagerly looking for marriage partners.
   b. enjoying the single life-style.
   c. planning to marry.
   d. associating with bad crowds.

_____ 2. The crowd gathers
   a. at favorite single spots.
   b. at local clubs only.
   c. more in the city than in the suburbs.
   d. at lectures once a week.

PRACTICE Outline the following selection and answer the questions that
follow.

OUTLINE

I. EXTENDED DATING

Strong bonds can exist in dating relationships. My cousin Candice and
her friend Louis started dating casually last year. As the months passed,
they began seeing only each other, and
now they enjoy a close relationship.
They are neither married nor engaged
but are constant companions and consider each other best friends. Candice's friends think of them as a couple
and recognize their special relationship.

Both Candice and Louis have made
commitments to each other. They
think of themselves as a couple. How-

ever, each has the freedom to develop new friends, to seek separate social activities, to build separate careers, and to have his or her individual needs fulfilled.

II. LIVING TOGETHER

Living together can be the transition from extended dating to marriage. Just recently, Louis and Candice decided to live together. They are not sure about marriage and want to try living together first. Louis has many divorced friends who had rushed into marriage. He doesn't want to make a similar mistake. He knows that living together will not be easy, but feels he has few alternatives. Friends and family will exert pressure on the couple to get married. Louis knows that this is the worst reason to get married. He believes that living together will provide Candice and him with an opportunity to see how well each can adjust to the other's feelings and living styles. He hopes they will discover whether they are compatible.

Louis moved into Candice's apartment this weekend. Books, records, and clothing fit in nicely. Of course, they will have to decide what to do with two couches, two beds, twenty-two pots and pans, and duplicates of all kitchen and bath items. They have settled in as an unmarried-married couple and will have to make the same adjustments as any newlyweds.

VOCABULARY EXERCISE   Find each of the following words in the story. Can you derive a meaning for each word as it appears in the story? Write the meaning next to the word.

1. casually _____

2. relationship _____

3. companions _____

4. respective _____

5. commitments _____

6. alternatives _____

7. compatible _____

8. duplicates _____

LITERAL COMPREHENSION EXERCISE Match the information in column A with the information in column B.

COLUMN A	COLUMN B
____ Louis and Candice decided to live together.	1. this weekend
	2. now
____ They started dating casually.	3. just recently
	4. as months passed
____ They see more of each other.	5. last year
____ They enjoy a close relationship.	

COLUMN A	COLUMN B
1. Louis	____ knows people who rushed into marriage.
2. Candice	____ has friends who think of Louis and Candice as a couple.
	____ has friends who know about their special relationship.
	____ has a fairly large apartment.
	____ knows that the worst reason for getting married is group pressure.

GENERAL COMPREHENSION EXERCISE Use the information in the story to decide on the answer.

____ 1. Candice and Louis' special relationship
  a. allows each person unlimited freedom.
  b. is an arrangement each agreed to.
  c. will probably anger most of their friends.
  d. has already proven their compatability.

____ 2. Living together
  a. is fairly common among singles.
  b. is practiced by relatively few.
  c. will involve both good and trying times.
  d. is sinful.

232   *If I Had It to Do All Over Again . . .*

CHAPTER 33

RECOGNIZING SUFFIXES:
Noun Endings

.

SULY: Maria, now that you understand adjective suffixes, you will want to know about **suffixes used to signify a noun.**

MARIA: Please give me an example.

SULY: Listen to these sentences:

EXAMPLE

Eileen hired a **teenager** to babysit for her children.

Our stereo system has a powerful **amplifier.**

The **investigator** checked the couple's credit references.

Bob was accused of being a **sexist** because he wouldn't hire women in his business.

QUESTIONS

1. What are the suffixes in each of the boldfaced words?

_____ _____ _____ _____

2. What does each word mean?

_____

_____

_____

_____

A "teenager" is one who is in the teenage years.

An "amplifier" is a thing that amplifies or makes loud.

An "investigator" is one who investigates.

A "sexist" is one who discriminates on the basis of sex.

The noun suffixes **-er, -or,** and **-ist** mean **one who** or **that which.** Drop the final **e** on the basic word if the suffix begins with a vowel.

EXERCISE Match the meanings in column B with the words in column A. The first one is done for you.

COLUMN A	COLUMN B
_4_ player	1. a person who teaches
_5_ antagonist	2. a machine that transmits
_6_ visitor	3. a person who plays the organ
_1_ professor	4. a person who plays games
_2_ transmitter	5. a person who opposes or argues
_3_ organist	6. a person who visits

PRACTICE Use one of the following noun suffixes to complete the underlined word: **-er, -or, -ar, -ist.** Use your dictionary to check the spelling.

1. A person who does research is called a <u>research<i>er</i></u> .
2. A person who operates a machine is called a <u>machin<i>ist</i></u> .
3. A kitchen appliance that toasts bread is called a <u>toast<i>er</i></u>   .
4. A machine that generates power is called a <u>generat<i>or</i></u> .
5. A machine that makes things go faster is called an <u>accelerat<i>or</i></u> .
6. A person who advises is called an <u>advis</u>   or a <u>counsel</u>   advisor
7. A person who types is called a <u>typ<i>ist</i></u>.
8. A person who collects things is called a <u>collect<i>or</i></u> .
9. A person who studies different cultures is called an <u>anthropolog<i>ist</i></u> .
10. A kitchen appliance that keeps things cold is called a <u>refrigerat<i>or</i></u> .

Courtesy of Queensborough Community College

FINAL PRACTICE READING

Untitled

Susan and her dearest friend Tracy sat down for a heart-to-heart° talk.   °intimate
Tracy said, "I am really confused about using the pill."

Tracy stated that last year she had seen a doctor and had been using the
pill ever since. Susan asked about the possible negative effects associated
with using birth control pills.

"Tracy, haven't you read the articles about all the risks involved, such as
heart attacks, circulation problems, and cancer?"

Tracy said, "I don't believe any of those claims."

Susan and Tracy talked for hours about the pros and cons° of using the   °reasons on both sides of
pill. Finally, Tracy admitted that she really didn't want to use the pill, but   an issue
had to. When Susan asked why, Tracy said that her boyfriend insisted that
she take the pill.

°secondary; unplanned
results

°birth control

"And, besides, what else can I do?"

Susan asked if Tracy had told her boyfriend about the possible side ef-
fects° of taking the pill.

"Yes, but he still says I must do it," answered Tracy.

Susan asked, "Tracy, why don't you show him today's article about male
contraceptive° pills. Scientists are perfecting these pills and need volunteers to help in the study. Ask your boyfriend to volunteer."

"He'll never do that."

Susan said, "Find out why not and tell him those are exactly the reasons
why you don't want to take the pill."

"I'll do that."

VOCABULARY EXERCISE Divide the following words into syllables.

confused   scientists   control
negative   associated   problems

SUFFIXES EXERCISE Write a sentence using each word.

SENTENCE

1. control: _____

    controllable: _____

2. reason: _____

    reasonable: _____

3. believe: _____

    believable: _____

4. use: _____

    usable: _____

Now add the suffix **-ed** or **-d** to each of these words and write a sentence
using that word.

SENTENCE

1. effect _____: _____

2. volunteer ____: _____

3. circulate _____: _____

4. claim _____: _____

If I Had It to Do All Over Again . . .

LITERAL COMPREHENSION EXERCISE Answer the following questions according to the story.

_____ 1. Tracy, who is taking the pill,
  a. argues with her boyfriend about it.
  b. visits her parents.
  c. has a friend named Susan.
  d. is divorced.

_____ 2. Susan
  a. knows about the side effects of the pill.
  b. tells Tracy to continue taking the pill.
  c. agrees with Tracy's boyfriend.
  d. doesn't read the newspaper.

_____ 3. Both Tracy and Susan
  a. have a boyfriend.
  b. discuss the pros and cons of contraception.
  c. use the pill.
  d. all of the above

_____ 4. Scientists are asking
  a. women to use the pill.
  b. for volunteers in a study of contraceptive methods.
  c. Tracy's boyfriend to volunteer for the study.
  d. both a and b

_____ 5. Tracy and Susan
  a. are not concerned about the negative effects of using the pill.
  b. insist that Susan's boyfriend use the pill.
  c. read an article about male contraceptives.
  d. have a heart-to-heart talk.

GENERAL COMPREHENSION EXERCISE Use the information in the story to answer each of these questions.

_____ 1. The best title for this passage is
  a. A Heart-to-Heart Talk.
  b. Susan's Boyfriend.
  c. Contraceptives for Men and Women.
  d. The Possible Dangers of Contraceptives for Women.

_____ 2. A "heart-to-heart" talk is a discussion
  a. about health problems.
  b. between friends.
  c. about birth control.
  d. that is direct and personal.

WRITING EXERCISE   Write a main idea sentence for each of the following topics.

Chaperones _____

Honeymoon _____

Wedding ceremonies _____

Groom _____

Elopement _____

Select two of the main idea sentences and develop each into a paragraph on separate paper. Use either an incident or several examples to support your main idea sentence.

UNIT VII:
WHO REALLY
WEARS THE PANTS?

Courtesy of Harry Greenberger.

In this unit, you will have a chance to learn about the differences between traditional family units and modern family groups. You will also practice new base word forms and learn to identify directional words in sets of special instructions.

DISCUSSION

How many people are in your immediate family?° With whom are you now living? How do you feel about this arrangement?

INITIAL READING

The Generation Gap

A few years ago it was fashionable to speak of a generation gap, a division between young people and their elders. Parents complained that children did not show them proper respect and obedience, while children complained that their parents did not understand them at all. What had gone wrong? Why had the generation gap suddenly appeared? Actually, the generation gap has been around for a long time. Many critics argue that it is built into the fabric of our society.

One important cause of the generation gap is the opportunity that young people have to choose their own life-styles. In more traditional societies, when children grow up, they are expected to live in the same area as their parents, to marry people that their parents know and approve of, and often to continue the family occupation. In our society, young people often travel great distances for their educations, move out of the family home at an early age, marry—or live with—people whom their parents have never met, and choose occupations different from those of their parents.

°moving up to an improved life-style

In our upwardly mobile° society, parents often expect their children to do better than they did: to find better jobs, to make more money, and to do all the things that they were unable to do. Often, however, the ambitions that parents have for their children are another cause of the division between them. Often, they discover that they have very little in common with each other.

Finally, the speed at which changes take place in our society is another cause of the gap between the generations. In a traditional culture, elderly people are valued for their wisdom, but in our society the knowledge of a

°outdated; useless

lifetime may become obsolete° overnight. The young and the old seem to live in two very different worlds, separated by different skills and abilities.

No doubt, the generation gap will continue to be a feature of American life for some time to come. Its causes are rooted in the freedoms and opportunities of our society, and in the rapid pace at which society changes.

QUESTIONS

1. How have you experienced the generation gap? _____

_____

2. Are there certain topics you cannot discuss with your parents or your children? _____

CHAPTER 34

FOLLOWING DIRECTIONS:
Introduction

*_**

You follow directions in all aspects of your life. For example, you follow directions when you try to locate an unfamiliar place or find the best route to school. You follow directions in your daily life when you use a recipe or put together a toy. Some directions affect your ability to read and understand many types of reading materials. Being able to understand and follow directions is a skill that enables you to follow the action in a story, complete text assignments, and do work according to the instructor's requests.

Understanding Signal Words: Quality and Quantity

Some words direct attention to quantity or quality.

EXAMPLE

1. <u>Most</u> children live with their families until they graduate from college.
2. The <u>average</u> family consists of a group of people living together: a father, a mother, and one or more children.
3. The <u>best</u> thing about Thanksgiving is being with my entire family.
4. The <u>finest</u> quality of the American family is its ability to cope with the stresses of modern life.

QUESTIONS

1. What does "most" tell about the number of American families discussed? _____

2. What does "average" tell about the number of American families described? _____

3. What does "best" tell about Thanksgiving? _____

_____

4. What quality of the American family is outstanding? _____

_____

The words "most," "best," "finest," and "average" are words that direct attention to a quantity or number and to a quality or type. Each word directly affects the meaning of the sentence. You know that the "majority" of students live at home, that "most" families consist of a mother, father, and one or more children, and that the "best" thing is being with the entire family. The trait being discussed as "outstanding" is the American family's ability to cope with the stresses of modern life.

Many words affect sentence meanings by **signaling a quantity** or **quality** of something. Here are several examples:

| best | least | every | weakest | finest | only | each |
| worst | most | none | strongest | poorest | some | all |

EXERCISE Highlight any signal words in the following sentences that direct attention to quantity or quality.

1. The *most* acceptable definition of a nuclear family is that it is a group consisting of a mother, father, and children.
2. *Some* people state that the American family structure is *weaker* than it once was.
3. *Others* say that the nuclear family is the *strongest* unit in American life.
4. *Every* country has different family arrangements.
5. *None* of the world's countries is *without* its own family structures.
   All

PRACTICE Answer the following statements True (T) or False (F). Be aware of any words that may affect the meaning of the entire statement.

F 1. The poorest example of a family activity is everyone watching television shows in different rooms.

F 2. The least frequently used explanation for having ten children is the high cost of living.

T 3. Critics of the nuclear family usually point to the fact that grandparents are excluded from the family unit.

F 4. Only the United States has nuclear family units.

F 5. Each of the following people belongs to the nuclear family: mother, grandmother, father, child, and cousins.

PRACTICE Complete each of the following statements. Be aware of any signal words that affect the answer.

___ 1. The strongest argument for maintaining the nuclear family unit is that
   a. it is expensive.
   b. it helps to maintain a close family relationship.
   c. it keeps older relatives separated from the family.
   d. it keeps older relatives close to the family.

___ 2. Every member of the nuclear family unit
   a. helps to support the family by working.
   b. is involved in community programs.
   c. contributes something special to the family.
   d. glows in the dark.

___ 3. Nuclear family units are found most frequently in
   a. colleges.
   b. communes.
   c. cities.
   d. retirement communities.

_____ 4. The person most likely to be included in a well-defined nuclear family unit is
   a. a cousin.
   b. an uncle.
   c. a stepfather.
   d. a grandparent.

_____ 5. The person least likely to be included in a well-defined nuclear family is
   a. a stepmother.
   b. an uncle.
   c. a sister.
   d. a brother.

PRACTICE   Read the following paragraphs carefully. Be aware of any signal words in the paragraphs or in the questions.

Paragraph 1   The nuclear family unit has done the most to preserve traditional American values. Comprised of° two parents and their children, the nuclear family unit has been a major force for maintaining religious, social, and ethical beliefs. Unlike some other countries in which children are raised apart from their natural parents, the American family has always stayed together until the children have grown.

°consisting of; containing

Answer the following True (T) or False (F).

_F_ 1. The nuclear family has contributed little to the continuation of the traditional American way of life.

_T_ 2. Most religious, social, and ethical beliefs have been transmitted through the generations by the family unit.

_T_ 3. American children usually live with their parents.

Paragraph 2   In all parts of the United States, there are people who belong to family structures that are larger than the nuclear family unit. The extended family,° for example, includes members other than the mother, father, and children. Additional family members may include grandparents, cousins, aunts, and uncles. Each member of the extended family unit has a special role within the group.

°a family unit consisting of all family members related by blood or marriage

Answer the following True (T) or False (F).

_T_ 1. Every part of the United States has people living in extended family units.

_F_ 2. The extended family must have more than two members.

_T_ 3. Most likely, the extended family will include the grandparents.

_F_ 4. When new people join the extended family, they will have no special place in the group.

_T_ 5. Most aunts and uncles are members of the extended family unit.

°bound by affection and loyalty

Paragraph 3   The <u>Old</u> West was settled by close-knit° family groups. For example, in 1870, the Stanton family arrived in Carsontown after a two-month trip in a covered wagon. They hoped to make this growing western town their home, and they were willing to work hard at it. Ed Stanton and his wife, Rebecca, decided to publish a newspaper, something that the town had never had. <u>All</u> the Stantons helped. The children, Jonathan and Elizabeth, sought new subscribers and advertisers. They were also responsible for reporting the school news. Grandpa Stanton wrote the editorals° and local news reports, while Grandma Stanton wrote about church, charity, and gardening events. Uncle William helped Ed and Rebecca set up the type, ink the presses, and bundle the newspapers. Jonathan was in charge of deliveries and asked friends to help. Together, the Stantons began to build a future as solid as their family ties.

°news columns expressing the views of their publishers or editors

Answer the following True (T) or False (F).

_F_ 1. The Stanton family unity was the <u>strongest</u> reason for their probable success.

_F_ 2. Every member of the family except Uncle William helped on the newspaper.

_F_ 3. The children were the only ones who wrote the news stories.

_F_ 4. The Stantons were the oldest family in Carsontown.

_T_ 5. Only the Stantons worked on the newspaper.

_F_ 6. Carsontown only had a monthly paper before the Stantons arrived.

°are successful; do well

Paragraph 4   Small businesses often survive and flourish° by the efforts of close-knit families. Aristotle Bita and his family are proof of this. They run the finest small grocery store in the neighborhood. Every day they awaken at 5:30 A.M. Aristotle leaves quickly for his morning errands. He visits many markets and selects the most desirable produce, meats, and fish. Meanwhile, Sophie busily gets the family ready for a long day. Sophie, her four children, and Grandpa arrive at the grocery at 7:00 A.M. and usually find at least two customers waiting for them. The children quickly sweep the store and arrange the milk, bread, and other daily deliveries on the shelves. They store all perishable° items in refrigerated cases. Grandma opens the front door and begins greeting customers. Soon Papa arrives and proudly displays the freshest food in town on the counters. The Bita family is now ready for the ten hard hours of work that lie ahead.

°likely to spoil

Answer the following statements True (T) or False (F).

_F_ 1. The family members awaken at 5:30 A.M. every day except Sunday when they sleep till 7:00 A.M.

_F_ 2. Aristotle has one favorite meat market where he gets the finest meats in town.

_F_ 3. There are never more than two customers waiting for the family at 7:00 A.M.

_F_ 4. Perishable items remain displayed on the counter.

_F_ 5. The Bita family does a fair job of running a grocery.

_T_ 6. Papa displays the freshest food in town.

CHAPTER 35
RECOGNIZING ROOTS

⁎⁎

MARIA: Wouldn't you know it! I always seem to miss an important class. Professor English discussed roots, and I don't have any notes. Can you help me?

SULY: Sure. A root is a stem or basic part of a word from which new words are formed. For example, **scribe** is a root meaning **to write.** You can add a prefix or a suffix or even both to a root, and new words are formed. If you add the prefix **sub-** to the root **scribe,** you will form a new word: **subscribe.** Similarly, if you add the prefix **in-** to **scribe,** you will form the word **inscribe.**

MARIA: Do you mean that knowing the meaning of the root of a word helps me to figure out the meanings of newer and harder words?

SULY: Yes and no. Knowing the meaning of the root and prefix or suffix is sometimes not enough to figure out the current meaning of a word. For example, if the prefix **sub-** (which means under) is added to the root **scribe** (which means write), the new word **subscribe** should mean **underwrite.** However, to subscribe to a magazine or paper means that you receive the publication regularly after having paid for it in advance.

MARIA: So, why should I learn roots?

SULY: Don't get frustrated, Maria. In other instances, knowing the meaning of the root can help you to determine the current meaning of a longer, more difficult word. For example, if you add the prefix **pre-** (which means before) to the root **scribe** (which means write), you form the word **prescribe** that means **to write out beforehand.** Even when the meaning of the root doesn't lead to the current or common meaning of the word in which it appears, knowing the meaning of the root gives a clue to the word's definition.

MARIA: Let's see how this works. The word **transport** consists of the prefix **trans-** (which means across) and the root **port** (which means to carry). The meaning of the word **transport—to carry across—** can be determined by knowing the prefix and the root. On the other hand, in the word **report** composed of the prefix **re-** (which means back) and the root **port,** knowing these meanings doesn't lead to the current meaning of **report,** that is, **a detailed account of an event or action.**

SULY: You've answered that perfectly.

The **base or stem** of a word is called a **root.** The root is the basic word part to which **prefixes** and/or **suffixes** can be added. Root meanings do not change when prefixes or suffixes are added. Rather, the prefixes and suffixes add additional information to them.

Recognizing Roots: Scribe, Script

Consider the underlined parts of these words having the root **scribe** or **script**, meaning **to write.**

<u>post</u>script   <u>in</u>scribe
post + script   in + scribe

QUESTIONS

1. Postscript means _____

2. What does inscribe mean? _____

The root **scribe** or **script** means to **write.**

EXERCISE   All the underlined words in this exercise contain the roots **scribe** or **script.** Select the correct meaning for each of the underlined words.

____ 1. Did Leslie get the <u>script</u> for the new play called "The Town I Love"?
   Script means
   a. a stage set.
   b. an actor's name.
   (c.) the written text.

____ 2. The <u>inscription</u> on the bracelet read, "All my love." Inscription means
   a. words written into something.
   b. a brightly colored cartoon.
   c. directions.

____ 3. The doctor <u>prescribes</u> medicine for sick people. Prescribe means
   a. gives out.
   b. writes direction to be followed later.
   c. asks for information about.

____ 4. Elyse received a <u>transcript</u> of her college grades. Transcript means
   a. an instructor's comments.
   b. the complete story.
   c. a copy in writing.

Recognizing Roots: Aud

Here is another commonly used root, **aud.**

> **Aud**ible: "The music was loud enough to be **aud**ible," or
> "The music was able to be **heard.**"

The root aud means hear.

EXERCISE Use the root **aud** to determine the meaning of the following underlined words. Write the meaning on the blank line.

1. The town meeting was held in the school <u>auditorium</u>.

   auditorium: _the part of a public building where an_

2. The <u>audio</u> system in the social hall was out of order.

   audio: _mechanical_

3. The little child had such a low voice that she was <u>inaudible</u>.

   inaudible: _not audible_

4. Bruce's father had the most <u>audible</u> voice in the room.

   audible: _heard or capable of being heard_

5. Did you have to take an <u>auditory</u> test in school?

   auditory: _relating to or experienced through hearing_

PRACTICE Select the correct general meaning of each word.

____ 1. An audience is made up of
   ✓ a. people who hear or listen.
   b. people who like to observe.

____ 2. Audiology is
   ✓ a. the science of hearing.
   b. the science of speaking.

____ 3. Audiovisual material
   a. relates to both tasting and seeing.
   ✓ b. relates to both hearing and seeing.

____ 4. An audition provides
   a. a chance to be excused.
   ✓ b. a chance to be heard.

____ 5. An auditor is
   a. a person who reports.
   ✓ b. a person who listens.

Recognizing Roots: Port

Another common root is **port.** Consider these words.

    export - carry out   de**port** - carry or send out

> The root **port** means to **carry or hold.**

EXERCISE Write the correct meaning for each of the underlined words in the space provided.

1. Sonia goes to school by public transportation.

   transportation: _transporting or being transported_

2. Gilbert is an importer of clothing from South America.

   importer: _a person in the business of importing goods_

3. My family does not own a portable television.

   portable: _that can be carried_

4. The newspaper reporter interviewed my brother and sister.

   reporter: _one who gathers information and writes reports for a newspaper._

PRACTICE Supply the missing word in each sentence by using one of the following words: **transportation, portable, porter, export, report.**

1. The _porter_ carried my mother's luggage to the train.

2. Max wrote a _report_ on his family's ancestry.

3. He can _export_ automobile parts to foreign countries.

4. I have a _portable_ typewriter that I take with me wherever I go.

5. Manuel can't afford the _transportation_ cost because of the new air fares.

Who Really Wears the Pants?

The Elderly

Old age in the United States presents many problems and opportunities. As a result of improved medical services, people live longer than they used to. This increase in longevity° creates a wide range of social needs that didn't exist when the average life expectancy was lower. The medical specialty of gerontology° has opened research areas and careers related only to the elderly.

°long life

°the medical study of aging

Because of changes in the family structure from extended to nuclear, the elderly have to create existences apart from basically small family units. This situation is complicated by the fact that many of their friends may have died and their children may have moved away.

The elderly person must set up a new life. Often, the elderly must rely on a fixed income—Social Security and pensions—and gradually diminishing savings. While some live with their children, many more live by themselves, with a friend, or in a nursing home.

small to small.

However, the increasing proportion of elderly people has given them a new political power. They have formed organizations such as the Gray Panthers to voice their own needs and concerns to local, state, and federal agencies. Lobbying° for such issues as increased Social Security benefits, better health care, income tax benefits, and rent controls has brought to the public an increased awareness of the determination of the elderly to assert their ability to deal effectively with their own lives.

°trying to influence legislators on behalf of a special interest

VOCABULARY EXERCISE   Use the following words in a sentence.

Gray Panthers: _sixty five or older_

longevity: _In my country in the New year's day people usually habla a longevity for another._ _The longevity of the college list 2 years._

gerontology: _____

LITERAL COMPREHENSION EXERCISE   Answer the following True (T) and False (F). Be aware of any signal words that affect the sentence meanings.

_F_ 1. First, the elderly start new life-styles, and then they receive improved medical care.

_F_ 2. Years ago, more people lived longer.

_T_ 3. As people grow older, they face new alternatives in life-styles.

_F_ 4. Old people start careers with fixed incomes and Social Security benefits.

_F_ 5. The old person's dependency on children remains constant in later years.

NOTE-TAKING EXERCISE In the space provided outline the Practice Reading entitled "The Elderly."

Outline Continued

CHAPTER 36
UNDERSTANDING
SIGNAL WORDS:
Sequence

⁎

Some words direct attention to a sequence of events. Read this paragraph.

EXAMPLE

Uncle Thomas began the day by washing, shaving, and getting dressed. Next, he went to the local market to do the food shopping for his family. After selecting the freshest bread, vegetables, and fish, he returned home and started cooking breakfast. By 8:00 A.M., he had completed his morning chores.

QUESTIONS

1. What did Uncle Thomas do before he went to the market? _____
   He began by washing, shaving, and getting dressed

2. What two things did he do while at the market? _____

   _____

3. Did Uncle Thomas cook breakfast before or after he washed? _____

4. What words in the paragraph signal the order in which the events happened? _____

5. List in order the things Uncle Thomas did:

   _____

   _____

   _____

   _____

   _____

It is necessary to understand the order of events in this paragraph to fully understand the passage. For example, it is not enough to know that Uncle

Thomas cooks breakfast and shops at the market. You need to understand that "first" he washes and "then" he goes to the market. He does not cook breakfast "until" he has selected the food at the market and has returned home.

Understanding the order of events leads to a more complete understanding of a passage. Several words signal the sequence of events: "began," "next," "by 8:00 A.M.," and "after." There are many more sequence–signal words that help you to understand a passage and also help you to answer questions about it. Here are some of them:

when	soon	later	finally	first	next
initially	to begin with	after that	then	beginning	last

EXERCISE Each of the following paragraphs contains words that signal a sequence of events. Read each paragraph and answer the questions.

Paragraph 1 Throughout the history of the United States, families have traveled across the country. In the early 1800s, for example, entire families including children, aunts, uncles, cousins, and grandparents loaded all their possessions into covered wagons and set out in search of new lands to settle. Today, however, smaller family units make the journey. Usually, a couple and their children fly or drive from one part of the country to another to visit relatives, such as grandparents. At holiday time, grandparents often make the return trip.

Answer the following statements True (T) or False (F).

__F__ 1. The first settlers visited grandparents living on the plains.

__F__ 2. Today, families travel in large groups composed of mother, father, children, aunts, uncles, cousins, and grandparents.

__F__ 3. Families seem closer today than they were years ago.

__F__ 4. Early settlers moved around more than modern families do.

Paragraph 2 People experience several distinct° stages of dependency° in their lives: first, the newborn stage; next, the childhood, early adolescent, and teenage stages; then, the young adult and adult stages; finally, old age. From the beginning, the infant is very dependent upon those around him or her. This dependency lessens as the child grows toward adulthood. A person experiences the greatest independence during adulthood. Finally, with the onset of old age, dependency on those around grows greater. This is a major reason why old age has been compared with infancy.

°separate; well-defined
°needing someone to care for one; trust

Answer the following questions.

1. List the major stages in people's lives from the last stage to the first.

_____   _____

_____   _____

_____   _____

_____

2. Place all the signal words that show sequence on the lines provided.

_____   _____   _____

_____   _____   _____

____ 3. The second major stage in people's lives is

    a. newborn.

    b. childhood.

    c. early adult.

    d. old age.

____ 4. The stages in which people experience the greatest dependency are

    a. old age and newborn.

    b. childhood and newborn.

    c. old age and adolescence.

    d. childhood and adolescence.

Paragraph 3 Today, new family arrangements are appearing all over the country. One major change has been brought about by increased divorce rates. For example, it is estimated that more than 50 percent of all American marriages end in divorce. Those individuals who are responsible for maintaining the family unity and structure after divorce are known as single heads of households.° Children living within such a family structure usually spend most of their time with one parent. They may visit their other parent on weekends and in the summer. More and more frequently, children are growing up in a single head of household family unit.

°single parents responsible for raising the children

Answer the following statements True (T) or False (F).

_F_ 1. More than 50 percent of all families in the United States are headed by single heads of households.

_F_ 2. Today, it is estimated that the majority of households in the United States are headed by previously unmarried persons.

_F_ 3. After children visit a parent during the summer months, the parents get a divorce.

_T_ 4. Before couples divorce, they are first married.

Paragraph 4 Paul and Sylvia are unsure as to whether or not they can afford another addition to their family. Their first child, Paul, Jr., is now twelve years old. Since his birth, the couple has had a baby every three years. Paul has been promoted from the rank of mechanic to machine shop manager. Sylvia also works and holds a responsible position as a travel agent. Both Paul and Sylvia must decide whether they can support another child.

Answer the following statements True (T) or False (F).

__T__ 1. Paul was three when the next baby was born.

__F__ 2. There are five persons in this household.

__F__ 3. Paul's first job in the shop was as manager.

__T__ 4. There are six years separating Paul, Jr., and the family's third child.

Understanding Signals of Sequence in Instructions and Questions

Sequence words often indicate the way to answer questions relating to a passage. Read the following paragraph.

EXAMPLE

This paragraph gives several instructions. First, circle all the signal words in the paragraph before you answer the questions. When you have finished the questions, highlight the words that you have circled.

QUESTIONS

1. When should you highlight the words? _____

2. When should you answer the questions? _____

3. Will you circle all the words in the paragraph? _____

4. Explain answer 3. _____

The directions indicate a precise order of activities. Specific signal words tell what that order is:

before you answer . . .
first circle . . .
when you have finished . . .

The instructor or the text often specifies a **definite order for completion of the work.** It makes sense to follow this order.

For example, it does *not* make sense to answer the questions before reading the paragraph.

In each of the following exercises, special instructions provide a guide to answering the questions. Be aware of any sequence words in each passage.

EXERCISE Each of the following statements is a direction. Do what the directions call for, in the order required.

1. First, underline the signal word "first" every time that it appears in this sentence and then cross it out.

2. List all signal words stated in 1 and then cross out this sentence. _____

_____

3. Before you write your name on this line, put your age at the beginning of the line. _48_ _____

4. Beginning with the first word in this sentence, write all the vowels appearing up to the word "with." _____

5. State the first and third classes in your schedule today. _____

_____

PRACTICE Read each of the following sentences carefully and then answer the questions.

1. The Untied States is approaching zero population growth.
   Do not circle the word "zero" if the word "United" is spelled correctly.

2. People in nuclear families usually have no cousins living with them.
   If you have a relative living with you, underline the word "cousins."

3. Elderly people often feel too proud to accept food stamps.
   Cross out every "e" in the sentence and circle the three words that contain double vowels.

4. Many elderly people do not want to retire at age seventy.
   If it is stated that elderly people want to retire at age seventy, place a check in front of the sentence.

5. In many American families, grandparents enjoy a place of honor in the home.
   Underline every suffix in the sentence.

6. The federal government is employing the services of retired business executives to help train young business people.
   Do nothing with the sentence above except put an "X" in front of it.

PRACTICE Read the following paragraphs and answer one of the questions about each.

Paragraph 1 As people approach seventy and forced retirement, they usually face difficulties in adjusting to the idea of retirement. For example, they may begin to experience feelings of uselessness. People who have built and maintained successful careers frequently feel this way. Even though they may want to continue working, they know that they will be forced out of their present jobs, and they are afraid to assert themselves. Also, those who are ill may start to feel that they are a burden to their families and friends. Another difficulty that they may experience is anxiety resulting from financial hardships, such as losing a monthly paycheck or having to get by° with only a Social Security check. And perhaps the most serious is the feeling they may experience that their lives are over. These feelings are all too often experienced by elderly people.

°manage barely

Understanding Signal Words   **261**

Answer True (T) or False (F) according to the passage.

_____ 1. The third difficulty stated in the passage discusses the relationship between older people and their families.

_____ 2. The passage states that people over seventy commonly experience many difficulties.

_____ 3. There are four major reasons why elderly people may feel insecure.

_____ 4. After older people are forced out of business, they will collect unemployment benefits.

Paragraph 2 Many immigrant families find themselves living in extended family home situations. Uncles, aunts, grandparents, and even cousins are living with the mother, father, and children. The extended family is one traditional family unit that maintains strong family ties. Also, each member contributes to the financial well-being of the entire group. Furthermore, each member contributes something unique to the whole. For example, the older members can transmit the cultural heritage° of the old country to the younger members, while the younger members can help the older generation adjust to their new country.

°traditions and ways of life of a particular group of people

Answer these statements True (T) or False (F).

_____ 1. Coming to the United States is an old family tradition.

_____ 2. The last statement concerns the transmission of cultural values to youth.

_____ 3. The first reason given for the extended family's existence is the maintenance of the family structure.

_____ 4. The extended family is made up of a mother, a father, and several children.

Paragraph 3 The single parent, whether mother or father, often tries to assume the responsibility of being both parents at once. Of course, this is not always easy to do, for the single parent has many interests and responsibilities. Work, friends, and education may take up time otherwise spent with a child. The wise single parent, therefore, must carefully balance family, career, and social life.

Follow these directions.

1. If the single parent is only concerned with the child, place a check at the end of this sentence.
2. Highlight the three factors that must be balanced by the single parent.
3. Underline in the paragraph any responsibilities that the single parent has.
4. If the single parent must put the child's interests ahead of all others, cross out the paragraph.

Paragraph 4 More and more, single people are adopting young children. My friend Cecilia is twenty-six, single, and has an excellent career in advertising. Recently, she applied to an adoption agency that specializes in the adoption of hard-to-place children. First, her financial qualifications were checked and approved. Next, four members of the staff interviewed her to determine whether or not she would be a good parent. They all agreed that she would. Finally, a representative of the City Department of Child Services met with her to discuss the child best suited for her. In a few weeks she will begin to share her home with a child whom no one else has wanted until now.

Complete the following.

1. If it is true that the first step in the adoption process involves meeting with city officials, place a check at the top of this page.
2. Circle the signal word in the third sentence of the paragraph.
3. Highlight none of the signal words in this paragraph except the one in the last sentence.
4. Reread the directions for the four paragraphs in this exercise. If you have followed those directions, write the number of answers you attempted here. 4

CHAPTER 37
RECOGNIZING ROOTS

Recognizing Roots: Duc, Duct; Mit, Miss; Vert, Vers

MARIA: Learning the meanings of roots has helped me to recognize the meanings of some difficult words without using a dictionary. I'm going to try to increase my vocabulary by learning the meanings of some more roots. Can you help me?

SULY: Sure, I'd love to. The roots **duc–duct, mit–miss** and **vert–vers** are roots that you should know. Pronounce these words aloud:

induce   conduct   abduct

QUESTION   Do you know what each of these words means? _____

_____

Each of the words contains the root **duc** or **duct**, which means **to lead or to draw.** The word **induce** means to lead or to draw into. The word **conduct** means to lead along. The word **abduct** means to lead away.

> The root **duc** or **duct** means **to lead or to draw.**

EXERCISE   Each of the underlined words contains the root **duc** or **duct**. Write a definition for each of the underlined words.

1. A good <u>introduction</u> to family responsibilities is to take over some of the chores.

   <u>introduction</u>: _something that introduce_

2. With the help of the police, the family recovered its <u>abducted</u> dog.

   <u>abducted</u>: _to lead_

3. Parents often try to <u>induce</u> their children to taste new foods.

   <u>induce</u>: _to lead_

4. Many housewives have full-time jobs at home, <u>conducting</u> household chores and family plans.

   <u>conducting</u>: _to act as leader or director_

5. Nelson's parents are <u>educating</u> themselves in English.

educating: _to lead_

PRACTICE   Choose the correct word from the list of **duc** or **duct** words to complete each sentence: **productive, product, produce, reduce, reduction.**

1. Fights between a husband and wife don't always _produce_ a divorce.

2. Good marriages are the _product_ of mutual respect and love.

3. Both housewives and working wives can lead _productive_ lives.

4. A _reduction_ in family size seems to be a trend in American families.

5. When both husband and wife are working, they can _reduce_ family financial burdens.

Consider these words: dis**miss** and trans**mit.**

QUESTIONS

1. What happens when you are <u>dismissed</u> from class? _____

_____

2. What does it mean to <u>transmit</u> news across the country? _____

_____

Both words have something to do with sending. **Dismiss** means to **send away,** and **transmit** means to **send across.**

> The root **mit** or **miss** means **to send.**

EXERCISE   Circle the correct word in each sentence.

1. Chung (admissed   admitted) to being the most intelligent child in his family.
2. Clara needs to get her parents' (permittion   permission) to get a job.
3. Mr. Lee is (committed   commission) to keeping his family together even though he is out of work.
4. The spies went on a (mission   mittion) for their government.
5. Ernesto had to (submiss   submit) his application to the license bureau.

Consider these words: **vers**ion and in**vert.**

1. What does a different <u>version</u> of a story mean? _____

_____

2. What happens to a cup when it is <u>inverted</u>? _____

_____

Both words have something to do with turning. **Version** means **a different** form, and **invert** means **to turn upside down** or **inside out.**

The root **vert** or **vers** means **to turn.**

EXERCISE Choose the correct meaning for each of the underlined words.

____ 1. A single parent often has to balance his or her time between a career <u>versus</u> time spent with children. <u>Versus</u> means
a. in addition to.
b. against.
c. before.

____ 2. Marlon tried to <u>divert</u> his brother's attention from baseball to homework. <u>Divert</u> means to
a. increase attention.
b. concentrate.
c. turn attention away from.

Recognizing Roots: Chron, Chrono; Gram, Graph; Cred

MARIA: Will you help me study for a quiz on roots? I think I need some help remembering some of the roots and words that Professor English taught us.

SULY: Do you know what roots you'll be quizzed on?

MARIA: Yes. I only need help with the roots taught when I missed class.

SULY: Okay, I'll help you. Just tell me what roots you want to learn.

MARIA: I'd like some work on **chron, gram, graph,** and **cred.**

SULY: Study the list of *chron* and *chrono* roots in words.

WORD	MEANING
anachronism	the placement of events or objects in the wrong time period
chronic	continuing for a long time
chronicle	a record of events in their time sequence; a history of events
chronological	arranged in order of time
synchronize	to arrange events so they occur at the same time

The root **chron** or **chrono** means **time.**

EXERCISE Select the correct word from the list to complete each sentence.

1. A _____ problem of adoption agencies is having too few children for the many people wishing to adopt.

2. My father kept a daily _____ of each day's activities.

3. Maritza's divorced father will _____ his visits to match his free time.

4. It is an _____ to say that the modern woman's job is in the home.

5. Tim related the story of his parents' separation and divorce in _____

_____ order of the events.

PRACTICE Fill in the missing letters of the word at the right. Each dash stands for one missing letter. Pronounce each word aloud.

DEFINITION	WORD
1. cause to occur at the same time	_ _ _ _ _ _ _ _ _ _ _
2. historical account of events	_ _ _ _ _ _ _ _ _
3. placement of events in the wrong time period	_ _ _ _ _ _ _ _ _ _
4. happening for a long time	_ _ _ _ _ _ _
5. recorded in time sequence	_ _ _ _ _ _ _ _ _ _ _ _

Study the list of **gram** and **graph** words and their meanings. Pronounce each of the words aloud.

WORD	DEFINITION
graphic	written or told in a clear manner; vivid
monogram	a person's initials
stenographer	a person skilled in the art of shorthand writing
typographical	occurring in written type or printing
mimeograph	a machine used to make copies of written material (noun); to make copies of written material (verb)
phonograph	a machine used to reproduce recorded sound
electrocardiogram	a writing or tracing made by an instrument that records electrical changes in the heartbeat

> The root **gram** or **graph** means **letter or writing.**

EXERCISE Select the correct word from the chart to complete each sentence. Read the sentences aloud.

1. After reading Gloria's _electrocardiogram_, the doctor told her that her heart was healthy.

2. Mario gave a _graphic_ description of his life with his mother and father.

3. Luis played the records on his _phonograph_ whenever he felt lonely.

4. The _stenographer_ took careful notes during the divorce trial.

5. All the towels with a ___monogram___ were given away after Oscar's divorce.

6. Clara and Orlando each used a ___mimeograph___ machine to make copies of their marriage license.

7. Yin made a ___typographical___ error as he typed a letter to his children.

Study the list of **cred** words with their meanings. Say each word aloud.

Word	Definition
credit	value, worth, system of later payment
discredit	to remove confidence from
creditor	one who lends money to another based on trust
incredulous	state of disbelief
incredible	not believable
creed	a set of principles or beliefs

The root **cred** means **to believe.**

EXERCISE Select the correct word from the chart to complete the sentences.

1. Anna and Mark were ___incredulous___ when their parents told them about their divorce plans.

2. Court attorneys try to ___discredit___ certain witnesses of questionable reputation.

3. Ed's family ___creed___ emphasized honoring one's father.

4. A ___creed___ must be paid before a person can do business again.

5. The growing number of single-parent families in this country will soon be ___incredible___.

6. It is difficult for newly divorced women who have never owned property and never held a job to obtain ___creditor___.

PRACTICE Fill in the missing letters of the word at the right. Each dash stands for one missing letter. Say each word aloud.

DEFINITION	WORD
1. not believable	_ _ c _ _ _ _ _ _ _
2. set of beliefs	_ _ e _ _
3. value, worth	_ _ _ _ _ _ t
4. to make unbelievable	_ _ _ _ _ _ _ d _ _
5. one who lends money	_ _ _ _ _ _ or

Untitled

Many changes are taking place in the way in which men and women look at their roles in society. We see these changes most dramatically° in job and business situations. It is no longer unusual to find a male nurse or a female construction worker. Years ago, however, a man who worked as a nurse would have been looked down upon for doing "a woman's job," and a female construction worker would have been hooted° off the construction site by her male co-workers. However dramatic these changes are, they are not as important as the changes that have taken place between men's and women's roles in family life.

°sharply

°shouted disapproval of

The fact that so many women today have entered the job market and are building independent careers for themselves has altered the traditional family structure in many ways. For one thing, household work that used to be done by women is now often shared equally by men and women. Men have discovered at last that they too are capable of preparing the family dinner, rather than thinking that they are only capable of taking out the garbage.

Perhaps the greatest change that has taken place in the family is in parents' new attitudes toward bringing up children. While it is true that only mothers can breastfeed their infants, nowhere is it written that fathers cannot bathe their own babies or change diapers. And more and more of them are doing just that. These days, being a full-time parent is a job that fathers and mothers both share.

As a result of these changes, men and women are now more aware of sexual stereotypes in their own lives. No longer do we insist that little boys play with trucks and grow up to be doctors, while little girls play with dolls and grow up to be housewives. Many men no longer feel that they must maintain a macho° attitude all the time, and many women no longer feel that they should be meek° and obedient. Changes like these do not occur overnight or even in a few years because they involve fundamental° changes in attitudes and behavior. Will events in the 1980s continue to build upon the changes that have already taken place, or will we see new directions in the ways in which men and women view their roles?

°masculine
°timid; shy
°basic

VOCABULARY EXERCISE Each of the underlined vocabulary words appears in the selection. If the word is used correctly in the sentence, write "Yes" on the line. If the word is used incorrectly, write "No."

_____ 1. Women's and men's roles in society are <u>dramatically</u> different from their roles fifty years ago.

_____ 2. The graceful dancer was cheered for his fine performance and then was <u>hooted</u> off the stage.

_____ 3. A <u>fundamental</u> difference between men and women is the ability to breastfeed a newborn baby.

_____ 4. Beautiful clothing, a soft expression, grace, and poise all give the woman a thoroughly <u>macho</u> appearance.

ROOTS EXERCISE The following roots appear in words in this unit. Each root should appear in **at least** one of the following sentences, and some roots appear twice. Note that in each sentence the prefix or suffix already appears. Write the root that correctly completes the sentence. The first one is done for you.

duc, duct = carry	**graph** = writing	**miss** = throw, thrown
scribe, script = write	**port** = carry	**vers** = turn

1. Men often <u>conduct</u> their business at home.

2. Women find the business world con_____ive to their new ideas about work.

3. Many women sub_____ to business magazines.

4. Many men eagerly give de_____ions of new recipes they've used.

5. Parents carry children to work in _____acribs.

6. Working in business requires writing many re_____s.

7. Both boys and girls listen to music on phono_____s.

8. Girls often play with toy _____iles.

9. Boys are very _____atile in their abilities to do household chores.

10. Everyone had a different _____ion of the accident.

LITERAL COMPREHENSION EXERCISE Match the information in column A with the information in column B based on your understanding of the passage.

COLUMN A	COLUMN B
_____ most dramatic changes	1. occur over a period of years
_____ independent careers	2. shared equally by men and women
_____ household chores	3. enjoyed by boys and girls
_____ nursing a child	4. jobs open to both men and women
_____ playing with trucks	5. only women can do this
_____ being macho	6. rejected by men
_____ fundamental changes in sexual stereotyping	7. altered family structure

GENERAL COMPREHENSION EXERCISE Complete the following statements, with the exception of the first one.

_____ 1. Today, little girls probably
   a. play with trucks more than with dolls.
   b. are becoming more macho.
   c. play with dolls and trucks.
   d. always play with dolls.

_____ 2. American women are developing
   a. new attitudes toward old-fashioned sexual stereotyping.
   b. interests that have usually been associated with men.
   c. new careers.
   d. all of the above

_____ 3. American men are finding that they can
   a. share in household chores.
   b. attend to a child's needs.
   c. breastfeed a child.
   d. both a and b

_____ 4. Sexual stereotypes are now
   a. completely disappearing.
   b. forcing little girls to play with trucks.
   c. slowly changing.
   d. remaining constant.

_____ 5. The best title for this passage is
   a. Changes in American Sex Roles.
   b. Changes in Women's Roles in Society.
   c. Changes in Men's Roles in Society.
   d. both b and c

WRITING EXERCISE Write a brief paragraph to support the following main idea sentence: Sexual stereotypes are (no longer) useful in society.

_____

_____

_____

_____

_____

_____

_____

WRITING PRACTICE Write a main idea sentence for each of the following topics:

Arranged Marriages vs. Free Marriages

_____

Nuclear Families and Single Parent Families

_____

Nuclear Families and Extended Families

_____

Attitudes toward the Elderly in the 1920s and 1980s

_____

Large Families vs. Small Families

_____

Select one of the main idea sentences in the previous practice and on separate paper develop it into a two-paragraph discussion comparing and contrasting the topics.

UNIT VIII
URBAN, SUBURBAN, AND RURAL:
Where We Live Now

Courtesy of D. Anthony English.

Americans live in cities, in suburbs, or on farms. Life-styles are different in each area. You will learn about the life-styles of the farmer, the suburbanite, and the city dweller° as you learn about multiple meanings of words and about techniques of taking tests.

°resident

DISCUSSION

What are some of the advantages of living in a city? In a suburb? In a rural area? If you could choose a life-style other than your present one, where would you like to live?

INITIAL READING

Modern Farming

Today, only 4 million people live and work on farms in the United States, but they produce more than enough food for 200 million Americans. They are able to do this because modern agriculture depends more on up-to-date machinery and scientific methods than it does on old-fashioned knowledge and human labor. These days, one man or woman spending an afternoon in an air-conditioned, stereo-equipped tractor can do the work that years ago would have required hundreds of hours of back-breaking drudgery.°

°dull, hard, unpleasant work

As a result of the modernization of agriculture, the farm of today looks a lot like a factory. When the farmer's hens lay their eggs, conveyor belts° carry the eggs off to be sorted and packed. If the farmer keeps pigs, those pigs will not be wallowing° in the mud, but lying around in sanitary pens.° And the farmer is likely to be found studying a computer print-out of long-range weather conditions. Why isn't the farmer milking cows in the barn? The answer is easy: A machine is doing it.

°mechanical belts for carrying things from one place to another
°rolling about / °clean enclosures or fenced areas

This reliance° on modern technology has its problems for farmers. The tractors that plow their fields, the combines° that reap° and thresh° the grain, and the silos° that store the grain for winter feeding are all very expensive. For example, a single tractor can cost as much as $50,000. Without this equipment, farmers could not run their farms profitably, but, to pay for it, farmers must take out large bank loans. A single bad season could put them deeply in debt. And, when the machinery wears out or becomes obsolete, the farmers must replace it with newer, more expensive models. Still, most farmers are willing to put up with these difficulties because their machines have freed them from the heavy labor and hard life that farmers had to endure in the past.

°dependence
°machines for cutting and sorting the crops in the fields / °cut or gather / °separate the seeds or grain
°storage towers

Not everyone is happy with the changes that have taken place on the farm. Some people say that the eggs that come from farm-factory chickens lack the flavor of the old-fashioned kind: The hens that lay them have become too civilized. Fruits and vegetables are no longer grown for flavor but for their ability to withstand mechanical harvesting.

No doubt there is some truth to these complaints, but the problem is not easy to solve. Giving up modern methods of agriculture would mean a return to a lower standard of living. The average dairy cow in the United

States produces nearly 15,000 pounds of milk a year; without modern methods, the figure would be only a tenth of that. The choice between old-fashioned flavor and modern abundance° is not an easy one to make.　　　°a full supply

QUESTIONS

1. What major crops does your country produce? _____ _____

_____ _____

2. What are the farms like in your country? _____

_____

CHAPTER 38
TAKING TESTS

.

We are continually faced with taking tests in everyday life. As children and young adults, we take formal tests in school. After that, each of us faces a variety of testing situations. Here are some.

EXAMPLE

> Taking a driving test to get a driver's license
> Taking an arithmetic test to qualify as a sales clerk
> Taking a civil service exam to qualify for the police academy
> Taking the test for U.S. citizenship

QUESTION List four tests that you have taken or expect to take shortly.

_____

_____

_____

_____

In Units I through VII you answered many types of questions including True–False, completion, matching, and multiple-choice items. These questions tested your ability to read and understand paragraphs and to apply specific skills to new information. When answering these questions you were not limited by time factors, and you could not prepare for the tests. You were able to discuss answers with other students or with your instructor, and you often completed the exercises in the comfort of your home or in the library.

When you take college quizzes, midterms, or finals, however, you must work within a specific time limit. You may not confer with anyone and must remain in a possibly uncomfortable testing room. How can you turn a difficult situation such as this into one in which you can really show what you have learned? The exercises in this chapter will offer approaches to taking tests that can be of help in any test situation.

Preparing for the Test

Many people find that they are nervous, poorly prepared, or confused in test-taking situations. Read each of the following selections carefully and answer the questions that follow each selection.

Selection 1 Malagre has attended every one of Professor Matthews' classes about rural America and has never been late for any lecture. She has listened to him discuss the American movement back to the simple farm life. Professor Matthews has carefully explained the true complexities of farm life and has made several comments about the reasons why people think that farming offers a simple way of life. Malagre has read the textbook chapters that explain that Americans want to grow crops themselves, work in the fields, and enjoy the alternatives to the fast-paced highly technical life that they lead in cities.

   Malagre understood all this, yet she worried about the announced midterm exam. She had always found tests frightening, and this one was no exception. She knew what she had to do for it, but where should she begin? Maybe Professor Matthews would ask about the increasing trend of young people staying on the farms rather than migrating° to the cities. Or he could ask about the need of young people to live simpler, less complicated lives.

°moving to a new place

   Malagre was so confused that she put off° studying until the night before the exam. Then she tried to learn everything about farm life in the United States in one evening. Malagre actually fell asleep at the kitchen table at 3:30 A.M. The next day, Malagre overslept. She rushed off to school without breakfast. She arrived fifteen minutes late and knew immediately that she could not complete the exam. She even had to ask the instructor for a pen.

°postponed; delayed

QUESTIONS

1. Does it appear that Malagre did well on this test? _____
2. Name six things that Malagre did completely wrong when preparing for the test.

   a. _____

   b. _____

   c. _____

   d. _____

   e. _____

   f. _____

3. Name three things that Malagre did right in class.

   a. _____

   b. _____

   c. _____

°think out; understand

Malagre was correct when she read all the chapter assignments and attended all the lectures. She was correct in trying to figure out° what Professor Matthews would ask. However, when she became nervous, she couldn't put those good actions and ideas to use.

Malagre approached the test in all the wrong ways. Here is a list of the good study habits that Malagre practiced and her poor study habits. See if your answers match the lists.

DO'S IN STUDYING

1. Read all chapters.
2. Attend all classes.
3. Figure out test questions.

DON'T'S IN STUDYING

1. Don't remember your past nervousness and automatically become frightened.
2. Don't put off studying because you don't know where to begin.
3. Don't cram all your studying into one night.
4. Don't stay up all night before the exam so that you risk oversleeping.
5. Don't skip breakfast or lunch.
6. Don't be late for the test.
7. Don't forget pens or pencils.

°gathering

°associations of U.S. farmers

Selection 2 Juan also studied for the exam on rural life in America. He missed six lectures in which Professor Matthews described the modern farmer's many activities, such as planting and harvesting° crops, tending livestock, maintaining machinery, and transporting crops to market. Because Juan was in Professor Matthews' 8:00 A.M. section, he was frequently late and missed the beginnings of many lectures. Also, he never bothered to get a copy of a classmate's notes and did not ask about any special assignments.

Juan sometimes read the text, but more often than not said, "Why bother, since Professor Matthews goes over the work in class?" And so Juan had very little text information about how the federal government sometimes pays farmers for not growing certain crops. In addition, Juan knew little about the social and economic activities of farmers, such as cooperatives and granges,° subjects touched upon only in class. Because he listened to the radio every day, Juan knew a lot about country and western music. But he mistakenly relied on that to give him a real understanding of rural life in America.

Juan was not nervous about the test. He studied the few notes he had taken a week in advance of the quiz and then decided to relax. He figured that Professor Matthews would ask about the difficulties of being a farmer, and Juan knew that he could make up a good answer for that question. Juan arrived early for the test and had all the correct supplies with him.

QUESTIONS

1. Does it appear that Juan did well on this test? _____
2. Name six things that Juan did poorly.

   a. _____

   b. _____

   c. _____

   d. _____

   e. _____

   f. _____

3. Name two things that Juan did well.

   a. _____

   b. _____

Juan was poorly prepared for this test. Although he was not nervous, he should have been. He did not follow most of these study guidelines.

DO'S IN STUDYING
1. Be on time for a test.
2. Bring the necessary supplies.

DON'T'S IN STUDYING
1. Don't overcut, that is, be excessively absent from your class.
2. Don't arrive late so that you miss part of every lecture.
3. Don't forget to make up all assigned readings.
4. Don't forget to get copies of the notes you missed.
5. Don't mistake general knowledge of a subject for true understanding of course content.
6. Don't study too far in advance.
7. Don't assume that an instructor will ask a question simply because you know the answer.

Malagre and Juan are extreme cases of students who are poorly prepared for a test. However, many students make some of the errors that Malagre and Juan made. Students should not feel overconfident if they are guilty of even one or two of the mistakes. Each mistake could mean the difference between passing or failing a test.

Selection 3 Amalia is another student in Professor Matthews' class. She has attended all classes but one and has never been late to lectures. Since she missed Professor Matthews' discussion on folk artwork and special crafts designed by members of farm communities, Amalia asked Greg for his class notes. She also asked if Professor Matthews had assigned any extra readings that day. Greg told her there was no special assignment but that there would be a quiz on the following Tuesday. Amalia made an appointment with Professor Matthews to find out which chapters he would be including on the quiz. And so she knew what to study.

Amalia read all the chapters that she had missed. She decided to start studying before the weekend. Each evening, after she had finished her class assignments, she studied a chapter. Soon Amalia knew definitions, specific facts, and general ideas about the recent growth of rural living in the United States. She knew that her major focus of study had to be the reasons why people are returning to rural and communal life-styles, and so she began to make up possible test questions. Amalia practiced the answers to many possible questions that weekend.

By Monday, Amalia had reviewed the chapters thoroughly and decided to spend a few hours on a final review. She finished early and then relaxed by watching television. The next morning she awoke refreshed, enjoyed a good breakfast, and had more than enough time to get to school. She made sure that she had a good supply of pens and even some candy with her. Amalia walked into the testing room confidently because she knew she had prepared as thoroughly as possible.

QUESTION   Highlight the proper study procedures that Amalia followed in preparing for the exam.

Amalia's method of studying serves as an excellent guide. Here are the DO'S taken from her technique.

> ### DO'S IN STUDYING FOR AN EXAM
> 1. Attend all classes.
> 2. Arrive on time for class.
> 3. Copy class notes and get special assignments when you miss a class.
> 4. See the instructor before class, after class, or by appointment if you have a special question about an exam.
> 5. Read all assigned chapters and outside readings.
> 6. Start reviewing early.
> 7. Study general ideas, specific facts, and definitions.
> 8. Try to reason out possible questions and practice answering them.
> 9. Have a final review before the exam.
> 10. Leave some time for relaxing before the exam.
> 11. Have a good meal before the test.
> 12. Bring necessary supplies to the testing room.

Allotting Time on a Test

Consider the following example.

EXAMPLE

Phillip studied thoroughly for his final exam. He carefully reviewed a chapter every evening and concentrated on understanding the modern techniques of farming and their applications to modern farm situations. Phillip arrived early for the exam, fairly relaxed, and well-supplied with pens. He received the exam booklet and began writing immediately. Some short answer questions puzzled him, and Phillip spent a lot of time figuring them out. He had only completed half the test when he heard the instructor say, "Time is up. Please turn in all exam booklets." Phillip couldn't believe what he had just heard. He thought, "I know all the work, but the instructor didn't give me enough time!"

QUESTIONS

1. Name the ways that Phillip prepared thoroughly for the exam.

   _____   _____

   _____   _____

2. What problem did Phillip experience at the end of the test? _____

   _____

3. Why did he have that problem? _____

   _____

No matter how correct Phillip's answers were on the first part of the exam, he could not receive any credit for questions that he had never attempted. Phillip never had the chance to show how well he could do because he did not budget his time. He spent too much time on the short answer questions and left no time at all for the second half of the test.

> When you receive the test, look through it to **determine the point value** of each section. **Determine how much time** you should spend answering each section and **allow a few minutes at the end for review.**

EXAMPLE

Professor Matthews' quiz on farm life will last two hours. The three-part test is divided as follows:

Part I: 10 points, definitions
Part II: 30 points, multiple-choice questions
Part III: 60 points, two essays

QUESTIONS

1. How much time should you spend on Part I? _____

2. How much time should you spend on Part II? _____

3. How much time should you spend on Part III? _____

Simple arithmetic tells you to divide the test as follows:

TIME	PART	POINTS	% OF TOTAL TIME	= TIME ALLOWED
120 minutes	I	10	10% of 120 minutes =	12 minutes
	II	30	30% of 120 minutes =	36 minutes
	III	60	60% of 120 minutes =	72 minutes
		100 pts.	100% of 120 minutes =	120 minutes

The figures should serve as a guide throughout the test. You should spend approximately ten minutes writing definitions, thirty minutes answering the multiple-choice questions, and sixty minutes writing the essays. This time allocation provides twenty minutes for review. Remember, these are general guidelines. If you finish the definitions in five minutes, go right on to the next section. Do not, however, spend twenty minutes on the definitions, sixty minutes on the multiple-choice questions, and only forty minutes on the all-important sixty-point essays.

EXERCISE Professor Matthews is giving several tests this term. Tell how much time you should allow for each section.

1. Professor Matthews' First Quiz: 30 minutes, 25 True–False items

    Time for each item = _____

    Review time = _____

2. Professor Matthews' Second Quiz: 1 hour
   50 points: 25 True–False items, 50 points: 1 essay

    Time for True–False part = _____

    Time for essay part = _____

    Review time = _____

3. Professor Matthews' Midterm Exam: 1 hour
   20 points: 5 fill-in sentences, 30 points: 10 multiple-choice questions, 50 points: 2 essays

    Time for fill-ins = _____

    Time for multiple-choices = _____

    Time for each essay = _____

    Review time = _____

4. Professor Matthews' Final Exam: 2 hours
   Part I—20 points: multiple-choice questions
   Part II—30 points: short essays
   Part III—50 points: 10 problems

   Time for Part I = _____

   Time for Part II = _____

   Time for Part III = _____

   Review time = _____

PRACTICE Tell how much time you should spend on each section of each of the following tests.

1. A 50 minute quiz: 50 points: 20 definitions, 50 points: 2 short essays

   Time for each definition = _____

   Time for each essay = _____

   Review time = _____

2. A final exam: 2 hours, 10 essays

   Time for each essay = _____

   Review time = _____

3. A driver's test: 20 minutes, 10 True–False items

   Time for each item = _____

   Review time = _____

4. An arithmetic test: 30 minutes, 100 addition and subtraction questions

   Time for each problem = _____

   Review time = _____

Answering Test Questions

Consider this example:

EXAMPLE

When Phillip received the test booklet, he immediately began answering questions. He worked very hard on the True–False items, taking twenty minutes to answer them. Several of the statements were complex and Phillip thought about each one for several minutes. He finally finished this section of the test and was starting the first twenty-five point essay when the instructor announced the end of the exam. Phillip was very upset because he had not finished either of the required essays.

QUESTIONS

1. Why did Phillip lose time on the first section of the test? _____
   _____

2. If Phillip had answered the True–False items correctly, could he have passed the test? _____

Phillip spent too much time on the True–False questions. He read and reread the very difficult statements and neglected to consider the other portions of the exam. Since the exam had at least two twenty-five-point essays, and since Phillip had never attempted those essays, he could not have passed. Even a perfect score on the True–False section would not have given him enough passing points.

> If several questions appear very difficult, omit them for the present. Concentrating for too long on difficult questions uses up valuable time. **Answer the remaining questions** and then **return to the difficult ones.** If you are still having trouble with the answer, don't leave it blank. **Guess if you must, but be sure that there is no penalty for guessing.** Remember, your instructor cannot mark as correct a blank space. Guessing gives you a chance at the correct answer. You have no chance if you leave the answer blank.

EXERCISE In this True–False exercise, first answer the questions that you are sure of. Leave the difficult questions until you have finished the items that you know. Then go back and attempt the difficult ones. You have **five minutes** to complete this exercise.

Starting Time _____   Ending Time _____

____ 1. Communes are made of groups of people living together.

____ 2. Everyone on a commune works.

____ 3. The largest commune in the United States is in Hoboken, New Jersey.

____ 4. On a commune, some people are richer than others.

____ 5. Everyone shares equally in a true commune.

____ 6. The major tax advantage for communal residents is incorporation for personal income tax purposes.

____ 7. Communal residents often sell organically grown vegetables.

____ 8. Most communes elect a ruling council.

____ 9. People from many life-styles enjoy communal living.

____ 10. Communes are a popular way of life in the United States.

PRACTICE   Answer the following True–False items in five minutes.

Starting Time _____   Ending Time _____

____ 1. Commercially grown tomatoes bounce.

____ 2. Organic foods are not sprayed with DDT.

____ 3. Communal living began in the eighteenth century.

____ 4. Bacon has no nitrites.

____ 5. People who eat only organically grown foods are sometimes called "health nuts."

____ 6. Consumer advocates have demanded that red dye #5 be eliminated from commercially produced foods.

____ 7. The financial success of a commune frequently depends on the sale of homegrown and home-baked goods.

____ 8. Homemade breads appear in many specialty stores.

____ 9. Consumers who purchase organically grown products often stop buying commercially produced goods.

____ 10. Commercially prepared foods are usually more expensive than organic foods.

Following General Directions on a Test

Read and do the following exercise.

DIRECTIONS Complete the following exercise in **two minutes.** Follow all specific directions and be sure to read each item thoroughly before answering it. In addition, read all the items before answering any of them.

Name _____

1. Write the name of this text on the line. _____

_____

2. Which reading skill has been most helpful this term? _____
3. Write your instructor's name at the bottom of this page.
4. Write your name at the top of this exercise on the line provided.
5. Circle the vowels in the word "syllable."
6. Underline the consonants in the word "syllable."
7. Cross out the odd numbers in this series: 1 2 3 4 5

8. Write your best friend's name on this line. _____

9. Write the number of credits that you are taking this term on this line. _____

10. Now that you have read items 1 through 10, do not write anything on this page.

If you had read the directions carefully, you would have written nothing in that exercise. Go back to the directions, and to item 10, and highlight the key phrases that tell you not to answer any of the questions.

EXERCISE In each of the following sets of directions, highlight the key phrase that indicates specifically what is expected of you. Then answer the question.

1. In the following list, several phrases describe farms. Choose one and write a complete sentence about it on the line below.

farm machines	automated vs. old-fashioned methods	horses
silos	storage of crops	farmers
acreage	a few hundred acres	chickens

_____

2. Two of the following topics include the other items. Circle them.

rural living	apartment houses	subways	business suits
farm houses	acres	overalls	city living

3. Cross out the poorest example of the reasons why people move to rural areas.

money   fresh air   simple living   love of animals

4. Which two of the following organic items are very popular? Check them.

____ shampoos ____ steaks ____ bread ____ spaghetti

5. Place the following events in their correct sequence by numbering them.

____ Children moved to the cities.

____ Cities became huge and complex.

____ Settlers worked the farmlands.

____ Grandchildren moved to the farms.

PRACTICE Read the following paragraph. Do not outline it.

 Organic farming is a modern development that consciously relies on old-fashioned techniques. Farmers whose produce is organic do not use chemical fertilizers because they believe that these products eventually wear out the soils that they are supposed to enrich. Instead, they rely totally on natural, organic fertilizers to build their soil. Similarly, they avoid chemical pesticides.° They believe that these chemicals, when they are sprayed on fruits and vegetables, are dangerous to the people who consume them. Instead, they rely on the natural enemies of insects such as mice, snakes, and birds to protect their crops. As organic foods become more popular, farmers are rediscovering the old-fashioned methods.

°chemicals used to kill insects

OUTLINE

_____

_____

_____

_____

_____

_____

_____

_____

_____

_____

PRACTICE Highlight the word or phrases in each sentence that direct you to do a specific task on a quiz.

1. Answer one of the five essays.
2. Describe the least important aspects of farm life.
3. Circle those words that call attention to the reasons for the renewed interest in communal living.
4. Choose five of the ten topics listed and write a paragraph about each.
5. Consider all choices given. Select the one that best restates the main idea sentence.
6. Write about either the advantages or disadvantages of eating organic foods.
7. Answer any ten of the twenty-five multiple-choice items.
8. Do not answer the question that involves math skills.
9. This exam is divided into four sections. Spend an equal amount of time on each part.
10. Do not leave an answer blank. You will not be penalized for guessing.

CHAPTER 39

USING THE DICTIONARY:
Multiple Meanings of Words

* *
*

You have learned how to use the dictionary to locate a word's history or etymology, parts of speech, special uses, synonyms and antonyms, and various meanings. The following is a typical dictionary entry.

EXAMPLE

reg·u·lar (reg′yə lər), *adj.* **1.** usual; normal; customary. **2.** evenly or uniformly arranged. **3.** characterized by fixed principle, uniform procedure, etc. **4.** recurring at fixed or uniform intervals. **5.** adhering to a rule or procedure; methodical. **6.** being consistently or habitually such: *a regular customer.* **7.** conforming to some accepted rule, principle, etc. **8.** *Informal.* real; genuine: *a regular fellow.* **9.** (of a flower) having the members of each of its floral circles or whorls normally alike in form and size. **10.** *Gram.* conforming to the most prevalent pattern of formation, inflection, construction, etc. **11.** *Math.* **a.** governed by one law throughout. **b.** (of a polygon) having all sides and angles equal. **c.** (of a polyhedron) having all faces congruent regular polygons, and all solid angles congruent. **d.** (of a function of a complex variable) analytic (def. 5). **12.** *Mil.* noting or belonging to the permanently organized, or standing, army of a state. **13.** *Internat. Law.* noting soldiers recognized as legitimate combatants in warfare. **14.** *Eccles.* subject to a religious rule, or belonging to a religious or monastic order (opposed to *secular*): *regular clergy.* **15.** *U.S. Politics.* of, pertaining to, or selected by the recognized agents of a political party. **16.** (of coffee) containing an average amount of milk or cream. —*n.* **17.** a habitual customer or client. **18.** *Eccles.* a member of a duly constituted religious order under a rule. **19.** *Mil.* a professional soldier. **20.** *U.S. Politics.* a party member who faithfully stands by his party. **21.** a size of garment designed for men of average build. **22.** an athlete who plays in most of the games, usually from the start. [ME *reguler* < MF < LL, L *rēgulār(is)* = *regula* ruler, pattern + -*āris* -AR¹] —**reg′u·lar′i·ty, reg′u·lar·ness,** *n.* —**Syn. 2.** even, formal, orderly, uniform. **4.** habitual, established, fixed. **5.** systematic. **6.** habitual.

QUESTIONS

1. What language gives us the word "regular"? _____

2. What parts of speech are listed for the word "regular"? _____

_____

3. What special uses are given for the word? _____

_____

4. What are the synonyms and antonyms for the word? _____

_____

5. How many numbered meanings are there for the word? _____

Using the Dictionary   **291**

The word "regular" comes into current use through the Middle English form. The word is defined as both adjective and noun and has several special uses: Informal, Gram., Math., Mil., Internat. Law, Eccles., and U.S. Politics. Synonyms for "regular" include "formal" and "even." Twenty-two major meanings are given.

Now you will learn how to use a dictionary entry to determine which definition is appropriate in the **context** of the sentence that you are reading. Read the following dialogue.

MARIA: I've learned some interesting things about the dictionary in Professor English's class. When I read, I find that many of the words have more than one meaning. When I look up a word in the dictionary, I find several meanings. How can I find the correct meaning quickly?

SULY: First, consider the sentence or context in which the word is used. Decide what part of speech, special use, or restrictive use you need. Then, read quickly through the entry to locate that part of speech, special use, or restrictive use.

MARIA: In other words, by knowing more exactly what type of meaning I need and eliminating all the others, I can save time. That's much quicker than reading through every meaning in an entry. Give me a word and let me try to get the meaning.

EXAMPLE

reg·u·lar (reg′yə lər), *adj.* **1.** usual; normal; customary. **2.** evenly or uniformly arranged. **3.** characterized by fixed principle, uniform procedure, etc. **4.** recurring at fixed or uniform intervals. **5.** adhering to a rule or procedure; methodical. **6.** being consistently or habitually such: *a regular customer.* **7.** conforming to some accepted rule, principle, etc. **8.** *Informal.* real; genuine: *a regular fellow.* **9.** (of a flower) having the members of each of its floral circles or whorls normally alike in form and size. **10.** *Gram.* conforming to the most prevalent pattern of formation, inflection, construction, etc. **11.** *Math.* **a.** governed by one law throughout. **b.** (of a polygon) having all sides and angles equal. **c.** (of a polyhedron) having all faces congruent regular polygons, and all solid angles congruent. **d.** (of a function of a complex variable) analytic (def. 5). **12.** *Mil.* noting or belonging to the permanently organized, or standing, army of a state. **13.** *Internat. Law.* noting soldiers recognized as legitimate combatants in warfare. **14.** *Eccles.* subject to a religious rule, or belonging to a religious or monastic order (opposed to *secular*): *regular clergy.* **15.** *U.S. Politics.* of, pertaining to, or selected by the recognized agents of a political party. **16.** (of coffee) containing an average amount of milk or cream. —*n.* **17.** a habitual customer or client. **18.** *Eccles.* a member of a duly constituted religious order under a rule. **19.** *Mil.* a professional soldier. **20.** *U.S. Politics.* a party member who faithfully stands by his party. **21.** a size of garment designed for men of average build. **22.** an athlete who plays in most of the games, usually from the start. [ME *reguler* < MF < LL, L *rēgulār(is)* = *regula* ruler, pattern + *-āris* -AR¹] —**reg′u·lar′i·ty, reg′u·lar·ness,** *n.* —**Syn. 2.** even, formal, orderly, uniform. **4.** habitual, established, fixed. **5.** systematic. **6.** habitual.

Early morning chores are a <u>regular</u> part of a farmer's routine.

QUESTIONS

1. What part of speech is the word "regular" as it is used in the sentence? _____

2. What type of definition will you look at in the entry? _____

3. How many definitions for this part of speech appear in the entry? _____

4. Which definition is most appropriate? _____

Since the word "regular" is used as an adjective in the sentence, you can eliminate definitions 8 as well as 10 through 15 because they refer to special uses of the word. Definitions 9 and 16 are too specific. The entry contains many definitions for the word "regular" used as an adjective. Only number 1 refers to something that is part of a normal routine—the context of the example.

> To locate a specific meaning of a word, decide whether you need a general meaning or a restrictive meaning, and part of speech you need. Then look at the specific type of meaning you need in the entry and select the one that is most appropriate.

EXERCISE The right-hand column contains dictionary entries. The left-hand column contains the word used in a sentence. Answer the questions that follow each sentence.

SENTENCE AND QUESTIONS   DICTIONARY ENTRY 1

1. This year's corn <u>harvest</u> was poor because of the spring floods.

   Special use: _____

   Part of speech: _____

   Number of best definition: _____

   Explain why you chose the definition: _____

   _____

har·vest (här′vist), *n.* **1.** Also, **har′vest·ing.** the gathering of crops. **2.** the season when ripened crops are gathered. **3.** a crop or yield of one growing season. **4.** a supply of anything gathered at maturity and stored: *a harvest of nuts.* **5.** the result or consequence of any act, process, or event: *a harvest of impressions.* —*v.t.* **6.** to gather (a crop or the like); reap. **7.** to gather the crop from: *to harvest the fields.* **8.** to gain, win, etc. (a prize, product, etc.). —*v.i.* **9.** to gather a crop; reap. [ME; OE *hærfest* autumn; akin to HARROW[1]]

DICTIONARY ENTRY 2

2. Farmers use a <u>combine</u> to harvest crops.

   Special use: _____

   Part of speech: _____

   Number of best definition: _____

   Explain why you chose the definition: _____

   _____

com·bine (*v.* kəm bīn′; *n.* kom′bīn), *v.*, **-bined, -bin·ing, *n.* —*v.t.* **1.** to bring or join into a close union or whole; unite; associate; coalesce: *She combined the ingredients to make the dough.* —*v.i.* **2.** to unite; coalesce: *The clay combined with the water to form a milky suspension.* **3.** to unite for a common purpose; join forces: *After the two armies had combined, they proved invincible.* **4.** to enter into chemical union. —*n.* **5.** a combination. **6.** *U.S. Informal.* a combination of persons or groups for the furtherance of their political, commercial, or other interests. **7.** a machine for cutting and threshing grain in the field. [late ME *combynyn* < LL *combīnāre* = com- COM- + bīn- (s. of *bīnī* two by two) + -ā- v. suffix + -*re* inf. ending] —**com·bin′a·bil′i·ty,** *n.* —**com·bin′a·ble,** *adj.* —**com·bin′er,** *n.* —**Syn. 1.** compound, amalgamate. **6.** merger, alignment, bloc. —**Ant. 1, 2.** separate.

3. Farmers' wives stock their shelves with fruit and vegetable <u>preserves</u>.

Special use: _____

Part of speech: _____

Number of best definition: ____

Explain why you chose the definition: _____

_____

pre·serve (prɪ zûrv′), *v.*, **-served, -serv·ing,** *n.* —*v.t.* **1.** to keep alive or in existence; make lasting: *to preserve our liberties.* **2.** to keep safe from harm or injury; save. **3.** to keep up; maintain: *to preserve historical monuments.* **4.** to keep possession of; retain. **5.** to prepare (food or any perishable substance) so as to resist decomposition or fermentation. **6.** to prepare (fruit, vegetables, etc.) by cooking with sugar. **7.** to maintain and reserve (game, fish, etc.) for private use in hunting or fishing. —*v.i.* **8.** to preserve fruit, vegetables, etc.; make preserves. **9.** to maintain a preserve for game or fish, esp. for sport. —*n.* **10.** something that preserves. **11.** something that is preserved. **12.** Usually, **preserves.** fruit, vegetables, etc., prepared by cooking with sugar. **13.** a place set apart for the protection and propagation of game or fish, esp. for sport. [ME *preserve*(*n*) < ML *praeserv*(*āre*) (to) guard (LL: to observe), L *prae*- PRE- + *servāre* to watch over, keep, preserve, observe] —**pre·serv′a·bil′i·ty,** *n.* —**pre·serv′a·ble,** *adj.* —**pres·er·va·tion** (prez′ər vā′shən), *n.* —**pre·serv′er,** *n.* —**Syn. 1.** conserve. **2.** safeguard, shelter, shield. See **defend.** —**Ant. 1.** destroy.

4. In rodeo competitions, cowboys <u>rope</u> steers.

Special use: _____

Part of speech: _____

Number of best definition: ____

Explain why you chose the definition: _____

_____

rope (rōp), *n.*, *v.*, **roped, rop·ing.** —*n.* **1.** a strong, thick line or cord, commonly one composed of twisted or braided strands of hemp, flax, wire, etc. **2.** a lasso. **3.** the sentence or punishment of death by hanging. **4.** a quantity of material or a number of things twisted or strung together in the form of a cord: *a rope of tobacco.* **5.** a stringy, viscid, or glutinous formation in a liquid: *ropes of slime.* **6. at the end of one's rope,** at the end of one's endurance or means. **7. know the ropes,** *Informal.* to be completely familiar with the operation or conduct of something. —*v.t.* **8.** to tie, bind, or fasten with a rope. **9.** to enclose, partition, or mark off with a rope or ropes (often fol. by *off*). **10.** to catch with a lasso; lasso. —*v.i.* **11.** to be drawn out into a filament or thread; become ropy. **12. rope in,** *Slang.* to lure or entice, esp. by deceiving. [ME; OE *rāp*; c. D *reep*, G *Reif*]

5. In the northern parts of the country, a farmer often grazes the cattle on the <u>slope</u> of a mountain.

Special use: _____

Part of speech: _____

Number of best definition: ____

Explain why you chose the definition: _____

_____

slope (slōp), *v.*, **sloped, slop·ing,** *n.* —*v.i.* **1.** to have or take an inclined or oblique direction or angle considered with reference to a vertical or horizontal plane; slant. **2.** to fall obliquely or at an inclination: *The land sloped down to the sea.* —*v.t.* **3.** to direct at a slant or inclination; incline from the horizontal or vertical: *The sun sloped its beams.* **4.** to form with a slope or slant: *to slope an embankment.* —*n.* **5.** a portion of ground having a natural incline, as the side of a hill. **6.** inclination or slant, esp. downward or upward. **7.** the amount or degree of deviation from the horizontal or vertical. **8.** an inclined surface. **9.** Usually, **slopes.** hills, esp. foothills or bluffs. **10.** *Math.* **a.** the tangent of the angle between a given straight line and the x-axis of a system of Cartesian coordinates. **b.** the derivative of the function whose graph is a given curve evaluated at a designated point. [abstracted from ASLOPE]

Urban, Suburban, and Rural:

PRACTICE Use the dictionary entry in the right-hand column to locate the appropriate meaning for the underlined words. Then answer the questions.

SENTENCE AND QUESTIONS	DICTIONARY ENTRY 1

1. Hard work and initiative can turn <u>barren</u> land into fertile farms.

   Part of speech: _____

   Special use: _____

   Number of best definition: ____

bar·ren (bar′ən), *adj.* **1.** not producing or incapable of producing offspring: *a barren woman.* **2.** unproductive; unfruitful: *barren land; a barren effort.* **3.** without features of interest; dull: *a barren period in American architecture.* **4.** destitute; bereft; lacking (usually fol. by *of*): *barren of tender feelings.* —*n.* **5.** Usually, **barrens.** level or slightly rolling land, usually with a sandy soil and few trees, and relatively infertile. [ME *barain* < AF; OF *brahain* < ?] —**bar′ren·ly**, *adv.* —**bar′ren·ness**, *n.* —**Syn. 1.** childless, infertile. **2.** ineffectual, ineffective. —**Ant. 1–4.** fertile.

DICTIONARY ENTRY 2

2. Apartment dwellers can sign one-, two-, or three-year <u>leases</u>.

   Part of speech: _____

   Special use: _____

   Number of best definition: ____

lease (lēs), *n., v.,* **leased, leas·ing.** —*n.* **1.** a contract renting land, buildings, etc., to another; a contract or instrument conveying property to another for a specified period or for a period determinable at the will of either lessor or lessee in consideration of rent or other compensation. **2.** the property leased. **3.** the period of time for which a lease is made: *this lease is up in December.* **4. a new lease on life,** a chance to improve one's circumstances or to live more happily because of some good fortune. —*v.t.* **5.** to grant the temporary possession or use of (lands, tenements, etc.) to another, usually for compensation at a fixed rate; let: *She planned to lease her apartment to a friend.* **6.** to take or hold by lease: *He leased the farm from the old man.* —*v.i.* **7.** to grant a lease; let or rent: *to lease at a lower rental.* [late ME *les* < AF (OF *lais*, F *legs* legacy), back formation from *lesser* to lease, lit., let go (OF *laissier*) < L *laxāre* to release, let go. See LAX] —**leas′a·ble,** *adj.* —**leas′er,** *n.* —**Syn. 5, 6.** rent, charter, hire.

DICTIONARY ENTRY 3

3. <u>Natural</u> foods are grown without chemicals.

   Part of speech: _____

   Special use: _____

   Number of best definition: ____

nat·u·ral (nach′ər əl, nach′rəl), *adj.* **1.** of or pertaining to nature. **2.** existing in or formed by nature. **3.** in accordance with the principles of nature. **4.** as formed by nature without human intervention. **5.** in accordance with human nature. **6.** in accordance with the nature of things; to be expected or reckoned with. **7.** without affectation or constraint. **8.** inborn; native: *natural ability.* **9.** being such because of one's inborn nature: *a natural mathematician.* **10.** reproducing the original or the original state closely: *a natural likeness.* **11.** of or pertaining to the natural sciences. **12.** having a real or physical existence. **13.** based upon the innate moral feeling of mankind: *natural justice.* **14.** related only by birth; of no legal relationship; illegitimate: *a natural son.* **15.** unenlightened or unregenerate: *the natural man.* **16.** *Music.* **a.** neither sharp nor flat; without sharps or flats. **b.** changed in pitch by the sign ♮ . **c.** (of a horn or trumpet) having neither side holes nor valves. —*n.* **17.** *Informal.* any person or thing that is well-qualified in some way. **18.** *Music.* **a.** a white key on a piano, organ, or the like. **b.** the sign ♮, placed before a note, canceling the effect of a previous sharp or flat. **c.** a note affected by a ♮, or a tone thus represented. **19.** an idiot. **20.** *Cards.* blackjack (def. 5b). **21.** (in craps) a winning combination of seven or eleven made on the first cast. [ME < L *nātūrāl(is)* (see NATURE, -AL¹); r. ME *naturel* < MF] —**nat′u·ral·ly,** *adv.* —**nat′u·ral·ness,** *n.*

4. The spies <u>planted</u> a listening device in the hotel room.

Part of speech: _____

Special use: _____

Number of best definition: ____

plant (plant, plänt), *n.* **1.** any member of the vegetable group of living organisms: *A tree is a plant.* **2.** an herb or other small vegetable growth, in contrast with a tree or a shrub. **3.** a seedling or a growing slip, esp. one ready for transplanting. **4.** the equipment and often the buildings necessary to carry on any industrial business: *a manufacturing plant.* **5.** the complete equipment or apparatus for a particular mechanical process or operation: *the heating plant for a home.* **6.** the buildings, equipment, etc., of an institution: *the sprawling plant of the university.* **7.** a person, placed in an audience, whose rehearsed or prepared reactions, comments, etc., are meant to appear spontaneous. —*v.t.* **8.** to put or set in the ground for growth, as seeds, young trees, etc. **9.** to furnish or stock (land) with plants: *to plant ten acres with corn.* **10.** to establish or implant (ideas, principles, doctrines, etc.): *to plant a love for learning in growing children.* **11.** to introduce (a breed of animals) into a region or country. **12.** to deposit (young fish, or spawn) in a river, lake, etc. **13.** to bed (oysters). **14.** to insert or set firmly in or on the ground or some other body or surface: *to plant posts.* **15.** to place; put. **16.** *Informal.* to place with great force or firmness: *He planted his fist in the palm of his other hand.* **17.** to station or post: *to plant spies.* **18.** to locate; situate. **19.** to establish (a colony, city, etc.); found. **20.** to settle (persons), as in a colony. **21.** to say or place (something) in order to obtain a desired result, esp. one that will seem spontaneous. [(n.) ME, OE *plante* < L *planta* a shoot, sprig, scion (for planting), plant; (v.) ME *plante*(n), OE *plantian* < L *plant*(āre) (to) plant] —**plant′like′,** *adj.*

5. A January <u>thaw</u> caused the early growth of the spring flowers.

Part of speech: _____

Special use: _____

Number of best definition: ____

thaw (thô), *v.i.* **1.** to pass or change from a frozen to a liquid or semiliquid state; melt. **2.** to be freed from the physical effect of frost or extreme cold (sometimes fol. by *out*): *Sit by the fire and thaw out.* **3.** (of the weather) to become warm enough to melt ice and snow: *It will probably thaw today.* **4.** to become less hostile, tense, or aloof. —*v.t.* **5.** to cause to change from a frozen to a liquid or semiliquid state; melt. **6.** to free from the physical effect of frost or extreme cold; bring to a more normal temperature, esp. to room temperature. **7.** to make less hostile, tense, or aloof. —*n.* **8.** the act or process of thawing. **9.** (in winter or in areas where freezing weather is the norm) weather warm enough to melt ice and snow. **10.** a period of such weather. **11.** a reduction or easing in tension or hostility. [ME *thawe*(n), OE *thawian;* c. D *dooien,* Icel *theyja*] —**thaw′less,** *adj.* —**Syn. 1.** See **melt. 2.** warm. —**Ant. 1.** freeze.

Courtesy of Gerald Kimmelman.

PRACTICE READING

Suburbs

In the United States today, nearly half of us live in areas that we refer to as the suburbs. Any dictionary will define the suburbs as those areas, usually residential, that lie outside cities and towns. But, for millions of Americans in the last thirty years, the suburbs have come to mean much more than that.

For those who moved to the developing suburbs after the Second World War, they represented an escape from urban congestion° to a home of one's own—preferably one with an attached two-car garage—on a little half-acre of tree-shaded land. It also meant daily commutation to work by railroad or expressway, a lawn to mow, and a mortgage to pay off over the years. °overcrowding

Nobody approves of life in the suburbs but the people who live there. Urban critics argue that suburbanites enjoy all the cultural, educational, and commercial advantages that cities offer without paying for them. Farmers worry about losing their farms to uncontrolled suburban sprawl.° The suburbs have also been criticized for the monotonous sameness of their design and for their ability to insulate° their inhabitants from the problems of the larger society in which they live.

°spreading out in all directions

°close off; protect

°including many things

On the other hand, defenders of the suburbs argue that the life-style that they offer is more varied and more inclusive° than the critics admit: There are many different kinds of suburbs and a variety of people living in them. While the development of the suburbs has created problems, it has also provided substantial modern housing for millions of people. Suburban living offers the best of two worlds—the city and the country—at a price that many are able to afford.

°calm; soothing

Many people will always prefer the hectic pace and excitement of life in the city, while others will want the more tranquil° pace of life in the country. But, for those in either city or country who are willing to compromise, the suburbs are waiting.

DICTIONARY EXERCISE Provide the required information for each word given.

	PARTS OF SPEECH	ONE GENERAL MEANING	ONE RESTRICTIVE MEANING	LANGUAGE WHICH GIVES US THE WORD
1. lie				
2. mean				
3. sprawl				
4. kind				
5. advantage				

FOLLOWING DIRECTIONS EXERCISE Answer each of the following questions and follow the directions carefully.

1. If suburbs developed after the First World War, place a check in front of the sentence.

2. The suburbs can be defined as those areas outside the cities. If this statement is true, underline the word "suburbs" in this sentence.

3. Farmers are unconcerned about suburban sprawl. Cross out the prefix in sentence 3 that makes the sentence incorrect.

4. Many different kinds of people live in the suburbs.

5. Suburban development has provided housing for millions.

   If sentences 4 and 5 are true, underline them both.

GENERAL COMPREHENSION EXERCISE Select the best answer for each statement.

_____ 1. The best title for this selection is
   a. Boring Commuters.
   b. How to Pay Off a Mortgage.
   c. Life in the Suburbs.
   d. Urban Congestion.

_____ 2. The strongest argument against the suburbs is that
   a. suburbanites enjoy the advantages of city life while paying for them.
   b. suburbs are all the same.
   c. suburbs are far away.
   d. suburbs have a lot of space.

_____ 3. Which of the following was not stated as a characteristic of suburban life?
   a. Daily commutation
   b. Mortgage payments
   c. Home ownership
   d. Apartment living

_____ 4. It is important to recognize that the author of this passage does not
   a. give equal treatment to city and suburban living.
   b. talk about the criticisms of suburban living.
   c. talk about the positive aspects of suburban living.
   d. none of the above

CHAPTER 40
TAKING OBJECTIVE TESTS
* *
*

Every time that you answered a True–False, multiple-choice, fill-in, or matching question in Units I through VII, you were responding to **objective questions.** That is, you were asked to recall a specific fact to answer the question. You may have given a definition, a fact from a passage, a main idea stated in a passage, or a general idea not stated but based on the passage.

EXAMPLE Answer the following statements.

_____ 1. True or False: Burgers are a very popular American food.

_____ 2. Television commercials influence children
   a. greatly.
   b. not at all.
   c. slightly.

_____ 3. True or False: Two boys reported on the uses of fantasy in advertising.

_____ 4. Singles in the United States are
   a. restricted in their travels.
   b. unrestricted in their mobility.

QUESTIONS

1. Are each of the examples objective test questions? _____

2. What kind of information does each question require? _____

3. Do the questions require you to organize ideas or write any thoughts on the subjects? _____

Generally, the term **objective testing** means that the questions require a student to **respond with a fact,** such as a definition, main idea, or detail, stated or implied in the passage. Objective test items may include True–False, matching, fill-in, and multiple-choice responses. The student is not required to formally organize ideas as in an essay but must display an ability to recall what was previously presented.

Following Signal Words: Objective Tests

In Unit VII you practiced recognizing sequence words, and, in the first part of this unit, you practiced the general rules for following directions. Objective test questions may have specific words that you must consider.

EXAMPLE

Ken eagerly began Professor Matthews' exam on urban sprawl and its effects on farmlands in the United States. Ken calculated his time, answered the easier questions first, and then returned to the harder questions. He thought that he had done everything correctly, and so he was amazed at the poor grade he received. What had gone wrong? When he went over the exam later, he saw what had happened. Here is one of the questions and the way in which Ken answered it:

Question: One reason for the lack of productive farmland is
> a. modern technology.
> b. the growth of the suburbs.
> c. both a and b
> d. none of the above

Ken answered the question "a." What important words in the question had he overlooked?

The question clearly asks for one important reason for a "lack of" farmland. Ken misread the question and thought it said "One important reason for productive farmland." The answer that he chose was correct, that is, "modern technology" is a reason for more productive farmland. The question, however, did not ask for that information.

Since you have already practiced recognizing words that signal quantity, quality, and sequence, the following brief review will remind you of the importance of those words. They are frequently used on objective tests, and their effect on sentences must be carefully considered.

EXAMPLE

T or F: The word negative is never correctly spelled with an X.
T or F: The earth is always in motion.
T or F: The earth is always in motion, but it never rotates.
T or F: The earth never stops spinning, and yet it is square.

The first two answers are always true. The second two answers contain parts that are true and parts that are false. They must be marked false. Be aware of words such as "never" and "always" when answering True–False questions.

Here are additional words that direct your attention to a quantity or quality and therefore affect your answers. You have seen these words before and will now have the chance to practice using them.

The following words direct your attention to quantity or quality and therefore affect your responses to questions:

never	**all**	**least**	**poorest**	**first**	**primary**	**best**
always	**none**	**most**	**strongest**	**last**	**secondary**	**worst**

EXERCISE Read the following paragraph and answer the questions True (T) or False (F) based on information in the paragraph. You are allowed five minutes for this exercise.

In most parts of the United States, wilderness areas are steadily decreasing in size because of the pressure of a growing population. Forests and deserts alike have turned into suburban housing developments. In some of the northeastern states, however, the reverse is happening. As unprofitable farms are abandoned, their pasturelands revert to forest. For example, fifty years ago, only 30 per cent of the land in Vermont was forest; today that figure is closer to 70 per cent. As a result, many animals that had declined in number or had disappeared completely from the area are now returning. Black bears, red wolves, beavers, and even coyotes from the western states can now be found in large numbers throughout northern New England.

Answer the following statements True (T) or False (F).

_____ 1. All of America's wilderness areas are steadily decreasing in size.

_____ 2. The primary reason for the loss of wilderness areas is the growing need for more housing.

_____ 3. Suburban housing has taken up all available lands.

_____ 4. Most farms are unprofitable.

_____ 5. Fifty years ago, most of America was forest.

_____ 6. Some animals were never found in Vermont.

_____ 7. Animals least likely to be seen in Vermont are suddenly reappearing.

_____ 8. Black bears, red wolves, beavers, and coyotes are animals only found in the western states.

_____ 9. Black bears are seen only in western states.

_____ 10. Seventy percent of Vermont's animals originated in the western states.

Following Directions: Doing What the Instructor Asks on Objective Tests

Many students find test directions confusing, and indeed they sometimes are.

EXAMPLE

DIRECTION In the following sentences, eliminate all negative sentences but the first.

QUESTIONS

1. What is the first part of the direction? _____

2. What is the second part of the direction? _____

A careful reading of the direction shows **two** linked instructions: **eliminate,** or cross out, any negative sentences, and **don't eliminate** the first negative sentence you read, that is, all but the first.

Reading directions carefully and making certain you understand them is necessary in any test-taking situation. Whenever you take a test, underline the word or phrase in the direction that tells you what the instructor wants you to do. If you are unsure, ask the instructor! Here are ten guidelines that should help you to follow test directions. Practice for each guideline will follow after all ten are presented.

GUIDELINES FOR TAKING TESTS

1. If the question requires a True–False response, make sure that the answer is always and completely true. Do not write Yes or No in place of True or False.
2. If the question requires you to choose one answer, you must choose only one. Do not put two answers in the space!
3. If the question requires you to match the numbers in column A with the letters in column B, do so. Do not match numbers with numbers in that case!
4. If you are asked to write a list, do so. Do not write a paragraph! If you are asked to write a paragraph, do so. Do not write a list.
5. Before you decide on the best answer, consider all possible choices. One choice may include all the others. Or perhaps the last choice is the best. You may never see it if you immediately select the first answer.
6. When the question asks "who" or "what," be sure to answer with "who" or "what" and not "when" or "why."
7. Follow directions stated by the instructor.

8. If the question requires a singular answer, do not pick the plural choice. If the question requires a plural choice, do not pick the singular choice.
9. If the phrase "all of the above" is a possible answer, be sure to read all of the other choices.
10. DO NOT LEAVE ANY ANSWERS BLANK. GUESS IF YOU HAVE TO!

Each of the following exercises illustrates one of the guidelines for test-taking. In each exercise, highlight the word or phrase that signals the specific instruction.

I: If the question requires a True–False response, make sure that the answer is always completely true. Do not write Yes or No in place of True or False.

EXERCISE Answer the following statements True (T) or False (F).

_____ 1. American farms are becoming more mechanized.

_____ 2. Many resorts are now located on big ranches, but no one visits them.

_____ 3. Some ranchers in the United States own more than 1 million acres.

_____ 4. Although there are some million-acre ranches in the United States, they are poorly run.

II: If the question requires you to choose one answer, you must choose only one. Do not put two answers in the space!

EXERCISE Select the best answer for each statement.

_____ 1. A burned-out forest can grow back in approximately
    a. 80 years.
    b. 2,000 years.
    c. 1 year.

_____ 2. A major cause of shrinking farmland in the United States is
    a. the declining population.
    b. the growing population.
    c. the higher number of U.S. citizens.

_____ 3. The average commuter lives in a suburb that once was
    a. inhabited.
    b. another smaller suburb.
    c. farmland.

_____ 4. Farmers often sell their goods at
     a. roadside stands.
     b. supermarkets.
     c. candy stores.

III: If the question requires you to match the numbers in column A with the letters in column B, do so. Do not match numbers with numbers.

EXERCISE Match the information in column A with the information in column B.

COLUMN A

_____ 1. American eagles

_____ 2. Polar bears

_____ 3. Pandas

_____ 4. Rattlesnakes

COLUMN B

a. found in the Arctic

b. poisonous reptiles

c. vanishing species

d. imported from China

IV: If you are asked to write a list, do so. Do not write a paragraph! If you are asked to write a paragraph, do so. Do not write a list.

EXERCISE List five reasons why people move from suburbs to farms.

_____

_____

_____

_____

_____

V: Before you decide on the best answer, consider all the possible choices. One choice may include all the others. Or perhaps the last choice is the best. You may never see it if you immediately select the first answer.

EXERCISE Choose the answer that best completes the statement.

_____ 1. As early settlers moved west, they
     a. encountered warlike Indian parties.
     b. immediately built cities.
     c. encountered peaceful and warlike Indians.
     d. moved into apartments.

_____ 2. American crafts include all types of
     a. bowls.
     b. vases.
     c. urns.
     d. pottery.

_____ 3. Woven blankets, pottery, and silverware are examples of
     a. glass items.
     b. handmade items.
     c. Indian crafts.
     d. inexpensive gifts.

_____ 4. "Getting back to nature" involves
     a. doing without machines.
     b. returning to simpler living.
     c. doing without the movies.
     d. eating less expensive foods.

VI: When the question asks "who" or "what," be sure to answer with "who" or "what" and not "when" or "why."

EXERCISE Read each of the following statements and answer the questions that follow.

1. George is joining a commune in the Berkshire Mountains.

   Where will George live? _____

2. While at the commune, he will help harvest crops this fall.

   When will George work? _____

3. George hopes to do well because he likes working in the outdoors.

   What does George like? _____

4. Kelly will join George on his trip to the mountains.

   Where will Kelly and George go? _____

VII: Follow directions stated by the instructor.

EXERCISE Follow the directions in each sentence.

1. Circle the third word in this group:
   communes nature organic healthy

2. Underline the vowels in the phrase "health foods."

3. Cross out any words that do not relate to rural life:
   apartments eggs chemicals fertilizers

4. Check the word that includes the others:

    tractors   combines   mechanical   machinery   computers   milkers

VIII: If the question requires a singular answer, do not pick the plural choice. If the question requires a plural choice, do not pick the singular choice.

EXERCISE Circle the word that best completes the sentence.

1. Chickens are brought to local (markets   store).

2. (Commune   Farms) are growing in numbers.

3. Organic foods (is   are) growing in popularity.

4. Healthy diets include a variety of (vegetables   vitamin).

IX: If the phrase "all of the above" is a possible answer, be sure to read all of the choices.

EXERCISE Select the best answer for each statement.

____ 1. A table set with a basket of organically grown foods can include
    a. tomatoes.
    b. rice.
    c. eggs.
    d. all of the above

____ 2. Organic foods have not been
    a. chemically sprayed.
    b. treated with dyes.
    c. sprayed with anything.
    d. both a and b

____ 3. Insects often act as
    a. organic substitutes for rice.
    b. transporters of sugar to the table.
    c. signs that foods are free from germs.
    d. none of the above

____ 4. People leave the suburbs because
    a. they want more open space.
    b. they seek a new life-style.
    c. they want a simple life.
    d. all of the above

X: DO NOT LEAVE ANY ANSWERS BLANK. GUESS IF YOU HAVE TO!

EXERCISE   Answer the following True (T) or False (F).

_____ 1. The average dairy cow in the United States produces 15,000 pounds of milk a year.

_____ 2. Computer print-outs record tornadoes and long-range weather conditions.

_____ 3. Without modern machinery an average dairy cow in the United States would produce one tenth of the milk it now produces.

_____ 4. The average farmer can reduce his or her labor-hour work ratio by 100 per cent by installing modern equipment.

CHAPTER 41

USING THE DICTIONARY:
Practice with
Multiple Meanings of Words

* *
*

You have used the dictionary to locate specific meanings of words appropriate to their use in sentences. Now you will practice reading sentences in which the same word is used in two different ways. Remember first to determine whether you will need a general meaning and specific part of speech, a restrictive meaning, or a special use of the word. Then, look in the dictionary entry for the word and focus on the type of meaning that you need.

EXAMPLE

    1A. The company's <u>staff</u> went on strike because it had no work contract.

    1B. The sheet of music was so carefully written that every note on the <u>staff</u> was clear.

QUESTIONS

1. Use your dictionary to determine the meaning of "staff" in sentence 1A.

    _____

2. Use your dictionary to determine the meaning of "staff" in sentence 1B.

    _____

The word "staff" in 1A is a noun referring to the employees who work in a company. The word "staff" in 1B has a restrictive use related to music. In the dictionary, there is a specific reference to music under the main entry for "staff." The word "staff" in 1B refers to the set of five horizontal lines and four corresponding spaces on which music is written.

EXERCISE Using your dictionary, select the appropriate meaning for each of the underlined words. Some of the words will have special or restrictive meanings.

1. Some suburban homeowners <u>tackle</u> home improvements on their own.

    <u>tackle</u>: _____

In the first half of the game, the <u>tackle</u> recovered a fumbled football.

tackle: _____

2. Many suburbanites face the daily problem of driving on <u>jammed</u> highways.

jammed: _____

The child <u>jammed</u> the controls when he dropped his pencil into the machine.

jammed: _____

3. The ship's <u>boom</u> held firm in the heavy thunderstorm.

boom: _____

The suburbs underwent a building <u>boom</u> in the 1950s.

boom: _____

4. Water is a <u>compound</u> of hydrogen and oxygen.

compound: _____

Heavy winds <u>compound</u> the difficulty of fighting forest fires.

compound: _____

5. The executive has a lot of <u>nerve</u> asking his secretary to serve coffee.

nerve: _____

Ever since the accident, Jane has had a problem with a pinched <u>nerve</u> in her neck.

nerve: _____

PRACTICE Use the dictionary to locate the appropriate meaning for each of the underlined words.

1. The college <u>faculty</u> celebrated the holiday at a special gathering in the president's home.

faculty: _____

The <u>faculty</u> of sensing hidden meanings is a wonderful trait.

faculty: _____

2. The <u>wings</u> of the seagull remained motionless as it glided in the wind.

wings: _____

The actress waited in the <u>wings</u> until she heard her cue to come on stage.

wings: _____

3. Let's all go for a <u>spin</u> in Joan's new car.

spin: _____

The astronomers used new instruments to calculate the earth's <u>spin</u>.

spin: _____

4. The doctor <u>stitches</u> the patient's wound carefully.

stitches: _____

For the entire performance, the comedian kept the audience in <u>stitches</u>.

stitches: _____

5. A fundamental physical property of a body is its <u>mass</u>.

mass: _____

A <u>mass</u> of people gathered outside the embassy when the dignitary arrived.

mass: _____

CHAPTER 42

TAKING ESSAY TESTS:
Introduction

**

In the previous units, you had a lot of practice reading and taking notes from paragraphs. As you apply these skills to your own textbooks, there will be additional requirements placed on you. Preparing for tests includes studying the notes that you have taken and allowing sufficient time to study class, lecture, and text notes as well. Your notes provide the basis for taking objective tests and essay tests.

Essay tests require an ability to **organize facts in a meaningful way,** that is, in a way that is clear and logical and reflects the information studied. There are several guidelines that should help you answer essay test questions.

Allowing Time for Essays

Since essay test questions require you to think about your response and organize your ideas, they are usually assigned a high point value on tests. Also, they require more time to complete than individual objective test questions do.

EXAMPLE

Dana took Professor Matthews' final exam on "The Growth of Suburbs in America." She allowed herself twenty minutes for ten multiple-choice items, twenty minutes for two twenty-five point essays, and twenty minutes for the long forty point essay. She began the exam at 9:00 A.M. By 9:30 A.M. she had completed the multiple-choice questions and was writing her first short essay when she noticed the time. She began to rush and was able to finish the second short essay by 9:45 A.M. Dana was just beginning to organize her ideas for the longer essay when Professor Matthews said, "Time is up."

QUESTIONS

1. If Dana achieves a perfect score on the multiple-choice section, how many points will she earn? _____

2. If Dana achieves a perfect score on the short essays, how many points will she earn? _____

3. What is the highest possible score Dana can earn on this test? _____

4. Explain answer 3. _____

   _____

5. Did Dana have an opportunity to reread her essays? _____

The highest that Dana can score on the final exam is sixty points. She spent too much time on the short answer section, wrote too much on the first essay, rushed through the second essay, and never attempted the major essay. Moreover, she never had the chance to reread any of her work.

> You should allow **sufficient time to think** through the essay question, **develop the facts** clearly and logically, and **reread** the essay.

EXERCISE Here are several essay topics and their point values as they appear on five separate exams. If each exam lasts one hour and is worth one hundred points, approximately how much time should you allow for each essay?

TIME	TOPIC
____ 1. 20 points:	The Advantages of Going to a Suburban High School
____ 2. 10 points:	A Description of a Typical Suburban Backyard
____ 3. 40 points:	The Reasons Why People Move to the Suburbs
____ 4. 5 points:	Some Problems of Suburban Living
____ 5. 50 points:	The Growth in Suburban Living Traced from the 1960s through the 1980s

Understanding Directional Words

Sometimes the instructor's general directions may appear confusing. Consider this incident.

EXAMPLE

When Sanford began reading Professor Matthews' instructions for the essay portion of the midterm, he was confident that he would get a high grade. Sanford read the five essay topics and decided to spend ten minutes on each. He finished the exam early and used the extra time to reread his essays. After changing a few words, Sanford was confident that he had done well.

Sanford was shocked to discover that he had failed the midterm. He read Professor Matthews' comments and soon understood the reason for his failure. Sanford had not read the instructions properly. Professor Matthews' instructions clearly required a choice of two of the five essays. Therefore, each essay was worth fifty points. Sanford had written briefly about all five essays and had not developed any two of them as fully as he should according to the directions.

QUESTIONS

1. Was Sanford able to show how well he knew the material for the essay? _____

2. Explain answer 1. _____

_____

3. What mistake did Sanford make? _____

_____

> It is necessary to **read the general directions** for the essay parts of tests. They provide clear information about the number of essays required, the type of response expected, and the limit or scope of the essay.

EXERCISE   Here are five sample essay topics. Read the test directions that follow and answer the questions about them.

Topics

Owning Your Own Land
Urban Congestion
Growing Earthworms for Profit
Building a Future in Suburbia
The Suburban Dream

1. Choose two of the essay titles and develop a short paragraph about each. How many short essays are required? _____

2. All but one of the essays focus on the suburbs. In a paragraph discuss the one that does not. Which essay should be developed? _____

   _____

3. Two of the essays relate to the land. Develop each fully. Which two essays should be developed? _____
   and _____

4. Two of the essays are related to people's hopes for the suburbs as an ideal place. Discuss them. Which two essays should be discussed? ____

   _____

   and _____

Following the Instructor's Directions

Too often, students fail to follow specifically worded essay question directions. Consider this example.

EXAMPLE

Selena is answering the following essay question: Discuss three reasons why people move to the suburbs. Here is her answer.

There are several reasons why people move to the suburbs. The suburbs have trees and a lot of space. I would like to live in a community that is surrounded by trees. There would be plenty of room to play games like stickball, and every afternoon I would play with new friends after school. The suburbs are spacious and beautiful.

QUESTIONS

1. What does the essay question direction ask for? _____

_____

2. Has Selena answered the question? _____

3. Explain answer 2. _____

_____

The essay question directions ask for two things: three reasons why people move to the suburbs <u>and</u> a discussion of each reason. Selena began her essay correctly when she said, "There are several reasons," and "The suburbs have trees and a lot of space." She did not continue correctly but, instead, narrated her own wishes throughout the rest of the paragraph.

Instructors use **special words to tell exactly what they require** in the essay answer. Here are several of the more frequently used directions:

SIGNAL WORDS	GENERAL MEANING
trace	Start at the beginning stages of a process and write about the major steps in its development.
illustrate	State an idea and give an example of its application in a specific situation.
discuss	Give all the important ideas relating to the topic or point that you are making.
compare or **contrast**	Show the similarities or differences between two or more persons, places, or ideas.

give the causes of	List the reasons for or the results of something.
give the effects of explain	State the idea and show your understanding of it by describing its basic parts.
summarize	Bring all the ideas about a topic together and present them briefly.

EXERCISE Here are sample essay topics. Read the instructions for each one carefully and then *briefly* tell how you would develop the topic. List the major points in your answer.

1. Most Americans dream of owning their own suburban homes. Explain why.

2. Suburban shoppers rely on shopping malls. Give several reasons for this.

3. Suburban living has more advantages than city living. Discuss these advantages.

4. Suburban schools are very different from city schools. Contrast the school systems.

5. Many people call the suburbs "the great American myth." Explain this statement.

6. The suburbs offer many positive experiences. Summarize these experiences.

7. Trace the development of the suburbs from 1940 to the present.

8. Some people claim, "The suburbs are the best places to raise children." Summarize their reasons for making this statement.

PRACTICE   Using the following signal words, decide which method of essay development is best suited for the groups of ideas in each exercise.

compare–contrast	**summarize**	**illustrate**
cause–effect	**trace**	**explain**

1. Type of Essay: _____

City schools are often overcrowded.
Suburban schools have few children in each class.
Suburban schools are located on large tracts of land.
Suburban schools try many new approaches to learning.
City schools maintain a standard curriculum.
City schools usually occupy a block in the neighborhood.

2. Type of Essay: _____

City dwellers are usually crowded into small apartments.
They desire the tax shelter that comes with a home mortgage.
City people want clean streets and more playgrounds.
City dwellers are afraid of crime in the streets.

3. Type of Essay: _____

"Suburbia" means many things to many people.
To some people, suburban living means that they will own two cars.
It may mean mowing one's own grass.
It could mean joining Little League with one's child.

4. Type of Essay: _____

Those who favor suburban living discuss the friendliness of neighbors and the easy access to commuter trains.
The pro-suburbia group talks with pride of the civic accomplishments and good schools in their communities.
Those against suburban living cite the high taxes required to pay for schools, police, fire, and other essential services.
The anti-suburbanites also cite high suburban crime statistics and a growing trend toward overcrowding.

5. Type of Essay: _____

When people first moved to the suburbs, they took over existing farmlands.
Soon builders arrived with blueprints for large housing developments.
°possibility
Investors saw the potential° for growth in suburban real estate and built huge shopping malls.
Soon, millions of people were lured by the promises of affordable homes, convenient shopping, good schools, and country-style living.

CHAPTER 43

UNDERSTANDING VOCABULARY:
Selecting the
Correct Meanings of Words

*_**

You have practiced locating the various parts of a dictionary entry and selecting appropriate meanings for words. Words with many meanings are common, and so the proper use of the dictionary is an important skill to know.

However, a dictionary may not always be available. Therefore, you must often use the context in which the word appears to decide its meaning. Read the following.

EXAMPLE   The sailor measured the depth of the river at mark five.

QUESTION   The word "mark" as it is used in the sentence means
- a. the grade on an exam.
- b. a measurement of the depth of water.
- c. a written or printed symbol.

ANSWER: _____

Although the word "mark" can, at times, mean any of the three choices, it has a specific meaning in the sample sentence: a measurement of the depth of water. By referring to the sentence, it is clear that "mark" indicates some kind of measurement. The word has a specific meaning and does not refer to a mark on a book page or a grade on an exam.

> The approximate meaning of a word can be determined by **context,** that is, by **the sentence in which the word appears.**

EXERCISE   Each of the following underlined words has several meanings. Read each sentence carefully to see how the word is used in the sentence. Then choose the definition that gives the best meaning.

_____ 1. Many city dwellers have their roots in rural areas. The word roots means
- a. the underground part of a plant.
- b. the origin or source.
- c. the basic grammatical part of a word.

Understanding Vocabulary   321

_____ 2. In every city, there is a wide <u>range</u> of housing, from highrise apartment buildings to one-family homes. The word <u>range</u> means

    a. a testing area for rockets.
    b. a cooking appliance.
    c. a variety.

_____ 3. People living in the wilderness <u>pool</u> their supplies in winter. The word <u>pool</u> means

    a. a special fund into which all people place a bet.
    b. a small pond.
    c. to combine resources.

_____ 4. A mayor is often the <u>head</u> of city government. The word <u>head</u> means

    a. the upper part of the body.
    b. a leader or chief.
    c. an ability to understand a certain subject.

_____ 5. The main street in town is sometimes the <u>scene</u> of a large parade. The word <u>scene</u> means

    a. a place where some action occurs.
    b. a division of a play or film.
    c. a view or picture.

PRACTICE Select the best meaning for each underlined word according to its use in the sentence.

_____ 1. Families living in the wilderness need to <u>master</u> the skills necessary for survival. The word <u>master</u> means

    a. someone skilled in a special trade.
    b. to become skilled at doing something.
    c. the captain of a ship.

_____ 2. It is <u>common</u> to find families living in apartments in most urban areas. The word <u>common</u> means

    a. coarse or vulgar.
    b. a frequent or usual occurrence.
    c. belonging to the entire community.

_____ 3. The general urged his men to <u>press</u> forward to meet the enemy. The word <u>press</u> means

    a. to compress or squeeze.
    b. to print.
    c. to advance eagerly.

___ 4. <u>Channel</u> 17 has a number of interesting programs about urban life.
The word <u>channel</u> means
   a. a body of water.
   b. a television station.
   c. a passage through which something may be directed.

___ 5. What's the <u>matter</u> with you? The word <u>matter</u> means
   a. difficulty or an unpleasant situation.
   b. a type of inorganic substance.
   c. a business affair.

PRACTICE Each of the following words has more than one meaning. Write two sentences, each one showing a different meaning of the word. Use your dictionary to help you.

   1. nuclear: _____

   _____

   2. fast: _____

   _____

   3. spice: _____

   _____

   4. trip: _____

   _____

   5. date: _____

   _____

   6. book: _____

   _____

   7. boil: _____

   _____

   8. agent: _____

   _____

   9. club: _____

   _____

  10. age: _____

   _____

Courtesy of Harry Greenberger.

Street Games

All over the world, children who live in cities play games that are unknown to their country cousins. Some of these are games that can only be played on concrete pavements: you can't shoot marbles, skip rope, or roller skate in a cornfield any more than you can play stickball where there are no sewer caps to use for bases.

Through their games, city children transform what is often a harsh and difficult environment into a place of wonder and fantasy. A rubble-filled lot between two vacant buildings becomes the landscape of the moon, a battlefield between two opposing castles, or just a good place for a game of hide-and-seek. No matter how old or rundown the city is, the imaginations of its children can make it new and exciting.

Many of the games played by children in the city involve singing, and, like the games themselves, the songs seem to be handed down from one generation of children to the next. Walk past a group of six-year-olds sitting like a tribe of pygmies on a brownstone stoop, and the chances are that you will hear them chanting one of their favorite songs:

First Child: Who stole the cookies from the cookie jar?
Second Child: Annie stole the cookies from the cookie jar.
Annie: Who me?
First and
Second Child: Yes, you.
Annie: Couldn't be.
First and
Second Child: Then who?
Annie: Sally stole the cookies from the cookie jar . . .

That particular song never ends. It goes around from one child to another, from one city to another, from one age to another. It will go on for as long as there are children to sing it and cities to sing it in.

Quiz on Practice Reading

Time Allowed: Two hours

PART I: 5 points   Time to Spend: _____

Directions Match the words on the left with their meanings on the right. You may choose five of the seven words to match.

_____ stickball   1. a small two- or three-story single house dwelling

_____ sewer caps   2. a simple melody sung in a sing-song manner

_____ rubble   3. covers for city sewers

_____ pygmies   4. a platform with steps leading to a house

___ brownstone   5. a pile of old broken items

___ stoop   6. a game like baseball

___ chant   7. little people

PART II: 20 points   Time to Spend: _____

Directions Choose five of the following statements and mark them True (T) or False (F) according to the story.

___ 1. You can't skip rope on a concrete pavement.

___ 2. Sewer caps are often used as bases.

___ 3. Children can transform a rubble-filled lot into the landscape of the moon.

___ 4. City children like to sing, but country children do not.

___ 5. Pygmy tribes chant songs in small villages and play stickball.

___ 6. The song described in the passage ends when one person forgets the words.

___ 7. Children of many cities have sung the cookie jar song.

___ 8. City children from many countries like stickball.

___ 9. Annie said she stole the cookie from the cookie jar.

___ 10. The cookie jar song has changed from one generation to the next.

PART III: 25 points   Time to Spend: _____

Directions Choose one of the following main idea sentences and place a check next to it. Then select a method of paragraph development from the list. Check that method. Finally, in the space provided, develop your main idea sentence into a paragraph.

MAIN IDEA SENTENCES
_____

___ City and country children play very different games.

___ Some songs have been sung by city children for generations.

___ City children enjoy many advantages that country children do not.

___ City children of all countries are alike.

METHODS OF PARAGRAPH DEVELOPMENT
_____

___ Example   ___ Incident   ___ Cause–Effect

___ Listing   ___ Sequence   ___ Comparison–Contrast

_____

_____

_____

_____

_____

_____

_____

_____

_____

PART IV: 5 points   Time to Spend: _____

Directions Paraphrase the dialogue from the selection.

_____

_____

_____

_____

_____

PART V: 45 points   Time to Spend: _____

Directions Write a paragraph about the games that you played as a child. Develop the paragraph by incidents or several examples.

_____

_____

_____

_____

_____

_____

_____

_____

DIRECTIONS   Write a main idea sentence for each of the following topics.

1. The positive (or negative) effects of suburban living on children

_____

2. The positive (or negative) effects of city living on children

_____

3. Why young married couples seek a suburban life-style

_____

4. Why adults with grown children leave the suburbs

_____

5. Why cities are stimulating environments for senior citizens

_____

Select one of the main idea sentences above, and develop it into a two-paragraph discussion of its causes or effects.

_____

_____

_____

_____

_____

_____

_____

_____

_____

_____

_____

_____

_____

_____

_____

_____

_____

GLOSSARY OF HOMONYMS

Homonyms are words that sound the same but differ in meaning and spelling. A list of frequently used homonyms and their general meanings follows. One of the words in the homonym groups may have more than one meaning. Whenever a homonym is a past or past participle form, the simple form of the verb appears in parenthesis following the definition.

aisle	a passageway between two sections
I'll	a contraction of **I will**
isle	another word for island
aloud	(1) in a loud tone; (2) spoken audibly
allowed	permitted (**allow**)
ate	consumed food (**eat**)
eight	(1) the number 8; (2) between seven and nine
board	(1) a sheet of wood; (2) a governing body
bored	(1) to be wearied from dullness or repetition; (2) made a hole in something (**bore**)
break	(1) to reduce to pieces; (2) to discontinue
brake	(1) a device for slowing or stopping motion; (2) to stop
Capitol	the building in Washington, D.C. in which the U.S. Congress holds its sessions
capital	(1) a town or city that is the official seat of government; (2) any form of wealth; (3) an uppercase letter such as A, B, or C
dear	(1) tenderly loved; (2) a loved one
deer	a four-legged forest animal
fair	(1) just or honest; (2) light in color; (3) a special gathering for buying and selling or for entertainment
fare	(1) a transportation charge or fee; (2) to get along
four	(1) the number 4; (2) between three and five
fore	in front
heard	perceived by the ear (**hear**)
herd	(1) animals that live and move as a group; (2) to gather into a group (usually animals)

here	at this place
hear	to become aware of sounds
knew	understood (**know**)
new	(1) bought or purchased recently; (2) not used before
know	to understand or to be aware of
no	(1) a negative response; (2) not so
male	referring to a man or boy
mail	(1) the letters or packages that are sent from one person to another; (2) to send something to another person
meat	(1) the flesh of animals as used for food; (2) the essential part of something
meet	to come together by chance or arrangement
our	a pronoun used to show possession
hour	(1) a specific time of day; (2) sixty minutes
passed	completed, or to have overcome (**pass**)
past	(1) a time before the present; (2) the name of a verb tense
pear	a fruit
pair	(1) two matching things; (2) two persons associated in some way
pare	cut off outer layer of something, usually a fruit
piece	a part or portion of
peace	(1) a time of calm; (2) the absence of war
plane	(1) a flat surface; (2) a shortened form of airplane
plain	(1) clear; (2) ordinary; (3) an area of flat land
pore	a small opening as in the skin
pour	(1) to cause to flow from one container to another; (2) to rain heavily
paw	an animal's foot
principal	(1) first or highest in rank or importance; (2) original amount of money before interest
principle	a basic rule or truth
right	(1) correct; (2) proper; (3) conforming to set standards
write	to set down or record, usually on paper

rode	traveled on or in something (**ride**)
road	a way made for traveling between places
scene	(1) a place where some event occurs; (2) a view or picture; (3) part of a play
seen	to have looked at or to have been noticed (**see**)
seam	a line formed where two surfaces meet
seem	to appear to be
shone	glowed with light (**shine**)
shown	pointed to, or illustrated (**show**)
so	(1) therefore; (2) in the manner described
sew	to stitch with a needle and thread
sow	to plant seeds
stationary	(1) not moving; (2) in a fixed position
stationery	writing materials such as paper and pads
steel	(1) a manufactured form of iron; (2) to strengthen
steal	to take without permission
sum	the total amount
some	(1) an unspecified number; (2) approximately
tail	the backmost or last part of something
tale	a story
they're	a contraction of **they are**
their	a pronoun used to show possession
there	at that place
threw	pitched or tossed (**throw**)
through	(1) to pass in one way and out the other; (2) successfully completed
throne	the raised chair occupied by a royal head of state or a bishop
thrown	tossed or pitched (**throw**)
tied	(1) fastened or bound together; (2) evened the score (**tie**)
tide	the periodic rise and fall of ocean water
to	in the direction of
too	(1) also; (2) very
two	(1) the number 2; (2) between one and three

way	(1) a method for doing something; (2) a path
weigh	(1) to measure according to a specific weight standard; (2) to consider carefully
waist	the narrowed part of the body just above the hips
waste	(1) to use carelessly; (2) to fail to use
weak	lacking in strength
week	a seven-day unit of time
weather	the state of the atmosphere relating to wind, moisture, and so on
whether	(1) used to introduce alternatives; (2) under whatever circumstances
where	adverb meaning at or in what place or situation
wear	to be clothed in
whole	(1) complete; (2) total
hole	an opening in or through something
whose	a pronoun used to show possession
who's	a contraction of **who is**
your	a pronoun used to show possession
you're	a contraction of **you are**

APPENDIX I: GUIDELINES FOR SPELLING: BASE WORD AND SUFFIX

Throughout the book you have learned to add a letter or letters to a base word. For example, you learned to add -s and -es to nouns to show plurality and to add -ed and -ing to verbs to express tenses. Suffixes such as -ible and -able can be added to base words to create new forms of the base word.

When endings are added to words, the base word often undergoes a spelling change. Several patterns that illustrate such types of spelling changes follow.

I. FINAL SILENT E AND SUFFIX

When a suffix beginning with a vowel is added to a base word ending with a silent e, usually the final silent e is dropped.

    advise + able = advisable
    advise + ed   = advised
    advise + ing = advising
    advise + or   = advisor

However, when a suffix beginning with a consonant is added to a base word ending with a silent e, usually the final silent e remains.

    care + ful = careful
    care + less = careless

II. FINAL Y AND SUFFIX

When a suffix beginning with a, e, o, u is added to a base word ending with a consonant + y, the y changes to an i.

    marry + es = marries
    marry + ed = married

    NOTE:

    marry + ing = marrying

When a suffix is added to a base word ending with a vowel + y, the y remains.

    delay   + ing = delaying
    monkey + s   = monkeys
    annoy   + ed = annoyed
    guy   + s   = guys

III. DOUBLING THE FINAL CONSONANT

When a suffix beginning with a vowel is added to a base word ending with a short vowel + a single consonant, that consonant is usually doubled.

jăm + ed = jammed
shŏp + ing = shopping
grăb + ed = grabbed
forgĕt+ ing = forgetting

When a suffix beginning with a vowel is added to a base word whose accent is on the last syllable, double the final consonant.

control' + ed = controlled
occur'   + ed = occurred
equip'   + ed = equipped

APPENDIX II: CONTRACTIONS

You have read contractions throughout this book, particularly in the dialogues. Contractions are common in speech and in informal writing and are becoming more acceptable in some formal writing situations. However, unless you are trying to imitate spoken English in your writing, you should use contractions sparingly.

A contraction means a shortening. Two words become one word. In written English, the contraction is signaled by an apostrophe that replaces the missing letter or letters.

I. Some contractions consist of a pronoun plus a shortened verb.

A. WORD + IS = CONTRACTION

he	+ is	= he's
she	+ is	= she's
it	+ is	= it's
here	+ is	= here's
that	+ is	= that's
there	+ is	= there's
what	+ is	= what's
where	+ is	= where's
who	+ is	= who's

B. PRONOUN + ARE = CONTRACTION

they	+ are	= they're
we	+ are	= we're
you	+ are	= you're

C. PRONOUN + HAS = CONTRACTION

he	+ has	= he's
she	+ has	= she's
it	+ has	= it's

D. PRONOUN + HAVE = CONTRACTION

I	+ have	= I've
they	+ have	= they've
we	+ have	= we've
you	+ have	= you've

E. Pronoun + Had = Contraction

I	+ had	= I'd
he	+ had	= he'd
she	+ had	= she'd
we	+ had	= we'd
you	+ had	= you'd
they	+ had	= they'd

F. Pronoun + Will = Contraction

I	+ will	= I'll
he	+ will	= he'll
she	+ will	= she'll
it	+ will	= it'll
we	+ will	= we'll
you	+ will	= you'll
they	+ will	= they'll

G. Pronoun + Would = Contraction

I	+ would	= I'd
he	+ would	= he'd
she	+ would	= she'd
we	+ would	= we'd
you	+ would	= you'd
they	+ would	= they'd

II. Another group of contractions consists of a verb plus a shortened form of not.

Verb + Not = Contraction

is	+ not	= isn't
are	+ not	= aren't
was	+ not	= wasn't
were	+ not	= weren't
has	+ not	= hasn't
have	+ not	= haven't
had	+ not	= hadn't
do	+ not	= don't
does	+ not	= doesn't
did	+ not	= didn't
will	+ not	= won't
would	+ not	= wouldn't
can	+ not	= can't
could	+ not	= couldn't
must	+ not	= mustn't
should	+ not	= shouldn't

III. A third group of contractions consists of a verb plus a shortened form of have.

VERB + HAVE = CONTRACTION

could	+ have	= could've
should	+ have	= should've
would	+ have	= would've

APPENDIX III: CERTAIN CONSONANTS AND VOWELS WITH THEIR PRONUNCIATION

Many letters have more than one sound or special sounds in English. To be able to identify words, you must recognize the various letter–sound relationships. Examples of these relationships follow.

I. CONSONANTS

A. The Letter C

Consonants are all the sounds in English except for the vowel sounds of a, e, i, o, u. Some consonants have two sounds. For example, **c** sounds like an "s" as in city. It also sounds like a "k" as in coat.

C

Followed by a, o, u Sounds like a "k" as in coat	Followed by e, i, y Sounds like an "s" as in city
carrot	celery
recall	recent
coffee	cinnamon
discover	acid
cucumber	cyclone

The consonant g has a hard and a soft sound. For example, **soft g** sounds like a "j" when it appears in the word ginger. If g is followed by an e or i, it usually has a "j" sound. A **hard g** sounds like the "g" in gas. If g is followed by a, o, or u, it usually has a hard "g" sound.

G

Followed by a, o, u Sounds like a "g" as in gas	Followed by i, e, y Sounds like a "j" as in ginger
gallon	germ
sugar	manager
gone	gin
forgotten	paging
gum	gym
disgust	biology

B. The Letters F, V, B, L, R

F, v, b, l, and **r** are sometimes difficult to pronounce. Practice reading these words aloud. Pay attention to the f, v, b, l, and r sounds in the following lists.

F		V	
fame	after	vase	review
fence	traffic	vest	revamp
fist	tariff	visit	avow
food	raffle	vowel	receive
fume	safe		

B		L	
bandaid	able	laugh	able
berry	cabbie	lemon	full
bite	neighbor	lime	silly
box	rebel	lox	self
bunch	symbol	lunch	slumber

R	
raisin	curry
red	after
ripe	favorite
rotten	reappear
rust	author

II. VOWELS

A. Long and Short Vowel Sounds

When you pronounce **long vowel sounds,** you say and hear the name of the letter. **Short vowel sounds** do not sound like the name of the letter.

ā	ē	ī	ō	ū
April	evil	ice	old	use
game	she	bite	stove	cute

ă	ĕ	ĭ	ŏ	ŭ
at	empty	in	odd	up
mat	set	lift	hop	fuss

B. Silent E and Long Vowels

> When a **final silent e** occurs in a word, the vowel before it has a long sound. When a word ends in a consonant, the vowel before it is usually short. Some exceptions are have, sore, come, give, and live.

a	e	i	o	u
tăp	thĕm	pĭn	hŏp	hŭg
tāpe	thēme	pīņe	hōpe	hūge

C. Two Vowels Together

> When **two vowels appear together** in a syllable or word, usually the first vowel has the long sound, and the second vowel is silent.

āi	āy	ēa	ēe	ōa
bail	stay	each	sweet	oat
remain	today	speak	resweep	toast

There are some exceptions: said, bread, lead, and read.

D. Two Vowels Together: IE, EI

> When **ie** appear together, they are usually pronounced like a long ē. When **ei** appear together, they are usually pronounced as a long ā. Sometimes the **ei** is pronounced as a long ē.

ie = ē sound	ei = ā sound	ei = ē
shriek	eighty	ceiling
niece	sleigh	deceive
believe	neighbor	receive

E. Special Vowel Combinations and Vowel–Consonant Combinations

When some vowels and consonants appear together, they have special sounds.

> When **a** is followed by **u, w,** or **l** as it is in caught, draw, and salt, it usually has the special *a* sound you hear in each word above. *All* these combinations sound alike.

> **OO** has many sounds, as in boot and took. The **oo** sound in boot is a long vowel sound, and the **oo** sound in took is a short vowel sound.

When **oi** and **oy** appear together they sound alike, as in toy and oil.

Ou and **ow** may sound alike as in house and brown. Sometimes these combinations have different sounds as in brought and slow.

au	aw	al	oo	oo
autumn	awful	always	ooze	good
daughter	straw	malted	spoon	book

oi	oy	ou	ow	ou	ow
oil	oyster	out	ow!	ought	own
broil	toy	house	flower	cough	flow

F. The Influence of the Letter R on Vowels

When a vowel is followed by an **r**, the vowel sound is neither long nor short. Very often, the **er, ur,** and **ir** sounds are alike in the way that you pronounce them.

ar	er	ir	or	ur
Arthur	Ernest	Irving	organ	urge
card	berth	skirt	short	purple

INDEX

G

Guidewords. *See* Dictionary

H

Highlighting
  guidelines for, 133
  main ideas
    in short passages, 108–113
    in single paragraphs, 82–90, 102–104, 123–127
  main ideas and details in note taking
    forming questions for, 133–135
    guidelines for, 160–162
    in longer selections, 143–151
    in single paragraphs, 135–137, 160–164
  See also Outlining
Homonyms
  definition of, 17
  dialogue introducing, 17–18
  selecting the correct, 18–20
  See also Glossary of Homonyms

L

Lists. *See* Details; Topics
Literal comprehension
  identifying who, what, 8–10
  introduction to, 3–4
  in longer selections, 24–29
  recalled facts in, 4–7
  in single paragraphs, 11–16
  in single sentences, 3–7
  See also details; Highlighting; Main idea sentence; Topics
Literal meanings. *See* Literal comprehension

M

Main idea sentence
  definition of, 82, 86
  highlighting, 82–90, 102–104, 108–113, 133–137, 143–151, 160–164
  introduction to, 81–82
  locating in longer selections, 143–151
  locating in short passages, 108–113
  recognizing the location in a paragraph
    first sentence, 90, 102–104
    middle sentence, 100–104
    last sentence, 99–100, 102–104

Main idea sentence [cont.]
  relationship to details of a paragraph, 81–89, 123–127
  relationship to topic, 81–85
  See also Note-taking; Outlining
Multiple meanings. *See* Dictionary

N

Negatives. *See* Appendix II; Prefixes; Test-taking
Note-taking. *See* Details: Highlighting; Main idea sentence; Outlining; Test-taking
Noun endings. *See* Suffixes

O

Objective tests
  definition of, 300
  guidelines for following directions and answering questions, 303–308
  introduction to, 300
    quality, quantity of, 301–302
  See also Following directions; Test-taking
Outlining
  in multiple paragraphs, 180–187
    guidelines for, 180–181
  moving from highlighting to written notes, 160–164
  in single paragraphs, 160–164, 170–174
    guidelines for, 162, 170
  in titled selections
    guidelines for, 198–199
    in multiple paragraphs, 215–219
    in short selections with subtitles, 223–232
    in single paragraphs, 198–202

P

Paragraphs. *See* Details; Highlighting; Literal Comprehension; Main idea sentence; Outlining; Topics
Parts of speech. *See* Dictionary
Prefixes
  common
    dialogue introducing, 175
  definition of, 165
  negative
    dialogue introducing, 165–166

Prefixes [cont.]
    anti-, dis-, il-, im-, in-, ir-, mis-, non-, un-, 165–166
    quantity
        dialogue introducing, 188
        bi-, mono-, multi-, poly-, semi-, uni-, 188–190
Pronunciation. *See* Syllables

Q

Questions. *See* Essay tests; Objective tests

R

Recall of facts. *See* Literal comprehension; Objective tests
Restrictive labels. *See* Dictionary
Roots
    definition of, 248–249
    dialogue introducing, 248–249
    recognizing common roots
        aud, 250
        chron, chrono, cred, 267–270
        duc, duct, 264–266
        gram, graph, 267–270
        mit, miss, 264–266
        port, 251
        scribe, script, 249
        vert, vers, 264–266

S

Signal words. *See* Essay tests; Following directions; Objective tests
Silent *e*, 204, 206
    See also Appendix III
Spelling. *See* Appendix I; Glossary of Homonyms; Silent *e*; Suffixes
Study skills. *See* Essay tests; Highlighting; Objective tests; Outlining; Test-taking
Suffixes
    adjective endings
        -able, -al, -ful, -ible, -ive, -y, 220–222
        dialogue introducing, 220
        guidelines for, 221
    definition of, 203
    dialogue introducing, 203
    noun endings
        definition of, 210

Suffixes [cont.]
    dialogue introducing, 210
        -es, -ies, -s, 210–211
    dialogue introducing, 233
        -er, -ist, -or, 233–234
    verb endings
        -d, -ed, -ing very forms, 206–207
        third-person singular
            -es, -s, 208–209
    verb suffixes
        to change part of speech, 203–205
        definition of, 203
        dialogue introducing, 203
        -en, -ify, -ize, 204–205
    See also Appendix I; Silent *e*
Syllables
    dialogue introducing, 114–116
    hearing, 114–116
    vowel and consonant rules
        consonant blends, 130
        single consonant between two vowels
            dialogue introducing, 114–116, 138–139
            V-CV, VC-V, 115–116, 138–140
    two vowel sounds separated by two consonants
        dialogue introducing, 152
        VC-CV, 129
    verbs ending in -ed
        dialogue introducing, 152
        pronuciation of, 152–153
    vowel sounds, 114
    words ending in -le
        dialogue introducing, 141
        dividing, 141
Synonyms. *See* Dictionary

T

Taking notes. *See* Details; Highlighting; Main idea sentence; Outlining; Test-taking
Test-taking
    allowing for time on a test, 283–285
        guidelines for, 283
    answering questions, 286–287
        guidelines for, 286
    following general directions on a test, 288–290
    introduction to, 278
    preparing for
        do's and don'ts in studying, 279–282
        charts of, 280–282
    See also Essay tests; Objective tests

Third-person singular. *See* Suffixes
Topics
    definition of, 37, 51, 54
    identifying
        in lists, 37–38
        in paragraphs, 54–57
    introduction to, 35–36
    naming
        in lists, 39–40
        in paragraphs, 50–53
    recognizing in longer passages, 64–70
    relationship to details, 81–85
    relationship to main idea sentence, 81–89
    selecting for lists of details, 41–43
    selecting for a paragraph, 54–58
    See also Main idea sentence

True-false questions. *See* Following directions; Literal Comprehension; Objective tests

V

Verb endings. *See* Suffixes
Verb suffixes. *See* Suffixes
Vowel sounds. *See* Appendix III; Syllables
Vowel and consonant rules. *See* Appendix III; Syllables

W

Written notes. *See* Outlining